TRUST
THE PLAN

Demand Management for Business Leaders

Greg Spira

ISBN: 978-1-60427-190-4

Printed and bound in the U.S.A. Printed on acid-free paper.

10 9 8 7 6 5 4 3 2

Library of Congress Cataloging-in-Publication Data can be found in the WAV section of the publisher's website at jrosspub.com/wav.

Phone: (954) 727-9333
Fax: (561) 892-0700
Web: www.jrosspub.com

CONTENTS

FOREWORD

By Colleen "Coco" Crum

Anthropologists cite the role that trust has played, since the first humans walked this earth, in sustaining the well-being of people as they interact with others, trade goods, and seek to borrow and loan something of value to one another. Adam Smith, the father of modern economics, wrote of the value of trust in economies and societies. "Without trust, nations and societies fail to thrive," he observed. Energy is consumed in just surviving, and there's little left to create the best opportunities for oneself and one's society and nation.

In this book, Greg Spira breaks new ground on creating trust within companies and business cultures. In essence, businesses are tiny economies. They produce and distribute goods in response to demand from consumers, which is the definition of economies. As such, the same economic principles for nations and societies apply to businesses as well, albeit on a much smaller scale.

When trust is lacking within the business culture, companies, too, fail to thrive. Business leaders spend an inordinate amount of time managing crisis after crisis, trying to achieve the next quarter's financial promises. They run hard—like a mouse on a treadmill with no exit in sight. Little time remains to develop strategies and tactics for increasing revenue and profits over the long term—or what Greg calls *focusing on the business*.

Economists attribute lack of trust to bringing down entire global economies, such as in 1929 and 2008. With the economies of companies, lack of trust is often the unacknowledged root of business failures. Few companies collapse as spectacularly as Enron. Most businesses disappoint their boards and investors in small ways that incrementally accumulate until lack of credibility brings them down. The board and investors simply do not believe the leadership team's explanations and do not have confidence in their plans to right the ship. Executives may be replaced. Companies may be acquired for far less than they might have been worth had trust existed. Or, sometimes, businesses cease to exist. And the mad scramble by business leaders to survive has been a massive waste of energy.

Greg takes a unique approach in this book. He narrows the issue of trust to the Demand Management of businesses. This focus makes sense considering that market-based economies *respond to* consumer demand. Within this context, Greg considers the impact on the business *as a whole* when demand plans or business forecasts are not considered credible or trustworthy.

Greg's focus on trust and Demand Management is not a theoretical pursuit. What makes this book particularly valuable for executives is its practical and actionable approach. Readers learn how to create credible demand plans through a wealth of examples that can be readily implemented. The behaviors Greg cites that are needed for all business functions to trust the demand plans should cause executives to pause and self-assess their actions and leadership.

While Greg's focus is on Demand Management, I hope you will widen your perspective and imagination for your business as you read his recommendations and real-life examples. The same principles and many of the approaches detailed in this book apply to other business processes as well, including the supply chain, product management, and Integrated Business Management. Making use of these approaches will keep your company's economy healthy.

PREFACE

Nearly 20 years ago, Colleen "Coco" Crum and George Palmatier wrote *Demand Management Best Practices: Process, Principles and Collaboration*. Before that, there were very few resources that comprehensively addressed the principles and best practices of Demand Management. That book established Demand Management as being more than just an activity within a company. It established Demand Management as a profession.

I began my professional journey around the same time that book was written. I was given a copy of *Demand Management Best Practices* when I took on the role of leading Demand Management at BlackBerry, and it has helped me tremendously in my career.

Over the past 20 years, the profession of Demand Management has continued to evolve. I have participated in that evolution firsthand—as a practitioner, coach, mentor, educator, and author. As a business advisor working with Oliver Wight Americas, I spend most of my time working with executives, coaching them on how to work together effectively as a team. I believe that while there has been much written about Demand Management for planners and practitioners, there remains an opportunity to address the topic in a way that is relevant to executives. That is what I aim to address with this book.

This book covers the best practices of Demand Management from the perspective of leadership roles, responsibilities, accountabilities, and behaviors. This book will not get into the nitty gritty of statistics or detailed performance measurements. Instead, it focuses on the key enablers of *trust*. Trust in the people, processes, and information being shared. Businesses achieve their goals through teamwork and teamwork is anchored in trust.

Greg Spira

ACKNOWLEDGMENTS

The inspiration, support, and experiences that have gone into the writing of this book have come from many sources. First and foremost are my clients and Oliver Wight colleagues, from whom I have been able to collect so many wonderful illustrations and examples. Jim Matthews, Mary Adamy, and Crystal Lee have supported and shaped my journey with Oliver Wight in ways that I am deeply thankful for.

One of my Oliver Wight colleagues, despite being in "retirement," has gone well above and beyond in supporting me on this journey. I initially approached Colleen "Coco" Crum for feedback on a first draft—which led to a year-long journey of revisions and improvements that have truly made this book something that I am extremely proud of. It has certainly been worth it, and I am extremely thankful for the time she has invested in helping to make this book what it is.

I would also like to thank my father, Allen Spira, and my colleague, Charity Lopez, for providing feedback and support on various drafts of the book along the way. I also owe sincere thanks to Timm Reiher, with whom I teach the Oliver Wight Demand Management course, for allowing me to use a few of his own stories.

Through my years in industry as a practitioner of Demand Management, I have had the good fortune of working with many talented leaders. Adam Michaels, Jay Cooper, Larry Di Nicola, Brian Forrest, and Pat Laflamme all deserve my sincere thanks for the impact they have had on my career experiences.

Last, and most important, I would not have been able to complete this endeavor without the support of my wife, Carol, and our two sons, Patrick and Christopher. They have supported me without question as I have invested countless hours in the writing of this book.

ABOUT THE AUTHOR

Greg Spira, a business advisor with Oliver Wight, is an expert in Demand Management and Integrated Business Planning. He has written and coauthored many whitepapers on Demand Management and is an instructor of the Oliver Wight Americas Demand Management course.

Greg has particularly deep experience in the consumer goods industry, having helped many well-known large food companies improve their planning processes. He has also supported companies in a wide range of other industries, including packaging, chemicals, healthcare, medical devices, and fashion.

Prior to joining Oliver Wight, Greg held several roles at Mondelez International, one of the world's largest snack companies. He established their Integrated Business Planning process in Canada and led the Integrated Business Planning process for the Nabisco business in the United States. He also had various roles leading forecasting and planning across North America.

Prior to joining Mondelez, Greg spent several years at BlackBerry where he led the global team responsible for planning smartphone demand. There he navigated a rapidly evolving environment with long lead times, short product life cycles, evolving business models, and intense competition. Greg also held roles as a controller and as an information technology manager with a midsize retail fixture company.

Greg received his MBA, CPA, and CMA from McMaster University, where he has since been a sessional lecturer.

Web
Added
Value™

This book has free material available for download from the
Web Added Value™ resource center at *www.jrosspub.com*

At J. Ross Publishing we are committed to providing today's professional with practical, hands-on tools that enhance the learning experience and give readers an opportunity to apply what they have learned. That is why we offer free ancillary materials available for download on this book and all participating Web Added Value™ publications. These online resources may include interactive versions of the material that appears in the book or supplemental templates, worksheets, models, plans, case studies, proposals, spreadsheets and assessment tools, among other things. Whenever you see the WAV™ symbol in any of our publications, it means bonus materials accompany the book and are available from the Web Added Value Download Resource Center at www .jrosspub.com.

Downloads for *Trust the Plan* include numerous whitepapers to enhance the adoption of world-class Demand Management best practices.

SMARTCORP ORGANIZATIONAL CHART

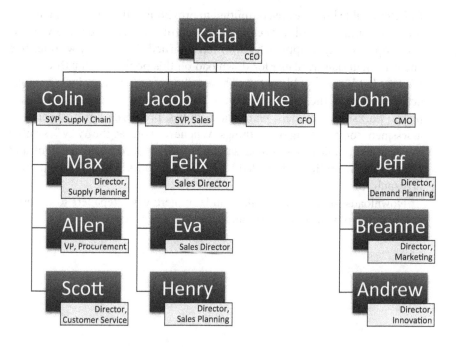

CEO – Chief Executive Officer
SVP – Senior Vice President
CFO – Chief Financial Officer
CMO – Chief Marketing Officer
VP – Vice President
CIO – Chief Information Officer

CHAPTER 1

PLANNING FOR SUCCESS

Let's start by exploring the fundamental premise that *planning is a good thing.* Some may ask: Why do we plan in the first place? Why not be carefree and deal with issues as they arise? This might sound a bit exaggerated, but I have encountered people who, frustrated with ineffective planning, focus their energy solely on improving their ability to react. Let's address the question of *why we should plan* by reviewing an example.

I recently enjoyed a tropical vacation with my family. Before leaving, my wife and I laid out a plan for the trip. We had a few constraints that impacted what we could and couldn't do—timing, duration, and budget—but otherwise, we were flexible. I'm sure we could have just showed up and figured out what we were going to do day by day, but that is not what we chose to do.

Even though *we* were flexible, that didn't mean that the activities that we wanted to do would be available on a whim. For example, we wanted to take a road trip, but we needed to be careful about weather conditions. We wanted to visit one of the national parks, but tickets were limited. Dinner reservations were needed in most cases, and activities like golfing, scuba diving, and surfing all had to be booked in advance.

So naturally, we put together a plan. We made reservations, scheduled activities, and enjoyed the trip. If I look back to what made the trip a success, however, I wouldn't say it was because we had scheduled our activities in advance. Sure, planning for the trip was important, but it wasn't the plan itself that was important. What mattered most was that we all had the opportunity to do the things that we really wanted to do. My youngest son wanted to try surfing. My oldest wanted to golf. I wanted to go scuba diving. My wife wanted to spend time relaxing on the beach. Our enjoyment of the vacation was measured by whether we got to do the things we wanted to do.

In the end, the discussions we had while planning the trip weren't really about logistics. They were about understanding everybody's goals and prioritizing accordingly. We shared what was important to each of us. We made sure everyone understood each other's desires, and then the scheduling became relatively straightforward.

Years before, we took a different sort of vacation. We drove across Canada from Ontario to British Columbia. We didn't know for certain how far we would want to drive each day. Instead of planning each hotel stop in advance, we booked hotels day by day. Our only requirement was that the hotels had a pool for the kids. Did we know where we would be on any given day? No. Did we have a plan? Absolutely. The plan reflected our approach to meeting our goals.

Even if there is no need to make advance bookings or reservations, planning is still important. If just one person is traveling, it's easy to have a conversation with yourself and prioritize. Once you expand to two or more people, communication becomes critical. Planning shifts from an activity that you do implicitly to one that is explicit and intentional. Planning includes communicating what our goals and objectives are and working together to find ways to achieve them.

Dwight D. Eisenhower is quoted as having said, "Peace-time plans are of no particular value, but peace-time planning is indispensable."[1] It's true—and not just for military leaders, but for business leaders as well.

Planning is indispensable, but it can also be challenging. In my experience, both people and organizations need to learn how to plan effectively—it doesn't always come naturally. This need is critical in larger organizations where many different people in different roles must come together to connect and align various plans.

To help illustrate some common challenges that business leaders experience in planning, let's look at the fictitious company SmartCorp. SmartCorp is like many actual companies, with a capable leadership team, smart employees, and products that customers want to buy. Like many other real companies, however, SmartCorp isn't perfect. As we progress through this book, we will use SmartCorp to illustrate common planning challenges that business leaders experience and how they can be addressed.

* * *

Let's take a look at the following situation from SmartCorp.

Katia, CEO of SmartCorp, is confused about the sales forecast, and she needs clarity quickly. She must present a financial forecast to the board of directors tomorrow.

"I don't understand the numbers," she says to Colin, the Senior Vice President of Supply. "What is shown here is a sales forecast of over $200 million for next quarter. We met with Jacob last week. He was clear that $165 million would be a stretch for the sales organization to achieve."

Jacob is the Senior Vice President of Sales. He is not participating in this meeting that Katia requested just this morning. He is making a sales call at RetailMart, SmartCorp's largest customer. He, along with Felix, the account sales leader, and John, the Chief Marketing Officer, are presenting an update on a new product. This new product will be released to the market in one month as part of Project Alpha. The sales strategy is for RetailMart to be the first customer to commit to buying the new product.

Katia's agenda for today's meeting includes reviewing a crewing plan to increase production capacity. She wants to hear Colin's proposal and needs Mike, SmartCorp's Chief Financial Officer (CFO), to weigh in on the financial feasibility.

SmartCorp has been growing rapidly for the past several quarters, driven by strong demand for their personal protective equipment products. Katia challenged Jacob in a one-on-one meeting last week when he reported strong competitive pressure was making it difficult to maintain their revenue growth trajectory. Katia expects him to propose a plan to overcome these competitive pressures.

Katia turns to Colin and asks, "Where did you get these sales revenue numbers?"

"From Jeff," Colin responds. Jeff is the Director of Demand Planning. The demand planning team meets with every account team monthly and collects their demand projections, item by item.

"I don't know why Jacob is being so conservative, but I've got all the detail and backup information behind Jeff's numbers," says Colin.

"I told you Jacob was sandbagging," Mike says. The CFO has a reputation for distrusting projections from both the sales and supply organizations.

"We have to send our plans to the board tonight for tomorrow's meeting," Mike adds. "I think we should go with the higher number. Colin has the details. Do we have enough capacity to deliver $200 million?"

"As long as we approve the crewing plan, including overtime, we should be able to hit $185 million," says Colin.

Katia pushes away from the conference table. "Great, let's do it," she says. "The plan is approved, and let's take $180 million to the board. That should give us a bit of wiggle room."

Fast forward three days. Jacob is visibly angry with his sales leadership team.

"Someone needs to explain to me how this happens. I just got a note from Katia that our target for next quarter is $190 million. I don't know how much clearer I could have been that it would be a stretch to achieve $165 million in sales revenue next quarter. But Colin tells me that my teams created that number!" barks Jacob.

"I don't like to be blindsided. No one brought the $190 million number to me," Jacob adds, clearly feeling his team undermined him.

Felix, one of the sales directors, musters the courage to respond. "Jacob, we've been talking about this problem for months now," he says. "We're chasing dozens of opportunities, and if we don't put them into the forecast file that we pass over to the demand planning group, manufacturing won't build the product. We can't sell it if they don't build it. It's as simple as that!"

"Even worse," chimes in Eva, another one of the sales directors, "the supply planners check every single order against the forecast. Almost every time we can't deliver something, I get blamed for not having forecasted it. We're so sick and tired of their second guessing that we include everything that is a potential sale in the plan. We don't have time to deal with these interrogations from the supply people."

"I get it, but now is not the time for excuses," Jacob says. "We now have a gap between what is feasible to sell and the revenue we are expected to produce next quarter. What are we going to do to close the gap?"

"Our best bet is to lean in on Project Alpha," Felix says. "You saw during our sales call at RetailMart how excited they are about these new devices. The Project Alpha products are supposed to be ready to ship to customers at the end of the quarter. One of our biggest opportunities is to sign an exclusivity agreement with RetailMart. I'm sure we can convince them to take product early to create inventory in their distribution centers in anticipation of sales the following quarter."

"I guess that's the only feasible shot we have. If you're telling me that it was covered in the plan that was sent to the supply people, then at least we won't have them saying it wasn't forecasted. Let's do it," says Jacob.

Fast forward to the end of the quarter. Katia is visibly frustrated with her team.

"I just don't get it," she says. "I'm really tired of having to go back to the board of directors to explain why we missed our numbers. They don't trust anything we tell them. Why don't we do what we say we're going to do?"

Katia is meeting with Jacob, Colin, and Mike to review the quarterly results. Revenue finished at $160 million, far short of the $180 that had been committed.

"We have orders for $185 million, Katia. We beat our projection by twelve percent!" says Jacob. "If Colin would have delivered all the product that was ordered, we wouldn't be in this mess. And let me be clear, I never signed up for $190 million. I told you we would deliver $165 million in sales revenue, and now my team is being penalized for doing an outstanding job."

"He's right, Colin," Katia says to her supply leader. "You said we could deliver $185 million in sales revenue. What happened?" asks Katia.

"This is silly. We received $25 million in orders for Project Alpha devices. We all knew that Project Alpha wasn't going to be ready to ship last quarter," says Colin. "I told you I could make $185 million in product, and that's exactly what my team did. It's not my fault that Jacob didn't sell it."

"Well, that's not the only problem," says Mike. "Of that $185 million in product that was produced, $20 million of that is unsold and now excess inventory. Since we've committed Project Alpha to RetailMart, they're not taking any of the old version devices."

* * *

You may see similarities between your own experiences and the events and behaviors that Katia and her SmartCorp team faced. I have certainly encountered similar situations myself.

Rarely would I describe the actions of the leaders I worked with as malicious. In almost every case, the road to hell is paved with good intentions. In our SmartCorp example, the sales directors are genuinely trying to close sales opportunities and delight their customers. Jacob is trying to make reliable commitments to Katia without overpromising what his sales team can achieve in sales revenue. Colin is working to ensure that he has a supply plan that can deliver the product that is needed. Even Mike, while calling Jacob a sandbagger, is likely doing so because he has rarely seen a sales team deliver the revenue it promises and believes that sandbagging is just the way the game is played.

One or two levels down in the organization, people tend not to have the same understanding and empathy for the challenges faced by the business leaders. It wouldn't be hard to imagine a demand planner, brand manager, or materials buyer at SmartCorp thinking that the leadership team is dysfunctional, unable to agree on a plan, and always blaming one another for disappointing performance.

I have frequently observed people lower in the organization questioning their business leaders' ability to work well together. The hard and soft costs associated with the lack of leadership trust and alignment are real and significant. When trust is lacking between leaders, it inevitably cascades down through their teams. Silos become strengthened, and the cross-functional collaboration at lower levels in the company becomes difficult, if not impossible. People shift their energy away from proactively solving problems to preparing explanations for why they weren't at fault. It can, in extreme cases, become outright combative.

My family vacation and SmartCorp's situation share some common traits—multiple people involved, each with their own goals and objectives. SmartCorp's challenge didn't come from people not caring or not being capable. Best practices for planning, collaboration, communications, and problem solving were missing. Open and honest discussion in scrutinizing and agreeing upon the sales plan did not occur. Jacob wasn't even included in the meeting to finalize the revenue projection that would be communicated to the board of directors! A common understanding of how the forecast of sales revenue would be achieved was not agreed upon. There was no discussion—let alone agreement—on the product mix, volume, and timing of production in support of the sales plan.

One fundamental principle that is not well understood nor embraced in many companies is that *we plan not for the sake of planning, but to achieve business objectives*. Customers don't buy products and services because a company has a plan, but planning is what enables companies to deliver products and services that customers want to buy, where and when they need them. Planning is the activity that brings together people within an organization to share objectives, prioritize, and create common understanding. This sharing includes communicating sales, new product, supply, and financial plans.

Plans are rarely stagnant. That's why planning is a continuous process that allows business leaders to recalibrate when things change. While goals and objectives may remain static over a longer period, business environments are dynamic.

For example, it's not sufficient to just tell the Sales organization to go and sell what was budgeted for the year. There might be some businesses somewhere that can set an annual plan or budget and then execute it without any deviation, but I have yet to find them.

Companies that achieve their annual goals and strategies have a different leadership mindset than in the SmartCorp example. Business leaders in high-performing companies understand that goals and plans are different. Goals are expressed as outcomes, and plans are expressed as actions that will deliver a result, such as achievement of revenue and profit goals. The leadership team also understands that goals can remain fixed over time. Plans, however, can and should change to adapt to new conditions that may impede achieving the goals and strategies.

Wise leaders ensure that conversations about plans include answering the following questions:

1. Do we still agree on the goals that have been established, or are changes needed?
2. Will our current operating plans enable us to achieve the stated goals?
3. If not, what do we need to change or do differently?

Using my vacation example, we knew that my youngest son wanted to try surfing. That was one of our stated goals. Surfing, however, depends on whether the *surf's up*. As the surfing date came closer, we checked the weather forecasts to make sure that our plan was still valid. If we had to change the date or time of the lesson, we could do that, but we would also have to consider implications on our other planned activities. Our planning process was continuous and routine—every day we checked the weather and made sure everything was on track.

High-performing organizations routinely discuss the answers to the aforementioned questions. They collect, evaluate, and respond to new information. They assess whether they are on or off track when it comes to achieving their goals. They make decisions regarding whether or not to change course. As a result, they have a better rate of success in achieving their goals than companies that have less formal planning processes.

In the SmartCorp example, business leaders confused goals and plans. Katia set a goal of achieving $180 million in revenue. The goal was not achieved, however, because there was no coordinated plan on *how* to achieve the promised sales revenue. The commercial organization focused on selling the new product; the supply organization focused on making more existing products available to sell. The result was a disappointed board of directors, a disappointed customer when product could not be delivered, and an increase in inventory for product that might not be sold.

In business, the confusion of plans and goals is unfortunately quite common. In fact, the language used to describe an annual target or objective quite often uses the word "plan." I vividly remember watching a heated, fist-pounding debate between two executives over which one was the real plan—the annual plan or the demand plan. The Chief Executive Officer was adamant that the annual plan was the only plan of relevance. The Senior Vice President of Operations believed that the demand plan was more worthy of attention because it included a documented action plan.

I chose wisely at that moment not to get in the middle of the debate, but the truth is that both leaders were right (to a degree).

In principle, an annual plan or budget is a goal. It is established and remains fixed over a period of time (often one or more years). It does not change in response to new information, such as changes in the marketplace or changes in internal capabilities, like an operating plan does. The annual plan is used as a benchmark or measuring stick. Business leaders compare the annual plan to the latest operational plans of the business. This comparison shows whether the annual plan will be achieved and whether financial promises to the board of directors and Wall Street will be met.

Organizations that consistently achieve or exceed their goals generally have business leaders who distinguish between operating plans and goals. They also routinely come together to adjust operating plans in pursuit of those goals.

Oliver Wight has tracked the performance of clients that we have helped to develop and improve their planning capability. On average, these companies have outperformed Standard & Poors 500 companies by 35 percent in terms of long-term operating income growth.[2] In our experience, when organizations routinely achieve or exceed their financial goals, they are more trusted by their board of directors. What they say and recommend is viewed as credible. This may sound like common sense—and it is, but just because something makes sense, doesn't make it easy.

The objective of this book is to show business leaders how to develop demand planning processes that increase the probability of achieving company goals and strategies. This book is also appropriate reading for business leaders from noncommercial functions. I hope it clarifies roles. I hope it creates a better understanding of what it takes to develop and execute credible demand plans. I also hope this book is useful for discussing within your company why it is necessary to trust those plans.

In the next chapter, we will discuss the roles in planning, including business leaders' roles. We will also uncover some challenges that leaders commonly face, and how these challenges apply specifically to Demand Management and planning.

SUMMARY

- We plan not for the sake of planning, but to ensure that we can achieve our goals and objectives.
- When planning involves more than one person or group, it requires each party to communicate their goals and objectives, and then work together as a group to achieve them.

- Planning is a continuous process. All businesses operate in a dynamic environment where things change regularly, requiring plans to be adjusted.
- Planning can be challenging and doesn't always come naturally to leaders.
- Plans and goals are different. Goals tend to remain fixed while plans change in response to changes in the market, customer's buying desires, internal capability, and other up-to-date information.

QUESTIONS TO ASK

- Are goals and plans clearly distinguished in your organization?
- Is your leadership team generally viewed as being high performing, dysfunctional, or somewhere in between?
- Is the process for making commercial decisions routine, coordinated, and planful?
- Are commercial decisions connected with the rest of the organization effectively?
- How broadly are commercial plans shared within the company?

ENDNOTES

1. Dwight D. Eisenhower. *The Papers of Dwight David Eisenhower, Volume XI: Columbia University.* Johns Hopkins University Press, 1984, p. 1516.
2. Nasdaq Data Link. https://data.nasdaq.com/databases/MF1/data.

CHAPTER 2

WORKING *ON* THE BUSINESS

When explaining the concept of business planning to a leadership team, my colleague Mary Adamy uses the metaphor of a bridge. On one side of the bridge are goals and objectives. The activity of setting goals and objectives is important and is linked to business strategy, vision, and mission. On the other side of the bridge is the day-to-day running of the business which includes developing new business, negotiating with customers, transacting sales orders, operating production lines, buying materials, accounting for and controlling company resources, and much more. These activities are important—you simply can't operate your business without doing them.

This metaphor signifies that the bridge itself is the midrange planning process known as Integrated Business Planning (IBP).[1] It's what executives traverse in order to connect strategy to execution (see Figure 2.1).

The question is: On which side of the bridge should business leaders focus their time and attention? If business leaders spend all their time executing, they will find themselves in the same situation as SmartCorp. The goals were set, but everyone executed in different ways that satisfied their near-term functional needs. Leadership teams can't skip planning and execute their way to achieving long-term goals. They need to connect execution to plans that support the business objectives and will bring an optimal financial result. They also need a routine process of recalibrating and synchronizing those plans across the organization to adapt to changes in the business environment, both externally and internally. Execution primarily occurs in individual business functions. Planning involves both individual business functions and collaboration across business functions.

I frequently observe the following behavior, most often in companies or business units that are growing and expanding and in companies with leaders who have spent most of their careers in high-growth environments. There is an attitude of *just work it out* when problems arise.

As a business grows, complexity increases. The culture of *just work it out* doesn't scale. The number of communication intersection points within a

11

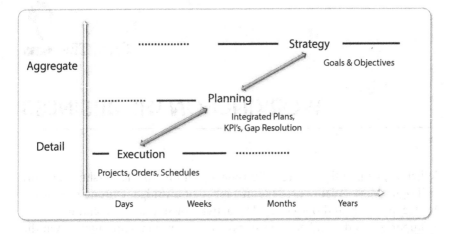

Figure 2.1   The Bridge Connecting Strategy to Execution. © Oliver Wight International, Inc. Used with permission.

company can grow exponentially if the expectation is that everybody establishes their own network. This lack of formality in problem solving often leads to what appears to be foolish or avoidable mistakes. One client used the sports analogy of increasing the number of unforced errors as complexity increases.

Much like with SmartCorp, common symptoms of informal decision processes include:

- The sales organization drives sales without alignment with what manufacturing can produce
- Decisions are made haphazardly, often with incomplete information
- Adherence to decisions is poor, and there is often confusion over what decisions have been made
- The finance team is often left deciphering misaligned information from across the business in an attempt to predict results
- People are tired and morale is low

The questions then are: Who is responsible for planning? Who should be on the bridge looking out for obstacles and steering around them, and who should be manning the oars?

A former Oliver Wight principal used to say: "If two people are trying to do the same job, fire the one who is more expensive." In other words, if the captain of the ship is manning the oars, he or she isn't really being a captain.

The leaders of an organization are chiefly responsible for planning. They certainly don't do this on their own. Chapter 4 covers in more depth the way in which plans are developed and shared in an organization. That being said, business leaders are put in their respective positions to direct the resources of their functions and make decisions. They are therefore accountable for the plans that their teams follow and the results that those plans deliver.

A commercial leader (for example, a Vice President of Sales or Chief Marketing Officer) is responsible for directing the commercial resources of an organization, such as making advertising investments, hiring salespeople, prioritizing the time spent by marketers, and setting the prices of products and services. That leader is therefore accountable for the plans that reflect those decisions.

I spent some time evaluating the planning processes for a client that operates a chain of restaurants. While assessing the behavior of the restaurant managers, a common trait emerged: When things started getting busy, the restaurant manager tended to help prepare the meals—or what they called "hop on the grill."

On the one hand, we might think that's an admirable trait—to get down in the trenches and work with the team to muscle through serving customers. On the other hand, if leaders are all working the grill, then who is looking out for and planning around the next wave of customers or other obstacles?

It is considered best practice for a leader's first priority to be working *on* the business, as opposed to working *in* the business. Before hopping on the grill or getting into execution activities, leaders must allocate an appropriate amount of their time to plan beyond the next few hours, 2–3 days, weeks, or months—and even years. Somebody must be thinking about what will or needs to happen 6, 12, 18, and 24 months from now.

Jim Matthews and Leon Dixon put it well in their whitepaper *Is your S&OP or IBP process delivering the results you expected?* They observe: "An executive may be able to 'help' or 'rescue' a situation by dropping down and overseeing detailed execution for a time, but the reverse is impossible. The execution level and middle management are not able to rise up and do the many mid- and long-term executive tasks that allow a company to prosper and avoid crises and firefighting in the first place."[2]

Those executive tasks include planning. Planning *is* working *on* the business. Business leaders plan so they can empower others to execute. Planning and execution are separate activities.

Think for a moment about your business. Can you clearly delineate planning activities from execution? Do long-term planning discussions inevitably devolve into what we need to do in order to deliver the expected results for the month or quarter ahead? Do you regularly jump on the grill, so to speak?

The most effective leaders empower their teams to work *in* the business, executing the plans that they have set. They trust their teams to execute because:

1. They have confidence that their teams will follow the plan, and will escalate decisions up the chain of command when deviations to the plan are anticipated or occur.
2. They are confident that the plan they helped develop and approve can be executed.
3. The business leaders and their teams understand how the plans are connected across business functions and how the plans will enable them to achieve the company's business corporate objectives.

When any of these three elements are missing, leaders struggle to manage an appropriate balance of their time between planning and execution. As quarter-end or year-end approaches, does your leadership team tend to become more involved or less involved in the day-to-day execution activities? I can't recall a single executive saying that they wanted to be micromanaging at quarter-end, yet I have worked with many who felt they *had* to. The tendency to "hop on the grill" is often explained by the three enablers of empowerment as mentioned before, or rather by the lack of those enablers being in place.

Unfortunately, leaders often don't appreciate the negative behavioral consequences of being caught up in execution. They may see themselves through a positive lens of working shoulder-to-shoulder with their teams. In my opinion, this belief is often a delusion.

There's a reason my former colleague suggested that the leader should be fired when he or she is performing the same job as a lower-level team member. The reason goes beyond cost savings. This type of behavior can be very demoralizing to teams. Teams are deprived of the opportunity to succeed on their own.

Keep in mind, success can only truly be achieved when the chance of failure exists. In my view, leaders need to get out of the way and let their teams demonstrate their ability to succeed on their own. Planning helps leaders get out of the way. It gives leaders confidence that their teams have the tools to succeed and will ask for help if needed.

The distinction between working *on* vs. working *in* the business applies directly to Demand Management. Philip Kotler is considered the father of modern-day marketing. His book, *Marketing Management*, is the most widely used textbook on marketing around the world.[3] He is recognized for defining Demand Management as influencing the level, timing, and composition of demand to accomplish a company's business objectives and goals. The Kotler approach to Demand Management can be thought of as a holistic activity involving both planning and execution of demand (see Figure 2.2).

In order to make better decisions about demand and to manage demand well, it helps for business leaders to first establish the definition of demand in their business. The word *demand* is often used, but frequently understood differently by different people.

Demand is what your customers need, when and where they need it. This definition may sound overly simple, but it has several powerful implications.

First, the focus is on what a company's customers need, not what the company is capable of supplying. Given the definition of demand, the next step is that demand should be planned without being overly concerned about whether the products or services can be delivered by the supply organization. Separation of customer demand from supply capability is critical to better serving customers in the most profitable way. It enables the ability to identify gaps between anticipated demand and supply capability—and to resolve those gaps before they become problems or crises. This behavior is a best practice.

Defining what a customer needs can be a tricky exercise. A senior vice president of a chain of successful retail stores once pointed out to me that they didn't sell anything that anyone actually needed. Her definition of demand would substitute the word *want* for the word *need*. In my view, the difficulty with using the word *want* is that customers often don't know what they want.

---------------------------- **Demand Management** ----------------------------

Demand Planning	**Demand Execution**
• Plans all demand for products and services to support the marketplace	• Doing what is required to help make the demand happen
• Involves all functional areas that plan and execute demand-creating activities	• Prioritizing demand when supply is lacking
• Communicates the demand plan to those who need to know in order to perform their responsibilities	• Encompassing order entry, order promising, and prioritization
	• Measuring execution to better align plans and actions

Figure 2.2   The Difference Between Demand Planning and Demand Execution. © Oliver Wight International, Inc. Used with permission.

Nobody said managing demand was easy. As a marketer, influencing customers to buy a company's products and services is paramount. An excellent marketeer does the following well:

- Creates awareness of products and services with customers
- Demonstrates why customers should buy those products and services
- Explains why the marketeer's company is the best company to buy them from

Consider this quote from Steve Jobs: "We have a lot of customers, and we have a lot of research into our installed base. We also watch industry trends pretty carefully. But in the end, for something this complicated, it's really hard to design products by focus groups. A lot of times, people don't know what they want until you show it to them."[4]

I believe there is value in assessing both the wants and needs of customers. In either case, demand for a product or service reflects a customer wanting or needing it, and then acting accordingly to buy it.

It is important to note here that customers don't typically buy dollars, euros, or rupees (unless your company is a currency exchange). Customers buy products and services in a finite volume at an agreed upon price. That is why it is a best practice to express demand in both volume and value. Volume is a physical measurement, such as cartons, pounds, liters, or cases. Value is the corresponding revenue that will be generated from selling that volume of product at a specific price. This explanation may seem like a trivial point, but it is important to be explicit so that there is no confusion when demand is communicated.

As we have now started to illustrate, demand typically doesn't happen all on its own. This statement may be controversial for some people. I have worked with more than one cynic who thought that salespeople just stood around taking orders. It sometimes might appear that way, but in reality, there's nothing further from the truth. If you believe that salespeople do nothing, I suggest that you spend some time walking in their shoes, getting to know their day-to-day activities, and learning the challenges and obstacles that they face.

When I was responsible for Demand Management at a smartphone manufacturing company, it certainly felt like the orders just kept piling in regardless of what we did. But when I traced things back and kept asking why we were getting so many orders, I found there were many reasons why people bought smartphones; those reasons went far beyond the phones simply being available for sale.

A Vice President of Revenue Management at one of my clients said it well: "Sales don't materialize based on our declaration that we have inventory." At the smartphone company, the products fulfilled the needs that customers had expressed for secure mobile communications. The products also fit into the *wants* category, as having a smartphone was very much a status symbol at the time.

Knowing what consumers and customers want and need along with paying attention to how their desires shift over time is critical in planning demand. The degree of influence over demand may vary, but the premise that your company is doing *something* to create or influence the demand for your products is foundational. Demand doesn't happen without the efforts to influence people to buy your company's products and services.

With demand defined, we can now extend that understanding to a definition of a *demand plan*. Recall the differentiation between goals and plans—goals are results or outcomes, whereas plans are expressed as the actions that will deliver those results. The demand plan is therefore the set of planned actions that will create or influence demand for a company's products or services. It is the list of actions that the sales, marketing, and product management teams are going to take to influence customers to buy the company's products and services.

Appreciating that a demand plan can be thought of as a to-do list for sales and marketing can be a significant adjustment in the mindset of those who think of demand as just a number. Do you know what the product, sales, and marketing teams are doing to influence customers to buy your company's products and services, not just next week, or next quarter or this year, but next year and beyond? If you don't, you need to find out.

A demand plan communicates the actions that will be taken to influence demand as well as the expected result of those actions in terms of product or service volume and value. The inclusion of "when and where they need it" in the definition of demand is therefore critical.

To be actionable, a demand plan needs to be communicated over specific points of time with an appropriate level of detail—or what some people call *granularity*. This form of communication is termed a time-phased demand plan.

An "appropriate level of granularity" refers to specifying what is expected to be sold in a specific time period with enough detail to be useful. For example, the supply organization must plan to acquire materials and manufacture products in the near term. The supply plan may need to be time phased in daily or weekly points of time, or what is known as time buckets. The supply organization's need for this level of granularity in demand information over the short term may require that the demand plan likewise be communicated in that same level of granularity.

In the longer term—over the next month, quarter, or year—it usually is unnecessary to communicate demand plans at that level of detailed granularity. It is sufficient to plan at a category or product family level in monthly time buckets, or what is often called the aggregate level.

As for "where customers need the product," knowing the location to warehouse and ship the product can be essential. That is what enables planning the logistics of timely and most cost-effective delivery to customers.

The previously mentioned planning examples focus on the information in the demand plan that the supply organization needs in order to develop its own plans. Keep in mind that there are other stakeholders as well who use the demand plan to create their own plans. These stakeholders include the finance, product management, and strategy organizations. These other organizations may require that the demand plan be expressed at different levels of detail over different time horizons. The demand plan must serve the needs of all stakeholders (see Chapter 6 for more detail). This is a best practice.

The over-arching goal of Demand Management is to create a trustworthy demand plan, and then execute it. The best way to develop a credible demand plan is to base the plan on reality and reflect the truth. To create trustworthy plans, the commercial organization must ensure that the plans are unbiased and reflect the best estimate of what customers will order. The plan should not turn out to be consistently high or consistently low. The commercial organization should feel as likely to over-deliver a demand plan as to under-deliver it.

When a demand plan has a bias (consistently high or consistently low when compared to actual sales), it creates a strong incentive for other stakeholders to second-guess or disregard it. Second-guessing undermines the value of cross-functional planning. Finance will be tempted to create its own forecast, for example, and so will the supply organization. These forecasts will suffer from lack of ownership by the commercial organizations. The forecasts inevitably will be misaligned with other functional plans, as was the case with SmartCorp. The importance of cross-functional planning will be explained in more detail in the next chapter.

With a better understanding of demand and the users of the demand plan, it is time to consider the definition and best practices of demand planning.

A best practice demand planning process involves developing, influencing, reaching agreement, and communicating what the commercial organization intends for customers to buy. The most effective demand planning processes consider what is likely to happen in the future that will result in demand for a company's products and services. This view of the future usually considers:

- Various perspectives of the marketplace
- Knowledge of competitors' pricing and product plans
- Understanding a company's own internal strategies, capabilities, and actions to generate demand

Understanding what is likely to happen (or is desired to happen) in the future requires collecting information and creating assumptions about what the company will offer and what customers are expected to buy in the future. The information and assumptions should not be taken at face value. They should be evaluated, cross-checked with members of the commercial team, and discussed. This analysis and discussion should lead to agreeing to a set of actions, responses, and expected results that optimize how products and services are commercialized, marketed, and sold.

Demand Management, critically, involves the commitment to follow the demand plan and execute it accordingly. Recall that Jacob, the Senior Vice President of Sales at SmartCorp, was not committed to executing the demand plan that Colin, the Senior Vice President of Supply, convinced Katia, the CEO, to approve. Also, recall the result: SmartCorp did not achieve the expected sales revenue.

This is why I am very careful not to confuse the term *forecast* with plan. People feel much more accountable to execute a plan than to make an accurate prediction or forecast. It is true that the demand plan will include some degree of forecasting. Not every assumption in a demand plan is completely within the commercial team's control. But agreeing on the plan means agreeing to execute the plan—and communicating when conditions change that put that commitment at risk. This is a best practice.

At one point during my time with a food manufacturer, I was responsible for planning demand for cough drops. Of the factors that influenced customers to buy our company's cough drops, two factors stood out: first, the price of the cough drops. Second, the level of seasonal cold and flu sickness. At the time, a single case of the flu would, on average, create demand for eleven cough drops.

The level of seasonal cold and flu sickness was completely outside our control. We did, however, make an assumption as to what the sickness levels would be. This assumption was derived from historical trends. Once the assumption was agreed upon, we monitored actual cold and flu sickness levels and adjusted our assumptions and resulting projections accordingly.

The price of cough drops, by contrast, was completely within our control. It was up to us to set the price. We made assumptions about our competitors' pricing, and our pricing decisions were influenced by the competitive environment.

The point of this example is that the demand plan must consider what is in a company's control and what is outside a company's control. Along with the demand plan numbers and time phasing of that plan, a demand plan should clearly convey both types of assumptions (we will talk more about assumptions in Chapter 7).

According to the definition of demand, a demand plan should also include the activities of developing new products and services. In practice, however, these activities are often split into separate but connected portfolio plans.

A portfolio plan defines the activities and expected results of evolving the portfolio of products and services that are offered to the market over time. The time horizon for a portfolio plan typically covers two to three years, but in some cases may be much longer, depending on industry circumstances. This plan includes new products being introduced; existing products being changed, repositioned, or sold into new geographies or channels; and existing products being removed and discontinued. The portfolio plan identifies and allocates the required resources, which might include investments in capital, research and development, regulatory, legal, quality, and other factors.

A portfolio plan has at its core a list of every project or initiative that is being actively worked on by the business that would impact the product portfolio (see Figure 2.3). This list is often referred to as the project master plan. New products are a vital part of the portfolio plan, but other types of projects or initiatives are as well. Some examples include projects that require substantial investment in time and money to reduce product costs, adjust product formulations to meet compliance requirements, retire or discontinue products, modernize critical production assets, and secure regulatory approval to launch an existing product in a new market.

Having a project master plan is the first step in developing a portfolio plan. I have, on more than one occasion, worked with companies to develop the project master plan and found business leaders surprised at what was being worked on. Typical reactions included: "Didn't we cancel that project three months ago?" or "Why are we working on a cost reduction for a product that we're about to discontinue?" These types of questions (and issues) surfaced simply by putting together the list and sharing it with business leaders.

Establishing integrity of the project master plan is the second step of portfolio planning. The timelines, milestones, volumes, margins, and other key data points associated with each of the projects must reflect reality—at least the most realistic assumptions that are available. For example, the projects and timelines in the portfolio plan must be balanced against the resources to deliver them, such as research and development capacity. If the project master plan lists 10 projects to be delivered next year, but the research and

Project	Family	Type	1st Year	Q1	Q2	Q3	Q4	Q5	Q6	Q7	Q8
Sierra	Family A	NPD	$52MM								
Blue	Family A	NPD	$1.5MM								
Continental	Family B	VE	$450K					NEW			
Purple	Family A	NPD	$30MM							NEW	
Tiger	Family A	VE	$150K								
Lexington	Family C	EPD	$200K								
Sunrise	Family C	EPD	$300K				NEW				NEW
Mustang	Family C	NPD	$140K								
Total Number				0	1	1	3	1	0	1	1

NPD	New Product Development
VE	Value Engineering
EPD	Existing Product Development

- OK
- ISSUE BUT CAN BE RESOLVED
- ISSUE BUT NEEDS TO BE RESOLVED

Figure 2.3 Example of Project Master Plan. © Oliver Wight International, Inc. Used with permission.

development team only has the capability to deliver five of them, then it isn't a valid plan. Similarly, if the projects themselves tend to be biased—either overly optimistic or pessimistic in terms of the volume or margin that they will deliver—then the plan won't be trusted.

Once the project master plan is validated, it then becomes a reliable input to both demand and supply planning. The commercial and supply sides of the business can rely on the project master plan for the latest information and see what is planned well beyond 12 months. This knowledge significantly reduces the churn and surprises that inevitably come from a portfolio plan that is anchored more in hope than reality.

Creating a *reliable* portfolio plan is not always easy. A common problem is that the same people who are being asked to create a sufficient pipeline of innovation are also establishing the volume and price projections that drive the business cases for new products. This overlap of duties can create an incentive for new product business cases to become overly optimistic. At one client, optimistic business cases were so chronic that the new president reduced volume projections in all new product business cases by 25 percent. The percentage of reduction coincided with the historical level of bias and underperformance in sales. The president's actions exposed another problem for the product development and commercial teams. They needed to develop additional products to create 25 percent more sales revenue or develop different strategies to boost the sales of the company's other new and existing products.

A key objective of Portfolio Management is to address the linkage of the portfolio plan with the company's strategy and goals. This linkage helps to ensure that the overall portfolio of products, services, and capital investments are aligned with the long-term strategic objectives of the business.

For example, Mondelez International established a strategic objective to achieve half of its revenue within five years from products that consumers considered healthier. This strategic objective was monitored through their Portfolio Management process. Attention focused on ensuring sufficient investment in initiatives that would create healthier snacks.[5]

Some people ask why portfolio planning is a separate and distinct activity from demand planning. The answer is that it reflects a company's organizational structure. Commercial activities for existing products and activities involving the development of new products are usually led by different executives. Here's an extreme example of this leadership separation in a high-technology business: the two activities were led by different CEOs, whereas in most companies, the leaders are vice presidents. This organizational distinction makes sense, whether at the CEO or vice presidential level. The required skill sets for new product development and commercial development involving sales and marketing are distinctly different.

To be clear, these activities are highly codependent, and should be integrated. One of the defining characteristics of IBP is the connectivity between Portfolio Management and Demand Management (see Chapter 4). That being said, plans must be owned by the executive leader who will direct the company resources to execute the plans. It would be futile to put a sales executive in charge of a portfolio plan if he or she did not have the authority to direct research and development activities.

I am frequently asked: Who should own the demand plan? Hopefully by this point, the answer is clear—a commercial leader in the organization must own the demand plan. Given that the demand plan reflects the planned sales and marketing activities of the organization, and that there must be commitment to execute that plan, only a sales or marketing leader could be accountable for it.

I am also being very intentional in saying that a commercial leader must own the demand plan. Sometimes, in the case of companies with different leaders of sales, marketing, and product management, there is a question as to which commercial leader that should be. The executive leader of the business must decide which commercial leader should own the demand plan. While the demand planning process requires multiple inputs and consensus, there must be one accountable owner of the plan.

I have seen organizations try to split ownership of the demand plan into different time horizons. For example, some people would argue that the top sales executive should own the near-term demand plan because the selling organization is closest to the customer. Therefore, the sales team should have the best perspective on what the customer will buy in the upcoming months. Similarly, some people believe the top executive for marketing or product management should own the long-term demand plan because these organizations have better insight into the long-range plans of the commercial side of the business.

This delineation of responsibility inevitably leads to problems. It fragments the planning process, leading to time and effort spent trying to figure out why planned demand in the two separate time horizons are inconsistent. When the short-term and long-term plans are joined together, it often becomes evident that different approaches, inputs, and assumptions are used by the different groups. Simply connecting the plans leads to something that makes little sense and is difficult if not impossible to explain. Worse, splitting the ownership accountability encourages behavior that is counterproductive and degrades collaboration and teamwork. Often, the two groups spend more time complaining about or blaming the other than reaching consensus on the plan for their horizon of responsibility. The following paragraph describes a case example.

At one client company, the Vice President of Sales was given ownership of the first two months in the planning horizon. The Vice President of Marketing was given ownership of everything beyond two months. When the demand plan transitioned from month three into month two of the sales horizon, the sales team frequently complained that the plan being handed over was unrealistic and inflated. It was not a plan that the selling organization could commit to executing. The marketing team, in response, complained that the sales organization wasn't pulling its weight and feared that the near-term plans would drive the wrong supply chain actions in response. Both groups spent more time criticizing the demand plan in the horizons that they did not own than they did focusing on the demand plan in the horizons that they did own.

It is worthy to consider why commercial business leaders decided to separate the two horizons in the first place. I think it's not too dissimilar from when my two boys would fight as children. My default response was to separate them and send them to their bedrooms. The problem with that approach is if you stop there, it doesn't teach them how to resolve their disagreements. Best practice is for leaders to work *on* the business together, as a team. That involves resolving disagreements rather than finding convenient ways to avoid conflict and live with a lack of consensus.

It is true that the sales organization generally is more focused on the near term—closing sales to customers (unless the company has extremely long lead times for selling; think of airline manufacturers and defense companies). This near-term focus naturally results in the selling organization generating many of the near-term assumptions, such as executing promotions, gaining distribution, securing contracts, etc.

Likewise, the focus of the marketing and product management organizations is frequently on the longer term. Their efforts to influence demand have longer lead times (think of the time it takes to design new products or developing branding and other marketing campaigns). This longer term focus naturally results in the marketing and product management teams generating many of the assumptions covering the longer term.

One commercial leader in the business must be assigned accountability bringing it all together. That leader is responsible for:

- Ensuring that assumptions are collected and incorporated into the demand plan decisions

- Making sure that consensus is reached on the demand plan over the entire planning horizon
- Making sure that there is commitment by the executives of sales, marketing, and product management to execute the demand plan

Choosing the business leader who should be accountable for, or owns, the demand plan is not always straightforward. The decision is often influenced by company strategy and the degree to which different commercial functions impact demand. It is also influenced by where decision-making authority is placed in the organization.

For example, in a company where growth is primarily being driven by geographic expansion led by the sales team, the Vice President of Sales would be the natural owner of the demand plan. Alternatively, in a product-driven company where growth is primarily the result of new product innovation, the product management leader would be a better fit.

It is not uncommon to find the role of demand planning being thought of as a supply chain activity. In many companies, demand planners are part of the supply chain organization. The demand planning function being in the supply organization isn't the result of someone having done something wrong per se. Often it reflects an outdated view of demand planning—one that is more heavily (or exclusively) based on forecasting than planning.

When the commercial side of the business fails to take responsibility, for whatever reason, for creating a robust demand plan, the supply side of the business often takes control out of necessity. There are two problems with that approach.

First, the supply organization is often detached (both organizationally and physically) from the functions responsible for marketing, product development, and sales. The supply organization is not accountable for generating demand and is not involved in knowing the actions that the commercial teams are taking to influence and generate demand.

Second, given that detachment, a demand plan generated by the supply organization often relies heavily on historical data and statistical modeling. The problem with this approach is that history doesn't always repeat itself. Models based on history alone rarely deliver a plan that meets business objectives. Models based predominantly on history and statistics do not consider the business decisions and commercial activities that will generate new demand in the future.

Also remember that you shouldn't have to forecast that which you already know. I often find demand planners spending more time predicting the behavior of salespeople than they do predicting the behavior of customers or consumers. One of these is a value-added activity and one is not when it comes to developing trustworthy, credible demand plans.

There may be many reasons why there is little appetite to shift the demand-planning function to the commercial side of the business. If that's the case, it is nonetheless important that the demand planners be perceived as part of the commercial team. Something as simple as having the demand planners physically located near their sales or marketing counterparts helps establish that relationship. It also facilitates demand planners to more easily know the commercial activities that are planned and how these activities will result in generating demand.

It is important to distinguish between being the accountable owner of the demand plan and being responsible for supporting the demand planning process by maintaining and updating the demand plan. A team outside of the sales or marketing functions may play the role of supporting the process. In fact, they may be best equipped to document the assumptions, perform analysis, and develop and update the time-phased plan. This is especially the case when an outside team has technical and analytical skills that the sales and marketing functions have not developed.

It is possible, and in many cases advisable, to achieve this best-of-both-worlds by the sharing of skills. For this arrangement to work, the team responsible for the process must remain properly equipped and supported to deliver what the relevant stakeholders need. This team also must be thoroughly trusted by the sales and marketing teams. A commercial leader of the business must accept accountability for owning the demand plan, and all commercial executives must accept accountability for reaching consensus on the plan and executing the plan.

Chapter 1 pointed out that plans need to be revisited and updated on a routine basis. It is common to be asked how frequently a demand plan should be updated. A demand plan is a living document and should be updated as needed to reflect new information and changes to assumptions. The frequency of your demand planning process should therefore follow the frequency with which new information is received.

Different time horizons may warrant updating the demand plan with different frequencies. Typically, a mid- to long-term demand plan, covering 4 to 24 months, is updated monthly. This frequency coincides with many inputs that tend to change monthly, such as:

- Month-end close reports where the prior month's sales volume and revenue are confirmed
- Receipt of syndicated point-of-sale data (such as Nielsen or IRI)

- Updates from the sales and marketing organization on customer plans and planned promotional activities
- Updates to customer relationship management systems to reflect new tenders or contracts
- Publication of industry reports and macroeconomic indicators

Updates of the demand plan in the near-term horizon, typically between one and three months, may be more frequent. Depending on the industry and circumstances, the demand plan within this horizon may need to be updated weekly, or even daily by exception.

Deciding on an appropriate frequency for updating the demand plan over specific planning horizons is a bit of a balancing act. On the one hand, it is important to know about new inputs as soon as possible to provide as much lead time as is necessary to digest and decide whether to adjust the demand plan. On the other hand, the cost versus the value of changing the plan must be considered, especially in the near-term horizon. Capturing planning inputs requires time and effort. Given supply lead times for making changes in the near term, it may be more practical to not alter the plan and manage delivery promising dates. Thinking about sales inputs, the trade-off of asking the sales team to spend time communicating changes to assumptions and numbers must be weighed against spending their time interacting with customers.

Considering how frequently to update plans is where the distinction between planning and execution becomes important. The planning activities for the longer term have a lower level of urgency, and it is usually sufficient to collect and review new information and update the plan on a monthly cadence. Changes that are within the execution horizon, typically between one and three months, can then be managed on an exception basis depending on the level of significance.

It is important to delineate between information and data—and how both are put to use in creating a credible demand plan. Technology makes it possible to acquire a growing amount of data that can be used in planning. As a result, more companies are attempting to consume large volumes of data on a more frequent basis, ostensibly for helping inform their decision making. Keep in mind, though, that just because we can, doesn't mean we should.

One example is the ability to perform *social listening*. Social listening technology collects data from various social networks in real time to monitor consumer sentiment and trends. Social listening certainly can serve as a helpful way to keep the consumer top of mind—but in a planning context, it has its drawbacks. Companies need to balance the availability of data with the capability to process and do something useful with it. Tracking consumer sentiment daily or hourly is not necessarily helpful for a process that updates its plans monthly. The value of a piece of information should be based on its ability to influence a decision. Gathering data and processing it into information that does not impact a decision is, therefore, a waste of energy and resources.

The smartphone maker dealt with these kinds of trade-offs as well. The primary attribute of its products was the speed with which email and other communications could be sent and received. The company's culture expected real-time visibility to everything. The company's demand-planning tools were initially configured to send a new demand plan to the supply planners four times per day. The result, in my view, was chaos. Imagine a conversation between a demand planner and supply planner: "Was that promotion accounted for in the demand plan at 9 a.m. on Tuesday or 12 p.m. on Wednesday?" The supply chain planners largely ignored the changes to the demand plan.

The company shifted from updating the demand plan four times per day to a weekly cadence and established demand/supply governance around that process. Despite fears that real-time visibility and, consequently, agility would be lost, performance to the demand plan improved. The company later shifted from weekly to monthly communication of demand plans, with communication of exceptions during the month as deemed appropriate. Again, performance improved.

The key to how frequently the demand plan changes were communicated was in determining the cadence at which the supply chain team could reasonably digest and respond to the demand plan. An important change in mindset also occurred. The company's leaders stopped fooling themselves into thinking they were more agile than they were. Changing a plan faster than you can execute those changes is futile. Doing so only introduces noise and confusion to the process and inhibits decision making and execution.

This book chiefly covers the process of developing a credible demand plan that is trusted by a company's business leaders and stakeholders. When consensus is reached on a demand plan that is considered credible, all stakeholders are expected to follow it. This is a best practice. The appropriate commercial actions are taken to generate demand and achieve the results articulated in the plan. The supply organization, in turn, takes the appropriate actions to deliver the volume and product mix within the timing communicated in the demand plan. This, too, is a best practice.

The best practices outlined in this book are anchored in the understanding that demand leads and drives the business. Hence the term *demand driven*, which is commonly used to describe best practice business models. In demand-driven businesses, demand planning requires cross-functional collaboration, alignment of plans, and teamwork. These, too, are best practices—and are the subject of the next chapter.

SUMMARY

- Leadership teams can't execute their way to achieving long-term goals; planning and replanning is required.
- The leaders of an organization are chiefly responsible for planning.
- Demand is what your customers need, when and where they need it.
- The demand plan has the following attributes:
    - A documented plan of actions that the commercial organization will take to drive or influence demand.
    - The communication of assumptions about what will influence customers to buy a company's products or services; these assumptions are a mix of what is within the control of a company and what is outside of the company's control.
    - A time-phased view of what a company's customers will order as a result of the aforementioned—expressed in both volume and value, and at an appropriate level of detail for the time horizon.
    - This time-phased view is unconstrained by what people in the commercial organization think that the supply organization is capable of delivering.
    - An unbiased view of demand; the demand plan numbers are not adjusted based on making corporate or the board happy, or pleasing one's boss—the demand plan is based on reality and what is most likely to happen.
- The demand plan is owned by a commercial leader, typically a sales or marketing executive.
- The demand plan is updated regularly to reflect the latest information, but not more frequently than necessary to be useful for decision making.

QUESTIONS TO ASK

- Where does your leadership team spend most of its time? Planning or executing?
- How often are your company's operating plans checked against business objectives? How often against strategy?

- How executable are your company's operating plans? Is there trust that the operating plans will be followed and will deliver the expected results?
- Is ownership of the demand plan clear? Do sales and marketing leaders take accountability for executing it?

ENDNOTES

1. George Palmatier and Colleen Crum. *The Transition from Sales and Operations Planning to Integrated Business Planning: Practices and Principles, Second Edition.* J. Ross Publishing, Inc., 2022.
2. Jim Matthews and Leon Dixon. *Is Your S&OP or IBP Process Delivering the Results You Expected.* Oliver Wight Americas. www.oliver wight-americas.com.
3. Philip Kotler. *The Father of Modern Marketing.* pkotler.org.
4. Interview with Steve Jobs. BusinessWeek. May 25, 1998.
5. "Mondelez to Boost Ad Spending, Healthier Offerings." CNBC, September 10, 2015. https://www.cnbc.com/2015/09/10/mondelez-to-boost -ad-spending-healthier-offerings.html.

CHAPTER 3

WORKING AS A TEAM

Take a minute to think about your favorite team sport. If you don't have a favorite, I, as a Canadian, would suggest ice hockey, but the specific sport doesn't really matter. What matters is that we think about what distinguishes the best teams from the mediocre teams. Do the best teams have the most-skilled players? Do they have the best equipment and facilities? What really makes a great team great?

Sure, having skilled players is important; but putting together a great team takes more than what any individual player brings to the table. Consider these quotes from respected sports figures:

"Talent wins games, but teamwork and intelligence
win championships."[1]

—Michael Jordan

"Individual commitment to a group effort—that is what makes
a team work, a company work, a society work, a civilization
work."[2]

—Vince Lombardi

"I think that from the time you start playing sports as a child
you see that your responsibility to your team is to play the
best that you can play as an individual . . . and yet, not take
anything away from being part of a team."[3]

—Wayne Gretzky

"No cricket team in the world depends on one or two players.
The team always plays to win."[4]

—Virat Kohli

Successful teams work together to achieve common goals. This statement is just as applicable in business as it is in sport. Every member of a team has a position to play. If team members don't play as a team or if team members decide to play someone else's position as well as their own, the success of the team degrades and the team will be outmaneuvered by the competition.

In Chapter 1 we established the distinction between plans and goals. Plans are what enable goals to be achieved. This concept is widely accepted, but that leads to the question: Which goals are we trying to achieve?

In business, as in sport, establishing and understanding common goals is critical to success. Think back to my family vacation example in Chapter 1. Planning the family trip together was a way for us to share our individual desires and establish some common goals. We were able to achieve everyone's individual goals without much conflict. That made it easy to declare the vacation a success.

In business, the process of goal setting is not always so easy. Lack of conflict can seem the exception rather than the rule. Goals must strike a balance between being achievable and being challenging. When that balance isn't achieved, performance suffers. Individuals will decide on their own whether the juice is worth the squeeze, so to speak. If goals are too aggressive, people will opt out. If goals are too conservative, people may not be sufficiently incentivized to perform their best.

With a family vacation, the family sets the goals. In business, some goals may be self-established, others may be negotiated, and some may be handed down and assigned. Goals, therefore, must be communicated, understood, and respected in order for them to drive the right behaviors.

Tension or conflict between a broader team's goals and the goals of individual team members is common. When conflicts occur, the most effective teams put the team's success first. To do so, all team members need to understand the team's objectives and how these objectives may differ from their own personal objectives. That way, they can understand where there might be misalignments and how they may need to adjust.

Let's use an example from a company that asked me to help them improve their planning capability. Speaking to the sales and marketing teams, I asked how they were involved in the demand planning process. The answers were consistent. They met with the demand planners to set a forecast for what products should be made available for them to sell. The forecast, which included volume and timing, was based on the sales and marketing plans. The revenue growth goals were well understood. The sales and marketing teams knew that to achieve the growth goals, the manufacturing organization would have to deliver the product when and where it was needed. They had concerns about the manufacturing organization's ability to ensure the right product was available in the right mix, volume, and timing. This concern caused them to increase the volume in the demand forecast. That way, in their minds, they could ensure that product availability would never run short.

I then spoke to the demand planners. They knew that the forecasts coming from sales and marketing were typically inflated. One planner put it succinctly: "I'd rather be slapped for missing the inventory target, than shot for missing a sale."

In other words, when orders were cut or shorted, the sales leaders expressed their dissatisfaction. The demand planners spent a lot of time and energy responding to the sales leaders' questions and criticisms.

The demand planners rarely felt the same discomfort when it came to missing inventory targets. They were conditioned to believe that the company's top objectives were to maximize revenue and customer service. Working capital, cash flow, and profits were secondary considerations.

I then spoke to the head of manufacturing, who expressed frustration. He told me that his team had to second-guess the demand plan because it was so inflated. He didn't have a blank check to buy and store inventory.

"It's not like supply is an open bar," he said. But the escalations from sales leaders when an order was fulfilled late were real and painful.

The head of manufacturing's solution highlighted the misalignment between the business functions. He knew he was accountable for achieving an inventory goal, but came to believe it only really mattered once a year. In December, the finance team scrutinized inventory investment. That's when they would measure inventory for external financial reporting. While the manufacturing leader knew that the demand plan was problematic throughout the year, he only had to tackle inventory head-on at the end of the year.

For eleven months of the year, the company operated with a mix of second-guessing, excess inventory, and less-than-ideal but not catastrophic service levels. In December, all hell broke loose. The factories were shut down to force achievement of the inventory goal to satisfy annual financial expectations. Customer service performance plummeted, and customers were furious. The head of manufacturing planned his vacation well in advance each year for the month of December.

In this example, who is at fault? Sales and marketing provided forecasts that they knew were inflated, but they were doing it to enable achieving their revenue goals. Manufacturing shut down the factories without notice, but it was to achieve their inventory goal. No one's hands were clean. Each player acted in their own self-interest, with little conscious consideration of the interest of the business.

In this case, like in many other companies, rules or guidelines for resolving conflicts between goals had not been established. It wasn't clear whether achieving inventory goals should be prioritized over the achievement of revenue goals.

Accountability for establishing these rules lies with the most senior leader of the business. In this case, it was the president. After the situation was explained to them, the president and executive team decided that they needed to change. They agreed to implement a more robust integrated planning process that would enable them to make the tough trade-off decisions.

Another lesson from this company's experience was that setting goals in functional silos and then hoping that everything would work itself out is usually not successful. It is possible for both business-wide and functional goals to be achieved. Many companies accomplish this feat routinely. But it does not happen without coordination. That coordination comes through collaboration and trust.

Just like players on a sports team, functional leaders must trust each other to share their plans for achieving both their personal goals and the business's goals. They must also trust that the plans that are being shared will be executed. Leaders must have confidence that their peers will *say what they do and do what they say*. The functional plans should be shared and reconciled with each other to ensure that the plans are compatible, and when executed, will achieve the company objectives.

Here's another example of the nuances of sharing and trusting functional objectives. A company has a goal to improve profit margins. That goal was established by the board of directors based on benchmarking of peer companies.

Increased profit margin can come from a variety of sources. One option is to influence the mix of products being sold, favoring those with higher profit margins. Another option is to reduce product costs without influencing or changing demand. In this case, the company president decided to assign the manufacturing organization the goal of reducing product costs. He left it to the manufacturing leader to decide the best way to achieve this goal.

The manufacturing leader decided to set a goal of improving manufacturing efficiency, but he knew that achieving this goal could not be accomplished by the manufacturing organization alone. The demand plan was chronically inaccurate. As a result, disruptions to the schedule hampered the ability to improve manufacturing efficiency.

The manufacturing leader turned to the leaders of the sales and marketing organizations to see if they had compatible goals. He specifically asked whether they were focused on improving demand plan accuracy.

After discussions, the sales and marketing leaders committed to a goal of improving demand plan accuracy. The manufacturing leader knew he would have to trust that the sales and marketing organizations would actively pursue achieving that goal. The sales and marketing leaders would also have to trust him to improve manufacturing efficiency. They knew that this was being done to achieve the company goal in order to improve profit margins, and the alternative would be for them to find ways to influence the mix of products being sold.

This type of activity, where the plans for achieving functional and company goals are reconciled, should occur at a minimum during the annual planning and strategic planning goal-setting process. When an annual budget is set, it is important to confirm that inventory, cost, revenue growth, and customer service targets are aligned. I have seen organizations set targets that are mathematically impossible to achieve. When this situation occurs, it almost always ends up pitting one function against the other. Setting unachievable goals causes infighting and shifting of blame. The company's business leaders spend too much energy focused internally on a self-induced problem. I firmly believe that the quickest way to hobble a company is to set unachievable goals.

While goals usually stay fixed over a longer period (years or more), goals and latest plans should be reconciled routinely (monthly). This is a best practice. As we noted in Chapter 1, business conditions change, both externally and internally. Over time, certain functional goals may become difficult to achieve for various reasons or the plans that one function creates to achieve its goals may create problems for another function.

For the company that had the goal to increase profit margin, here's what happened—the market conditions changed. It was more advantageous for the sales and marketing teams to pursue growth in other regions. Therefore, the drawback was that there would be more volatility in demand, which almost always creates challenges for demand plan accuracy.

The trade-off to pursue growth over improving demand plan accuracy was the right commercial (and sales revenue growth) decision, all things being equal. However, the decision limited the manufacturing organization's ability to increase manufacturing efficiency in their effort to improve profit margin.

As each function adjusts plans to achieve their goals, the recalibrated plans need to be coordinated and tested with other functional plans to ensure that all company goals are being met. The sharing and alignment of functional plans is a skill that is often lacking in companies. It also may be very uncomfortable to reveal the plans to those outside the business function.

The point I'm trying to make is essential to achieving business and financial goals. Business leaders can't simply put their heads down and focus only on their own departments. They must trust and work with cross-functional counterparts to synchronize plans. Doing so ensures that what they are doing as a team will enable business objectives to be achieved. It is often the difference between success and failure.

Recall the SmartCorp example from Chapter 1. Jacob, the Senior Vice President of Sales, changed his plan in pursuit of the goal that was assigned to him. He included sales of new product in the demand plan to achieve the financial goal. He did not communicate this decision and the revised plans to Colin's supply organization, however. The supply organization should have had the chance to evaluate and respond to the revised demand plan.

This chain of events started when Jacob's peers did not trust the demand plan that he had communicated to Katia, the CEO, in the first place. The most senior business leader is accountable for establishing compatible goals for the business. They are also accountable for ensuring that functional plans are aligned. When the plans are not aligned, they are accountable for making sure the trade-off decisions are made. In SmartCorp's case, Katia, as CEO, owned that responsibility, but failed to fulfill it.

Why do many companies struggle with sharing and aligning functional plans? One reason is that when plans are shared, leaders will sometimes be forced to face reality. They will have to make tough choices that sacrifice personal or functional goals in support of the broader business health. These are uncomfortable choices.

Using the team sport analogy, in ice hockey, players have a decision to make when the puck is passed to them. One choice is to take the puck down the ice on their own to attempt to score a goal. They may have significant incentive to do so. They may be close to breaking a personal record or may believe that better scoring statistics will make them more marketable as a player. They also may not trust their teammates' ability to score a goal. Another choice is to pass the puck to another player who is in a better position and can make a coordinated play.

Faced with this decision many times, how are players who always go it alone regarded by their teammates? Do the other players respect them? Will others pass the puck to them? How does this selfishness impact the team's win-loss record?

Consider this sports analogy in a business context. Collaborating with other business functions is often an adjustment for sales and marketing leaders. They cannot go it alone and expect to win the game. They often must consider broader implications when establishing commercial plans.

When focused on the betterment of the entire business, a shift in thinking occurs. Sales and marketing leaders become more mature in their thinking about the demand plan. They consider the demand plan a request for product that they are accountable for selling.[5] The manufacturing organization is rarely an open bar, so to speak. Supply planners should not be forced to guess which of the demand mix, volume, or timing in the plan is going to come true, and which are hedges against possible poor performance from the manufacturing organization.

Similarly, the supply chain organization's thinking shifts. They know the pitfalls of second-guessing the demand plan. The role of supply chain organization is to create a supply plan in response to the demand plan. This supply plan considers inventory, cost, and service level parameters that are deemed optimal.

Coordinating and synchronizing plans across functions enables coordinated responses to changes regarding both problems and opportunities. Doing so creates agility. When business leaders play their positions and trust their teammates to do what they say they are going to do in their plans, something else happens. Responding to change becomes much simpler, and in some cases, effortless.

Take, for example, an organization where the sales, marketing, and finance functions create their own separate forecasts. Imagine business leaders trying to decide whether or not to approve a customer promotion. The leaders will not understand whether the promotion is incremental to, or already included in, any of the different forecasts. They will not understand which demand forecast the supply chain used to develop its production plan. It becomes very difficult to make the investment decision, let alone predict the outcome of the promotion.

Business leaders also would find it difficult to effectively respond to competitors' moves. If competitors were to raise prices, introduce a new product, or exit a market, which forecast and information would be relied upon to assess the impact on the business? Which forecast would be used to understand the most effective actions to take in response? One forecast may have predicted the competitor's moves—another may not.

Situations like the one just described arise when functional leaders resist sharing and aligning their functional plans. What happens when the sales and marketing teams fail to share their commercial plans with the finance or supply chain organizations? Those functions are forced to develop their own forecasts of demand. What happens when the manufacturing or supply chain team fails to share its supply plan? The sales, marketing, and finance organizations are forced to create their own projections of what will be available to sell.

The result of failing to share plans is often a dangerous pattern of self-constraint. The sales team will hesitate to make commitments to customers when there is uncertainty as to what can be delivered. The supply organization hesitates to commit to making product when there is uncertainty as to whether the product orders will be received. The finance team will make their best estimates of sales revenue, margins, and cash flow—all of which may not reflect reality.

Whether or not any given plan is the best one, the team should never be confused over which plan is being followed or that there even is one. There should be one demand plan, to which the commercial leaders of the organization hold themselves accountable. There should be one supply plan, to which the supply chain leaders of the organization hold themselves accountable. Those plans should be published, shared, and aligned.

My colleague Jim Matthews often reminds me that we can afford to be wrong (in fact, at times, we most certainly will be wrong), but we can't afford to be confused. When something is wrong, we can work through the issue and get back on track. When a team or a business is confused, it can seem impossible to know what steps need to be taken to get back on track, like a mouse running through a maze and ending up on a wheel that goes nowhere. It certainly will be time-consuming to determine the best course of action.

Remember, too, that regular synchronization of cross-functional plans is also a key to empowering teams to execute. Recall from Chapter 2 that when business leaders are not confident that the plans that are being deployed by their teams will meet business objectives, they micromanage. They often are reluctant to step back and let their teams execute the plans. Their time is spent focusing *in* the business rather than *on* the business, which can marginalize future business performance.

Working together across functions to proactively identify and work through misalignments is a far more productive approach. It is much better than looking in the rearview mirror and trying to explain who was at fault for a failure (like in the SmartCorp example). So much so, that when executives who have become accustomed to a proactive, collaborative environment move to a new organization where trust and teamwork are lacking, they are often quick to give me a call.

Companies that develop a strong planning capability go beyond establishing just one course of action. When planning capabilities are strong, business leaders and their direct reports are liberated from dealing with day-to-day execution issues. They have the time and energy to regularly evaluate alternatives and contingencies. They can shift their focus to what might happen in the market, with their competitors, with their suppliers, and their internal capabilities. They can focus on how to best respond (as necessary) to changing conditions. They also can consider the best responses to stay on track in achieving business objectives.

Evaluating potential changes is sometimes called *what-if* planning or *scenario* planning. It is the antithesis to wishful thinking.[6] When scenario planning occurs regularly and with honesty, business leaders realize these advantages in focusing on the business. Responding to change becomes nearly effortless. Potential changes are anticipated, and the most appropriate response is agreed to *cross-functionally* in advance. The company can respond more swiftly to change, giving it a leg up on their competition. Scenario planning, and how it enables organizations to achieve their goals more consistently, will be discussed in more detail in Chapter 9.

When contingencies are planned, execution is much easier. Business leaders have provided their organizations a playbook that explains: if X happens, Y is our response. It is critical that the response is coordinated—we all move left or we all move right, but critically, we all move together. Consider the following example.

The Hershey Company had a choice to make. In the midst of a global pandemic, they had to decide how to approach the fall Halloween season. The uncertainty was unprecedented. Thankfully, The Hershey Company had implemented a robust Integrated Business Planning (IBP) process. They were able to use the process to align and synchronize plans, and evaluate different scenarios.

Without the discipline created by the IBP process, planning the highly uncertain Halloween season would have been an opportunity for confusion and misalignment to run rampant. Instead, The Hershey Company leaned on its rigor of being planful. This rigor allowed them to make a strategic decision on how to best service their customers during the uncertain Halloween season. That decision paid off not only because it was the right plan, but because all functions were aligned on the plan and were able to follow through in executing it.

Michelle G. Buck, President and CEO, commented while discussing the quarterly results: "Our decision to lean into Halloween ahead of the season supported consumers' desires to find new and creative ways to celebrate safely. Our team, advantaged brands, capabilities, and execution enabled us to deliver Halloween net sales slightly above prior year and estimated category seasonal share gains of over 400 basis points."[7]

In the following chapters, we will cover in more detail the Demand Management best practices that build trust. This trust encompasses the commercial functions of the business (sales, marketing, and product development) becoming trusted team players. It also encompasses working as part of the broader business team to achieve company goals.

SUMMARY

- Both goals and plans need to be aligned cross-functionally to ensure they are compatible and will deliver expected results for the business, not just for the function.
- Plans need to be recalibrated routinely (typically monthly), as each function adjusts their plans in response to changing business conditions while in pursuit of their functional goals.
- The most senior business executive (President, General Manager, or CEO) is accountable for resolving conflicts with functional goals and making appropriate trade-off decisions in pursuit of company goals.
- There should be only one demand plan, and this plan is owned by the commercial organization (sales and marketing). There should be only one supply plan, and this plan is owned by the supply chain organization. Those plans must be aligned to ensure that they will achieve the company's overall business goals and strategies.
- Companies that develop a strong planning capability go beyond establishing just one course of action and will consider different scenarios.

QUESTIONS TO ASK

- Are your business goals and objectives believed to be achievable when they are set?
- Do leaders from different functions trust each other to say what they do and do what they say?
- Does your company operate with multiple forecasts created independently by sales, marketing, finance, and supply chain?
- Are leaders reluctant to share their plans openly and transparently with each other?
- Are cross-functional trade-offs highlighted and decided on in a routine way?

ENDNOTES

1. Michael Jordan. *I Can't Accept Not Trying: Michael Jordan on the Pursuit of Excellence*. Harper, San Francisco, 1994, p. 129.
2. Vince Lombardi. Famous Quotes by Vince Lombardi, Family of Vince Lombardi. 2022. http://www.vincelombardi.com/quotes.html.

Working as a Team 41

3. Wayne Gretzky. Wayne Gretzky Quotes. BrainyQuote. https://www
.brainyquote.com/quotes/wayne_gretzky_454032.
4. Virat Kohli. Virat Kohli Quotes. BrainyQuote. https://www.brainy
quote.com/quotes/virat_kohli_623205.
5. Ron Ireland. "Demand Planning: Where Does it Fit in the Organization?" Oliver Wight Americas, 2013. www.oliverwight-americas.com.
6. Pamelyn Lindsey, R. Hirschey, and C. Groven. "Scenario Planning
Has Never Been More Important." Oliver Wight Americas. www.oliver
wight-americas.com.
7. Monica Watrous. "Hershey Outpaces Category during Tricky Halloween Season." Food Business News RSS, Food Business News, November 9, 2020. https://www.foodbusinessnews.net/articles/17246
-hershey-outpaces-category-during-tricky-halloween-season.

CHAPTER 4

GAINING ALIGNMENT THROUGH INTEGRATED BUSINESS PLANNING

Over the years I have worked with leaders having varying degrees of confidence and capability. There tends to be a pattern. The most capable leaders are not afraid to share their plans with their peers. One leader was so open to transparency that even his personal calendar was visible for everybody in the organization to see. He wasn't concerned with people questioning or challenging how he was spending his time.

Not everyone is that confident or capable, however. Sharing and aligning plans with leaders of other business functions can often be uncomfortable. Functional leaders may face questioning, and ultimately may have to make difficult decisions to align plans cross-functionally in support of company-level objectives. Functional (and often personal) sacrifices may need to be made for the greater good.

In some cases, leaders may simply lack the confidence to discuss options and then make the tough choices. Thus, they avoid sharing their plans. In other cases, the information being shared is not trusted. In situations where there is a lack of trust, people will question why a sacrifice or decision is necessary in the first place.

This was exactly the situation with a certain electronics manufacturer. This client operated in an extremely competitive market. Timelines for new product development were often compressed to ensure that they were first to market with an innovation. The timelines frequently were not based on what was achievable with the resources that had been allocated to the projects. Instead, timelines were often based on when product management leaders believed new products or technologies needed to be delivered to the market to remain competitive. The accelerated timelines were often unrealistic, and therefore, launch dates were routinely missed. There simply was not enough time and resources to release the products when promised.

Missed launch dates became the norm in the view of the sales team. Not trusting the promised launch dates, the sales team reduced their demand plan for new products. It wasn't that they didn't believe in the viability of the new products. They didn't believe that the product management team would launch them on time.

The sales team planned to sell more of existing, older products even when knowing competitors that launched new products on time would have an advantage. What choice did the sales team really have? They feared experiencing a double whammy. The new products would be late and not available to ship. If they trusted the launch date, they would not be able to include demand for the old product in the plan. There would be nothing to sell. Customers would become confused and probably impatient with the lack of product.

The finance organization also became concerned about the viability of the new products. They were well aware of the disconnect between the product plans and the demand plans. The volume demand plan was much lower than what had been initially communicated in the business cases prepared by the product management team.

The supply organization was equally concerned. Should the supply plans be based on the product management plan or the demand plan?

If honesty and trust had prevailed, all the functional leaders would have openly faced making tough trade-off decisions. To launch the new products on time and ahead of competition, they would have had to assess whether the compressed timelines could realistically be met. If the timelines could not be met, they would have to assess the viability of being second or third to market with the new technology.

No one, including the CEO, wanted to deal with the consequences of the tough decisions. The consequences clashed with the cultural mentality that *failure is not an option*. Nobody was confident enough to deal with the issue, nor capable of solving it on their own.

Ironically, that mentality led to repeated failures to launch products on time. Fear of failure cemented it. If they had addressed the issue and worked together as a team, they may have had a chance of solving the issues that caused the launch of new products to be delayed. Put another way, hope is not a good strategy.

I have guided business leaders of other clients where trust in the information was not a problem. They struggled with another impediment to decision making: the perception that trade-off decisions were made unfairly. This perception was compounded in several cases by an inflexible incentive or compensation model that directly rewarded the wrong behaviors.

One of my clients is organized by product brands. Each brand business is led by a different marketing director. All the brand businesses share a common production line.

In times of labor shortages in the production facility, decisions were made to allocate production between the brands. The supply organization did not make the allocation decision. The decision was made by the sales leaders. The sales organization's incentive program was based on achievement of revenue growth targets. Prioritizing production for the brands that were bought in the highest volumes allowed for more efficient use of the production line, resulting in greater sales revenue. These brands were called *power brands*.

The leaders of the lower volume, smaller brands believed prioritizing based on sales volume and revenue overlooked profit margins. The smaller brands often generated much higher profit margins than the power brands. The marketing director argued that the decision-making process was flawed and unfair. The fact that their brands were being marginalized did not just impact those brands. It also impacted cash generation for the business, given the favorable profit margins of the smaller brands.

The marketing director of the smaller brands responded in a way that I do not recommend, although I do understand the temptation. She resorted to gaming the system by inflating forecasts for the small brands in the hope that allocation decisions would give greater priority to the lower volume, higher margin brands. Increased allocation would also give her team a better chance to achieve bonus incentives. The marketing director inflated the forecasts with the belief that she was compensating for an existing, unfair process that was not in the best interests of the company, let alone her team.

This example highlights the problem of flawed incentive models and decision-making processes that appear unfair. When people game the system and purposefully share inaccurate information in the demand plan, business leaders lose trust in it. They eventually will realize the demand plan is biased.

I am often approached by functional leaders—usually from the supply chain—asking for help to solve the problem of plans that are not credible. Their seemingly straightforward request is typically, "Can you help me fix the demand planning process? I can't get the sales and marketing leaders to be honest with me."

Solving this problem is not straightforward. A lasting solution usually requires the intervention of the most senior leader. That is, the President, General Manager, or CEO. The most senior leader must take ownership and accountability for the process of routinely aligning and synchronizing plans.

Why can't this accountability be delegated? The reason is simple: when the business leaders don't trust one another to share credible information to run the business, it thwarts all sorts of collaborative efforts. Business leaders certainly won't trust one another to establish a cross-functional planning process that aligns and synchronizes plans. They also will hesitate or resist making functional sacrifices for the good of the business.

The challenges of trust are rooted in human behavior that often values self above all others. For example, supply chain leaders are often rejected when they try to work with other functional leaders. They are seen as *not minding their own business*. Sales leaders say they have no time for process improvement; supply chain leaders just need to get their own houses in order and deliver product to customers on time. Supply chain leaders counter that they have no problem fulfilling orders on time when they receive an accurate demand plan. It's a standoff that remains unresolved until the senior most leader in the business intervenes.

Thankfully, there is a way out for the senior executive, his or her leadership team, and their managers; it is called Integrated Business Planning (IBP). The IBP process is how business leaders routinely reach consensus on a single operating plan. The executive team first holds themselves accountable for reaching consensus on a plan. They then hold themselves accountable for allocating the critical resources of people, equipment, inventory, materials, time, and money so the plan can be executed.

For decades IBP has proven to be the most reliable way for the most senior executive of an organization to manage the business with his or her business leaders. An effective IBP process ensures that the executive team agrees on how the functional plans are aligned and synchronized. It also is how executives make sure that trade-off decisions are made with the broader organizational goals and objectives in mind. It is the way they can work *on* the business, and not get caught up working *in* it.

Done well, IBP is the formal way that the business is managed. Many executives and managers say they would not work in a company that does not practice IBP.[1] It is now common for Presidents and CEOs to implement IBP when they join companies that do not have the process in place.[2]

An effective IBP process enables a company leadership team to answer these vital questions every month:

1. Do we still agree on the goals that have been established, or are changes needed?
2. Will our current operating plans enable us to achieve the stated goals?
3. If not, what do we need to change or do differently?

The answers to the previous questions are made possible by updating functional plans and then aligning all the plans every month. Updating the plans and reconciling misalignments are what ensures that cross-functional issues are exposed and addressed. It also exposes gaps in business performance.

This approach for executives to manage the business is key to being able to respond to changes—both internal and external. It is also key to avoiding surprises that jeopardize business performance (see Figure 4.1).

When the senior most executive leads and owns IBP, trust is enhanced in the organization, from the leadership team all the way down the chain of command. With the President or CEO in the lead, their involvement diffuses, to a significant degree, the perception that the process is in service of one function or group. IBP doesn't solve the issue of lack of trust in an organization on its own. It does provide the forum to address where trust is lacking and where information being shared is not trustworthy.

Many of the key principles that underpin IBP result in establishing trust and credibility. These principles include:

- Portfolio plans that are checked and balanced against available resources to ensure that projects are completed on time and on budget
- Demand plans that are objectively measured and corrected to eliminate bias
- Supply plans that are based on realistic, demonstrated capacity and adherence is objectively measured

Figure 4.1   Integrated Business Planning Model for Aligning Company Plans Each Month. © Oliver Wight International, Inc. Used with permission.

- Financial projections that are based on the credible portfolio, demand, and supply plans—and not created independently

Each of these principles must be adopted by the executive team. Then, the President or CEO must hold both themselves and their functional leaders accountable for operating in accordance with those principles.

As the trust between business leaders improves and the information shared is more credible, here is what also happens: functional teams see the value of working collaboratively. They work together to propose solutions to misalignments in plans and business issues. They also work collaboratively to find the best ways to leverage business opportunities.

The behavior of the cross-functional leadership team is critical. These behaviors are destructive to leadership teams: second-guessing, withholding, or failing to share information; finger-pointing and blaming; and failure to take accountability. The senior most leader must not allow those behaviors to persist. No process will work effectively when leadership trust and teamwork are absent.

It's worth pointing out that grassroots efforts to create cross-functional collaboration rarely work for long. Without the aligned support of the executive leadership team, collaboration almost always breaks down. Inevitably, people receive direction from their boss that undermines the relationships built with cross-functional peers.

Let's think back to the SmartCorp example in Chapter 1. Recall the reaction of Jacob, the Vice President of Sales, when he learned of conflicting demand information being provided to Katia, the CEO. He had committed to Katia a sales revenue projection. His sales directors and the demand planning team, with encouragement from the supply organization, provided a different, higher sales revenue number. Jacob was not privy to the information shared by his team. Nor was he involved in the decision.

I have observed this same type of situation in practice. The executive's response often is to tell his or her teams not to share information without the executive's prior approval. The result of which is that information sharing becomes tightly controlled and restricted.

Lack of process and lack of proper executive behaviors and leadership led to the breakdowns described in the SmartCorp example. This situation, in my experience, inevitably leads to financial surprises at the end of the month, quarter, and year. It reduces the trustworthiness of the entire business in the eyes of the board of directors and investors.

IBP has proven an effective solution for creating trust, collaboration, and teamwork among the executive team and their managers. IBP works well when the complete process is implemented—without skipping process steps. When steps in the process are not utilized, it is like cutting Jacob out of the collaborative teamwork and decision making.

As illustrated in Figure 4.1, IBP consists of five steps. These steps all start with a business strategy (illustrated in the center of the graphic). As noted in Chapter 2, IBP is a bridge between strategy and execution. This bridge ensures that functional plans are regularly calibrated and aligned with strategic objectives.

When describing IBP, I start with the Portfolio Management Review (PMR), as it is a natural connection between business strategy and the plans for the products and services that will be brought to market to achieve that strategy over time. In the PMR, updates to the portfolio plan are reviewed, with a focus on how changes to the plan impact what will be available to sell and how revenue projections may need to change.

The executive owner of this review is often a Vice President of Product Management or Product Marketing. The owner is accountable for making sure that the results and outputs of all projects being worked on (new products, value-engineering, reformulations, renovations, etc.) will achieve strategic objectives. The portfolio is often measured in terms of sufficiency. It is essential to assess whether there are enough projects in the pipeline to deliver sufficient growth to meet expected revenue and margin over the next two to three years (possibly longer in some industries). In addition to reviewing sufficiency, it is also vital that the information shared in the review demonstrates that the portfolio plan is valid and properly resourced. The product plan should not be based on hope or wishful thinking; there must be a high degree of confidence that the portfolio plan can be delivered as planned.

The PMR is vital in ensuring that business leaders have options in what is often the most uncertain aspect of business planning. There is far less certainty in the development of new products and services than there is in the selling of existing ones. Without a PMR, companies can become distracted through the course of the year. Business leaders allocate time and resources to deal with near-term issues in delivering products and services. They do not invest enough time and effort on filling the funnel of future new product or innovation opportunities.

On many occasions executives have confided that they aren't confident that the right balance is being struck between supporting the existing portfolio and developing the future portfolio. They worry that their development teams respond to whoever shouts the loudest. They know the spark of inspiration that leads to the next big thing is rarely a loud voice in the room.

Without a robust funnel of projects, companies are forced to commercialize less than ideal options. Rules on hurdles are circumvented because there simply aren't any other better alternatives.

Companies with a robust PMR, by contrast, find they have developed more options and can be more selective in what they commercialize. The demand and supply organizations benefit from a much more reliable and sufficient portfolio plan upon which to base their functional plans.

The Demand Review (DR) follows the PMR. The DR is the culmination of the demand planning process where the commercial management team (sales, marketing, and product management) reaches consensus on the actions that will be taken to influence and generate demand. These planned actions consider the inputs and assumptions about external conditions that may impact demand, such as market trends and competitors.

The output of the DR is consensus on a projection of demand volume, revenue, and margin that the rest of the organization can rely on to develop their plans. The volume output of the demand plan serves as a request for product to be supplied in support of the plan and stated business objectives.

The DR also serves as a forum for deciding which commercial actions are the *correct* actions to take and invest in to achieve the company's stated goals (such as revenue, profit, or market share) and strategies (such as growing in a particular channel or segment). The correct actions may change over time and must be reevaluated and adjusted in response to changes in the internal and external business environment.

It is important to structure the DR so that the focus is on the result of plans for influencing and generating demand. The goal is to create and communicate a trustworthy plan based on reality and with a minimum of bias. The DR is *the* decision-making meeting and should not be preempted by other meetings.

Let's look at what can happen when multiple, misaligned meetings related to demand are conducted in a company. I worked with a large and complex medical technology client to implement IBP. In talking with a global product leader, he told me their division had an existing demand planning process that was run by supply chain. The supply chain-managed process focused on creating a demand forecast for use in supply planning. I subsequently discovered that in addition to the existing demand review meetings, separate meetings that addressed demand were being held between the global product organizations and the regional sales and marketing teams. When I asked the product leader why they didn't just have these discussions in the DR, they responded candidly that their meeting was to talk about demand-generating activities. My question in response was simple: "Why is the Demand Review called a Demand Review if it's not a place to discuss demand generation?"

I share this example because it is a common misconception. Consider the following questions and answers about plans in general: (1) Who follows a construction plan? Construction workers. (2) Who follows flight plans? Pilots. (3) Who follows production plans? Factories. Yet, when I ask: Who follows demand plans?—most people pause before providing a response. The sales and marketing organization is *not* the answer that I frequently receive. The pause, however, is indicative that by framing my questions this way, people realize that it's odd to think that a DR wouldn't be the forum where the sales and marketing business leaders will review their coordinated activities and the resulting demand projections.

The Supply Review (SR) follows the DR. The goal of the SR and its supporting processes is to say *yes* to the demand plan, while balancing trade-offs between cost, working capital, and service levels. Finding the optimal balance between investments in inventory, manufacturing costs, and customer service levels requires measuring the plans for each against stated goals and assessing whether trade-offs need to be made.

The output of the SR is the supply plan, which reflects the planned production and inventory levels, along with resource utilization, costs, and any other key assumptions needed to deliver that output. Just like the demand plan needs to be unbiased, the supply plan must be unbiased as well. Supply chain professionals tend to be optimistic. They want to succeed and be able to deliver what is being asked of them. The supply plan, however, must reflect the demonstrated capability of the supply chain. It must be reliable and trustworthy in the same way that the demand plan must be.

Here's an important distinction that some business leaders fail to consider or may not understand while trying to align plans in the IBP process; the demand plan and the supply plan don't have to be the same. In fact, the supply plan might encompass a wide range of considerations that go well beyond what would be contemplated in a demand plan, such as:

- The locations from which product and materials will be sourced and the lead time from each source (e.g., which plants will manufacture product and which suppliers will provide materials)
- Capacity constraints that might exist and ways to plan around them
- How goods will be moved through and positioned in a network of warehouses and distribution centers
- Optimal use of production facilities such as level-loading, where a consistent rate of production is maintained over time for efficiency

- What inventory levels, safety stocks, and other flexibility mechanisms will be used to respond to fluctuations in demand

In each of the first three steps of IBP, functional plans are updated to reflect the latest information. Those plans are then checked against goals. When the latest projections indicate that they will fall short of the business goals, it is called a gap. It also should require changes to those plans to course-correct where possible.

Note the caveat *where possible*. It is not always possible to identify or solve every gap within the Portfolio, Demand, and Supply Review steps. This is where the "I" in IBP comes into play. Each of the functional portfolio, demand, and supply steps are expected to identify gaps between their functional goals and plans. When those functional plans are brought together and aligned, further gaps or issues may be exposed. A demand plan might show, without consideration of supply, an ability to deliver enough revenue and gross margin to meet or exceed the annual budget. However, when aligned with the supply plan, a gap may be exposed showing that the requested mix of products cannot be supplied.

Integrated Reconciliation is a defining characteristic of IBP. Integrated Reconciliation is the continuous process where cross-functional plans are aligned, issues or gaps are identified, and solutions are proposed. It culminates in a checkpoint review meeting, called the Integrated Reconciliation Review (IRR), which occurs after the SR. Integrated Reconciliation is as much a mindset and approach as it is a meeting. In the Integrated Reconciliation process, the coordinators of the Portfolio, Demand, and Supply Review steps operate as a cross-functional team, sharing changes and assessing impacts.

The finance team plays an important role in the Integrated Reconciliation process, too. The finance team uses the functional plans to update pro forma financial statements that represent the expected financial results of those plans. Monetizing the functional plans avoids creating a financial forecast that is different from the functional plans. It also leads to tighter integration of the finance organization in general, with their role being more of a team player than simply a recipient of an output.

Integrated Reconciliation results in what is known as *one set of numbers* that explains the operational plans to invest and deliver revenue and profit while serving customers' needs. The associated pro forma financial statements provide a view that is vital to business leaders: How do the latest financial projections compare to the company's stated annual budget and business goals? This information is vital. It tells leaders where gaps exist and proposes actions to close those gaps. This is a topic that will be discussed in more depth in Chapter 9.

In the IRR meeting, issues arising from the earlier IBP steps are brought together and trade-off options and alternatives are developed. Critically, the issues and decisions assessed in the IRR are framed with appropriate supporting information. The IRR is preparation for the following—and last—step in the IBP process, which is the Management Business Review (MBR). The IRR team must be meticulous in what issues and information is brought forward to the executive team. It is not wise or productive to simply foist all the detailed plans on the executive team and expect them to figure out how those plans impact achieving corporate goals. As issues are identified, the relevant supporting information from the prior steps is selected and consolidated to appropriately explain each situation in a way that is easy to grasp and follow.

The IRR is also where functional goals themselves may be evaluated. As we illustrated in Chapter 3, conditions can change, making it impossible to achieve all functional goals. Trade-offs may need to be made. Relief may also need to be given on goals and objectives to ensure that the right overarching business decisions are made and followed.

For example, at one particular client of mine, the product portfolio was in good shape, meeting goals, and aligned to strategy. A launch of a significant new product release was planned in the first half of the next year, and it was on track and on budget. The demand plan was in good shape as well. Revenue was slightly ahead of budget with a few opportunities available in case demand in the current plan might fall short. The supply plan, however, was reflecting some business issues that made it difficult to achieve cost goals. There had been significant unexpected inflation, which caused cost overruns that were far greater than could be managed with improvements in productivity. The pro forma profit and loss statement showed a significant gap between the latest projections and the business goals for the bottom line.

The coordinators of the Portfolio, Demand, and Supply Review steps worked together to identify possible solutions. Several alternatives were considered, with the best option being to delay the new product launch. With the launch came a significant marketing expense that would be incurred in the first year. The team determined that since the new product had not yet been committed to customers and marketing plans had not yet been finalized, they would be able to delay the launch with little expense. They also evaluated and showed that the corresponding increase to demand on existing products could be supported.

In the end, the CEO approved the recommendation. A commitment was also made to not penalize the product portfolio teams for the delay of the launch when performance bonuses were awarded. The result was a compromise that made the most sense for the business overall.

This example highlights a key advantage to the IBP process spanning a longer term horizon—at least 24 months. With due diligence, potential problems can be identified and addressed well in advance. With advance notice, the pressure to make hasty decisions is diminished. There is time to develop sufficient information and consider cross-functional impacts. In this example, the team was able to not only identify the problem but evaluate the feasibility of the proposed solution.

Sometimes agreement can be reached immediately on the best option to take to align the portfolio, demand, and supply plans. It may be as simple as shifting a promotion from one product to another. When a decision does not have to be made immediately, it is often more prudent to assign the relevant functional managers action items to address the issue during the next monthly cycle of IBP. The best solutions often take time to develop.

As previously mentioned, the final step in the process is the MBR. This forum is chaired by the most senior business leader—the President, General Manager, or CEO. The participants typically include the executive leadership team, of which the executive owners of the Portfolio, Demand, and Supply Reviews are typically members. In this step the updated functional plans and pro forma financial statements are presented in a way that provide a succinct executive overview of where the business is heading.

In the MBR, the executive team is presented information on decisions needing to be made that was prepared in the IRR. The presentation on each issue includes sufficient information to make a well-informed decision. This is crucial, as it leads to decisions being made when they are needed instead of being *taken offline.*

Consider the earlier example of a new product launch being delayed. Each functional executive would have a different perspective on the decision, and accordingly, each may want to see different pieces of information. The marketing leader might want to understand the impact of the delay on market share. The sales leader would want to know if the delay would cause any concerns or issues with customers. Manufacturing would want to know that the shift of demand to existing products had been considered and wouldn't cause delivery problems. For significant decisions like this one, it is advisable for the Integrated Reconciliation team to brief their respective functional leaders in advance of the MBR in order to ensure that there are no surprise issues or question raised in the MBR.

The MBR is the keystone for the entire IBP process. The MBR is where trust between sales, marketing, finance, product management, and marketing leaders is put to the test. The objective measures for trustworthiness of plans must come together in the MBR, including such things as demand plan bias, adherence to manufacturing schedules, and the achievement of new product development milestones.

The President or CEO also observes and tests whether the leadership team trusts one another and is operating collaboratively. Behaviors, above all else, should be addressed and corrected through the MBR. When trust among executive leaders improves, the functional teams underneath them work far more effectively across the business functions.

At another client, early in their implementation of IBP, I briefed the CEO in advance of the MBR. The demand plan had chronic bias—it was overstated every month. The executive who was leading supply chain had confided in me that he was skeptical that the behavior would ever change. In my discussion with the CEO, I shared the data on bias, which had not been shown before. The executive team had seen various forecast accuracy numbers in the past, but it hadn't been framed in a way that showed what the numbers really meant. I also shared, discreetly, the distrust that the biased demand plan caused between the marketing and supply chain leaders, and the problems this distrust, in turn, caused.

The CEO recognized that the bias was, to some degree, a result of the executive team's own pressure to show stronger growth projections. When the bias measure was presented in the MBR, the CEO directly called out the head of marketing for the biased plan and tasked him with resolving it. He also admitted the executive team's own contribution to the problem and encouraged the leadership team to speak up if they were feeling undue pressure was being exerted to show growth that was not feasible.

This example illustrates how the MBR is the forum for the President or CEO to reinforce accountability to meet the following expectations:

- The sales and marketing leaders are accountable for developing an unbiased demand plan—and for executing the plan approved in the MBR
- The product management leaders are accountable for delivering portfolio initiatives on time and on budget
- The supply chain leaders are accountable for executing the supply plan within the agreed-upon parameters of inventory, cost, and customer service
- All of the company's senior leaders are accountable for communicating when conditions change that will impact execution of the previously approved plans

In order to meet this list of expectations, integration is key. The integrated model shown in Figure 4.2 provides a blueprint as to how business functions interact in a collaborative way. It illustrates the key leadership and management processes of a business. IBP sits at the top, and all of the steps are supported by underlying functional management processes.

The connectivity between the different functional management processes, as shown in the model, is vital to a business. Look at the connections between Supplier Management, Demand Management, and Project Management; note that the connections go both ways. Strong interconnectivity between the processes shown in the model encompasses teamwork at all levels, a collaborative culture, and expectation for a more reliable business performance.

IBP provides the framework for strengthening the business, as was described. Getting there may come in fits and starts as the abilities fostered by IBP evolve. Let's use SmartCorp's situation as an example.

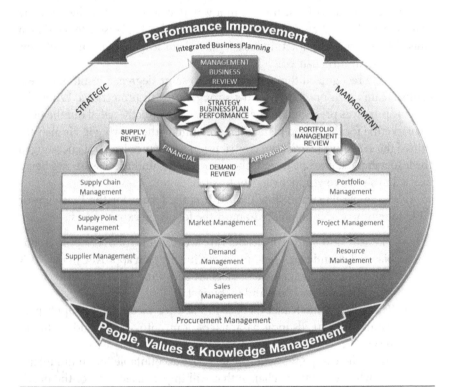

Figure 4.2   The Integrated Business Model. © Oliver Wight International, Inc. Used with permission.

* * *

Allen, the Vice President of Procurement for SmartCorp is dealing with a situation that is common with new product launches. Orders for a new product, Project Beta, are well below the planned expectations and inventory is higher than planned. Excess inventory for the new product has been identified as a risk in the SR meeting. Consistent with the Integrated Reconciliation philosophy described earlier, a small working group had been assigned to work together to recommend how best to address the inventory situation.

"My team has worked with our suppliers to mitigate any excess materials as much as possible. But I still think we're going to be on the hook for a lot of material and final product inventory," reports Allen.

"Thanks Allen," says Breanne, the Director of Marketing, "but I'm not sure that we need to be slowing down production yet. First, we need to understand *why* customers are ordering less of the new product than expected. I checked in with Scott in Customer Service this morning. He said we haven't received any orders from RetailMart yet. When those orders come in, that should get us back on track."

"RetailMart isn't taking Project Beta," says Jeff, the Director of Demand Planning, with trepidation.

"Wait, why isn't RetailMart taking Beta?" asks Andrew, the Director of Innovation. "They've been doing so well with Project Alpha." Andrew and his team are responsible for developing new product plans.

"That's exactly the problem," responds Jeff. "Felix, in Sales, says RetailMart doesn't see any real need to add to the portfolio with Alpha doing as well as it is."

"Why didn't we flag this possibility sooner?" asked Breanne. "This feels like something we should have been out in front of." She goes on to explain that had it been known that RetailMart wasn't going to take Beta, John, the Chief Marketing Officer, and Mike, the Chief Financial Officer, would not have approved the Beta product launch.

"We've had this discussion before, Breanne. My demand planning team isn't part of the new product process," says Jeff. His tone shifts from trepidation to frustration. "I don't know how I'm supposed to influence a process that I'm not involved in."

* * *

The situation at SmartCorp illustrates a company's progress in improving communication and collaboration as part of its IBP process. During the first few months of IBP being in place, communication starts to improve, and cross-functional issues become visible. In the SmartCorp example, the process exposed a problem that needs to be addressed. Before IBP, the problem of poor sales of a new product might have lingered for months before it was addressed.

In SmartCorp's case, the executive team members and business functions were aligned as part of the IBP process steps. This alignment enabled a cross-functional team of leaders who were one or two levels lower in the organization to work together in order to solve problems that were identified during the monthly process. Initially, as this case example illustrated, the focus is on identifying problems. Over time, the process and people reach a maturity where the discussions shift from problem solving to problem prevention. This shift of focus also results in greater concentration on responding to business opportunities.

For SmartCorp, the immediate problem was excess inventory, but the more consequential issue that Breanne raised was that it may not have been the right decision to develop the new product at all. Breanne rightfully recognized that the resources needed to develop new products are not infinite and should be allocated to optimize the balance between risk and reward. In SmartCorp's situation, critical information that would have enabled making better decisions was not being shared.

IBP provides a framework for sharing information. With IBP, business leaders and managers should know where and when key decisions are being made so that surprises can be avoided.

With a more mature IBP process, SmartCorp would have aligned the portfolio and demand plans sooner. Gaps, such as the one identified where RetailMart was not taking Project Beta, would have been identified through that process. Critically, the supply plan would be driven by the demand plan. Assuming the sales inputs into the demand plan had been shared with enough lead time, the excess inventory would not have been built. Surprises might still occur, but they wouldn't be the result of a lack of collaboration within SmartCorp. If the decision from RetailMart truly was a surprise to SmartCorp, the launch date of Project Beta could be delayed, giving the sales and marketing teams the time needed to influence different customers to buy the product.

IBP helps business leaders work together to better manage the existing portion of the product portfolio as well. The SR provides a response back to the commercial organization about how the demand plan will be fulfilled. This response is underpinned by trustworthy information. The sales organization, in turn, is better equipped to make reliable commitments to customers more confidently.

A regional managing director for one of my clients described the planning process that existed before IBP as being a "black hole." The prior process was primarily used for financial forecasting, and the only output was a set of financials to be communicated to the corporate leadership team. The regional leaders contributed various inputs into the financial forecast but received no feedback on the plan or their inputs. They were never sure if the demand plans that their teams were executing would be supported by supply and thus, were often surprised with shortages and backorders. One salesperson lamented that conversations with customers were "twenty-five minutes apologizing for poor performance and surprises, followed by five minutes of selling, if we're lucky."

Implementing IBP did not magically resolve supply constraints. It did, however, force the alignment of demand and supply plans and identifying where decisions needed to be made. IBP also set the expectation to provide a response back to the regions in the form of approved plans. Even if it wasn't good news, the sales teams could manage expectations with their customers. Credibility with customers dramatically improved, and customers were more willing to collaborate on plans that could be trusted and executed by both parties.

As maturity in the IBP process develops, the supply chain organization can and should respond to more than just the demand plan number. When risks, opportunities, and scenarios are openly shared and evaluated as part of the Demand Review, the supply chain organization is expected to perform its own analysis. There is often more than one way for the supply organization to respond to a given situation. The supply organization should be expected to propose alternatives that consider customer service, costs, revenue, and margin. As a result, the most effective responses can be planned.

Opportunities, such as tenders or new contracts, can be evaluated through IBP before making a commitment to customers. This evaluation allows the organization to understand if and how the tenders or new contracts can be supported, along with any implications to existing business. This often gives commercial leaders a more confident, if not stronger negotiating position.

I worked with one supply chain executive who had a very black and white view toward planning. Whenever he was asked if something could be supplied, his response was: "Just tell me what you're going to sell, and we'll figure it out." This attitude wasn't helpful to the sales directors. They, in turn, were being asked by their customers to provide some indications of possible volume and delivery dates before making a purchase commitment.

Working together with the demand and supply planners, we developed a way for sales opportunities to be shared and evaluated before adding them to the approved demand and supply plans. This approach gave the demand organization visibility of what *might* happen. With visibility to opportunities, the supply chain team could consider options earlier than usual and propose taking *some* risk. In one case, leaders approved (in the MBR) the ordering of raw materials prior to the confirmation of a significant marketing promotion. This action shortened the supply lead time and better aligned with the delivery time that the customer desired. It was an acceptable risk, as the raw material would be consumed even if the order was not received. The material was used in other products with substantial demand.

All of the newfound capabilities that were just described start with credible demand information that creates trust among business leaders. The result is enhanced business performance. Revenue growth is frequently cited as a key benefit that companies realize after implementing IBP.[3]

Benefits of a trustworthy, unbiased demand plan are tangible for the supply chain organization as well. It is not necessary to waste time and energy second-guessing or judging the demand plan. More time is spent improving the way in which the supply chain organization responds to the demand plan. Proper accountability is established for classic *hot potato* issues such as excess inventory or poor customer service levels that can consume energy because of blame shifting. Both issues can be caused by planning or execution failures in demand or supply. When demand plans and supply plans are trusted and measured, the failure point becomes clear and the appropriate corrective action can be taken. There are few or no arguments about who owns the problem.

As noted in Chapter 2, when the commercial side of an organization fails to take responsibility for demand planning—for whatever reason—the supply side becomes forced, out of necessity, to forecast demand. I have rarely encountered a supply chain leader who *wants* to forecast demand. There are those who are protective of it because the only thing worse than having to do it themselves would be to have to follow a biased or untrustworthy plan provided by somebody else. However, when given the option of being provided a trustworthy, commercially owned demand plan as an input versus doing it themselves, the former is always the better option. The reason is often simple. Without a commercially owned demand plan, when there is too much inventory, who is blamed? *Supply*. When there isn't enough inventory, who is blamed? *Supply*. IBP, at its core, is a mechanism for the executive team to work *together*, and accordingly it puts accountability where it belongs.

Business leaders, as a result, stay focused *on* the business. For example, should the unconstrained demand plan need to be constrained due to supply capacity limitations, business leaders spend time solving the problem rather than pointing fingers. They can provide credible information to the board on the impact to revenue and margin along with what to expect in future months. Expectations can be managed, and time and energy are spent productively.

With trust being a central theme, the next chapter will demonstrate what trust looks like (and similarly, what distrust looks like) in an organization. From there we will explore the various best practices that reinforce trust in a Demand Management process.

SUMMARY

- The most senior leader of an organization must take ownership and accountability for the process of routinely aligning and synchronizing plans.
- IBP is a best-practice way for business leaders to routinely reach consensus on a single operating plan.
- IBP highlights where trust is lacking and where information being shared is not trustworthy.
- There are five steps in the IBP process:
  - Portfolio Management Review (PMR)
  - Demand Review (DR)
  - Supply Review (SR)
  - Integrated Reconciliation Review (IRR)
  - Management Business Review (MBR)
- Integrated Reconciliation is a defining characteristic of IBP through which cross-functional plans are aligned, issues or gaps are identified, and solutions are proposed.
- IBP is a way to ensure that overarching business objectives are prioritized over functional ones and that the right trade-off decisions are made to achieve them.
- IBP puts accountability where it belongs and moves organizations from blame and finger-pointing to problem solving and problem prevention.

QUESTIONS TO ASK

- If you have a Sales and Operations Planning or Integrated Business Planning process in place today, is it owned and led by the most senior executive of the business?

- What routines or governance process does your most senior executive use to make decisions and run the business?
- Is the governance process routine and predictable?

ENDNOTES

1. George Palmatier and Colleen Crum. "Transitioning from Sales and Operations Planning to Integrated Business Planning." Oliver Wight Americas. www.oliverwight-americas.com.
2. "How Marzetti Navigates Good and Bad 'Weather' With Class A IBP." Oliver Wight Americas. www.oliverwight-americas.com.
3. James Correll and George Palmatier. "How Good Is Your Sales and Operations/Integrated Business Planning Process?" Oliver Wight Americas. www.oliverwight-americas.com. pp. 5–7.

CHAPTER 5

TRUST

Management guru Peter Drucker is widely recognized for observing that "culture eats strategy for breakfast."[1] His thinking is that regardless of the strength of a company's strategy, its culture will ultimately determine whether the strategy is successful.

This observation is not limited to strategy. In my experience, it's true for all aspects of planning. In the end, it's not the strategy or plan itself, it's the people implementing the plan who determine whether it succeeds or fails.

Take a minute to think about your company. How do things get done? What moves the needle? Are decisions influenced only by logic, facts, and data or are politics and informal networks involved? Have you ever taken an action because you believe it's the right thing to do, even though it would seem to contradict a standard process or policy?

If it's the people that matter, then a successful planning process must embrace people and the behavioral aspects of teamwork. What separates companies with exceptional planning processes from those that are regularly frustrated by their processes comes down to one word: *trust*.

Successful planning relies on many different aspects of trust:

- Trust that everyone understands the cross-functional processes and ways of working
- Trust that people will follow the process and play their positions
- Trust that people will do what they say they will do
- Trust that information being shared is credible and can be relied upon
- Trust that teams will execute plans that are agreed upon or communicate when they cannot
- Trust that the goals and objectives are clear and that the goalposts will not be moved

For a team to work well together, there must be trust in the people, process, and tools. It's a fundamental prerequisite to business success. People don't come to work wanting to fail. They naturally do what they *believe* will lead to the best result. Without trust, people compensate by building hedges, second-guessing, and double-checking. That creates waste and inefficiency, and ultimately undermines business performance. It also erodes the foundation of teamwork.

Early in my career I spent some time in accounting. I was a financial controller and was responsible for managing cash. I naively thought that the process would be straightforward: customers would pay their bills and we would pay our suppliers when our bills were due. Nothing could be further from the truth. I was constantly negotiating—not only with customers and suppliers, but with the owners of the company as well. Certain loan covenants had to be met, and the owners had a lot at stake personally. I was advised early on to create my own hedge. When the CEO signed checks for key suppliers, I held some of them back instead of mailing them all immediately. This gave me some negotiating leverage. When a supplier would call, I could promise to try to work something out with the CEO to have a check signed, when in fact it was already signed and all I had to do was send it.

What I know now—but didn't appreciate then—was just how much of my time and energy was spent managing the hedge instead of managing the business. The CEO knew that I was holding back signed checks but wasn't quite sure how many. That led them to second-guess my requests to sign more. That made my ability to get checks signed less reliable. That undermined my ability to make commitments to suppliers. It was a vicious cycle.

Dr. Paul Zak, a neuroscientist, created a survey instrument that quantifies trust within organizations. He used that survey to study several thousand companies. The following statement is a key finding from the survey that was published in the *Harvard Business Review*:

> "Compared with people at low-trust companies, people at high-trust companies report: 74% less stress, 106% more energy at work, 50% higher productivity, 13% fewer sick days, 76% more engagement, 29% more satisfaction with their lives, 40% less burnout."[2]

What would work life be for you if your company was able to lower stress levels and significantly improve productivity? What would it mean if most people were more engaged in their jobs, complained less, and did not quit their jobs because of burnout?

I quit my job as financial controller because of the stress. I've seen similar situations with family, friends, and colleagues. By contrast, when I look to those who I believe are truly happy, there is a common theme. They tend to work and live in environments where there is a culture of trust.

Trust is not simple to create and sustain, however. The *Merriam-Webster Dictionary* defines trust as "assured reliance on the character, ability, strength, or truth of someone or something."[3] In order to trust something, we must be prepared to rely on it. Relying or depending on a person or a piece of information means that we are prepared to be vulnerable and expose ourselves to the possibility of failure.

When I get into my car and drive to the airport, I am depending on the brakes, steering, and other critical components of the car to work. If the brakes were to fail while driving on the highway, I would certainly be in trouble. That being said, I am reliant on them. I trust that the design of the car and the maintenance performed on it will keep me safe. It saves me from having to become an expert mechanic myself and allows me to focus on what I want to accomplish—which is getting from point *A* to point *B* safely. I am not alone in this scenario. According to *CarsGuide,* more than one billion passenger cars were on the road throughout the world in 2018.[4] This means that nearly a billion people most likely have no idea how the brakes on their car work, but choose to rely on them anyway. They barely give the brakes a thought.

Relying on something is a choice. We choose to trust—in this case, our brakes—because the risk of failure is significantly less than the cost of not being able to rely on them. I rely on my car because I believe that the risk of the brakes failing is small relative to the cost of verifying that the brakes work by inspecting the brakes each time I use the car.

Equating this example to trust and reliance in business, people need to believe that relying on a person or piece of information is worth it. The risk of failure must be perceived as being lower than the cost of not relying on it.

Note I am using the terms *believe* and *perceive* intentionally. People will often need to be shown and convinced that the cost/benefit relationship of relying on teammates or information, such as a demand or supply plan, is positive.

To add to the complexity, the costs and benefits are not always easy to quantify or even visible to the person making the decision to trust. Consider a commercial leader who has been provided with a supply plan in response to their demand plan. The sales leaders should have enough confidence in the supply plan to rely on it to make promises and commitments to customers. If for some reason the supply plan is not executed, those customer commitments would be broken. That risk is very clear to the commercial leader.

The alternative to relying on the supply plan might be to hedge or work around it when making promises to customers. The examples of the lengths that salespeople will go to in order to speak directly to people in the factories and to get their own view of what promises can be made are legendary. So, too, are the lengths that salespeople will go to in order to make their orders top priority. As was shown in Chapter 3, the cost of this sort of misalignment is not solely born by the commercial leader.

A lack of trust has implications that go beyond the costs of misalignment in an organization. When there is a lack of trust, additional time and energy is wasted not only by second-guessing and hedging, but also by positioning and politicking. A colleague of mine was a regional general manager for a company that dealt with electronics manufacturing services. He often recounts the dynamics in the company when it appeared that their sales targets would not be achieved.

Sales targets were negotiated and set for the year. Sales executives at headquarters periodically checked with the regional general managers to validate they were on track to deliver those objectives. If the regional general manager responded that achieving the sales target was at risk, the sales executive at headquarters would become involved to provide help.

Unfortunately, this "help" required the regional leaders to fly to company headquarters and explain their plan to get back on track. Help was not really provided. The meetings with the senior sales executive mostly involved criticism and browbeating. It was like the saying, "The beatings will continue until morale improves."

This behavior did nothing to develop trust between the regional sales managers and corporate sales executives. The cost of honesty and transparency was very high and the benefit was very low. It was much more productive to remain in the region and work on the issues that were obstacles to achieving the sales targets. Many a regional general manager yielded to the temptation to not tell the truth until the end of the year. That way, they only had to take one beating per year.

The tendency of executives wanting to help regions or divisions get back on track is not uncommon. The type of intervention previously described poses additional risks, however. When trust is lacking between the board of directors and the leadership teams at headquarters and in regions, the result is often increased oversight and micromanagement. The focus shifts almost exclusively to delivering on short-term objectives, as that is seen as the way for leaders to rebuild trust with the board.

The problem is that a short-term focus on achieving sales targets takes away from planning how best to achieve future sales, strategies, and business objectives. It pushes leaders back to working *in* the business instead of *on* the business. A vicious cycle of trying to predict and deliver the next month or quarter prevails. Decisions that are needed to alter the trajectory of the business over the mid- to long-term horizon are not made. The root cause of this problem is not an inability to plan, it is a lack of trust.

In my experience, the better and more constructive intervention is for executives to genuinely help. Helping starts with having the interests and objectives of the person being helped in mind. In the example, the corporate executives were focused on themselves and meeting their own performance objectives. If instead the corporate executives believed that the regional and corporate goals and objectives were aligned, they would be more inclined to provide support. Instead of providing criticism, they could ask what they could do to assist in solving the problem. Then, with the near-term performance issue resolved, they could take the time to invest in helping the regional leaders avoid that problem in the future.

When trust is in place between the board of directors and the leadership team, a virtuous cycle of opportunity realization and growth can be found. Consider the following case in point regarding T. Marzetti, a maker of salad dressings and dips.

Capacity had long been an issue and a cause of frustration at Marzetti. The supply organization received short-term demand and innovation plans and did their best to fulfill customer orders despite capacity limitations. Longer term plans were rarely communicated.

Marzetti's CEO had previous experience with Integrated Business Planning (IBP). He made the implementation of IBP a top priority when he joined Marzetti. He knew the benefits and competitive advantages that would result from a better focus *on* the business, planning longer term, and cross-functional sharing and alignment of plans.

IBP spurred Marzetti to enhance its demand planning process. The goal was to consistently produce a demand plan that was continuously improving.

Meanwhile, the supply organization developed a structured way to evaluate production capacities. Having a better understanding of their supply capacities enabled the sales team to more confidently work with customers to plan for future growth.

These collaborative plans were backed by Marzetti's authorization for the capital expenditures that were needed to grow the business. The output of IBP was more credible plans that were executed as planned. Marzetti's board of directors trusted those plans. They would not authorize capital funding without great confidence in the credibility of Marzetti's growth strategy, market plans, and capacity plans and recommendations. In short, the board of directors trusted the recommendations of the leadership team when it came to growing the business.[5]

Trust can be strengthened in an organization by making the choice to share plans and information and to rely on teamwork more straightforward. Business leaders can do so by communicating the benefits of alignment and positively reinforcing trust and trustworthy behaviors. Leaders at all levels of the organization, including the board of directors, have a responsibility to drive a culture of alignment and teamwork.

The Marzetti experience illustrates how strong executive leadership creates ownership and accountability for aligning and synchronizing plans across the business. By making IBP a top priority, the CEO sent an important message to the organization that reinforced the idea that planning was to be the way forward. Addressing the perceived risks that individuals face when deciding to rely on each other, however, is something that *every* leader and function influences.

For example, one of my clients was dealing with excess inventory of a new product. In one discussion, a demand planning manager moaned to the team that "marketing is always optimistic" in their projections of demand for new products. That one remark, factual or not, was enough to undermine teamwork. I know this because it was recounted to me by a planner while explaining why they were second-guessing the information provided by marketing. They didn't trust the information at face value because they had been warned of its unreliability.

This isn't to say that we should simply rely on information that is unreliable. The better course of action would be for the demand planning manager to engage with his or her peers in marketing to help make those inputs more trustworthy, instead of disparaging the marketing team and sowing seeds of distrust.

Trust is a two-way street. We trust people who trust us. We don't trust people who don't trust us. We often use the phrase "trust is earned," but that's only partially true. The person from whom we're trying to earn trust must also be trusted by us.

Since trust is a two-way street, it can't be created unilaterally. The best that people can do is to look in the mirror and address the things that they are doing within their *own* function that will inspire trust and make relying on the information and plans that they share less risky.

Building trust certainly can be accomplished; it is not an exercise in futility. I regularly take on the challenge of building the trustworthiness and credibility of teams, and I regularly succeed. The key is to focus on what is within your control and what you can do to be more trustworthy.

On one of these occasions, I was tasked with building a team that was to be responsible for brand planning. Planning had historically been a responsibility of brand managers, but it had been consolidated into a central team of planning and forecasting specialists. When taking on the role, I knew that I would be starting from scratch to create a credible team in the eyes of the rest of the organization.

The first few months were painful. The team was still taking shape and had not yet earned the respect and trust of the organization. A lot of time was spent in reactive, fire-drill activities. I often felt personally attacked when the plans that were being put forward were challenged and torn apart by other stakeholders.

Six months into the assignment, I held an off-site event for the team. The theme of the meeting was credibility and trust. It was a milestone for my team that cemented how the team operated. We worked together to establish achievable goals and make commitments to the rest of the organization that we could keep. We openly shared what we could and could not deliver. We communicated openly with the belief that the benefit of transparency would, over time, outweigh the risk of disappointing our bosses if we had to deliver *bad* news. We knew there would be backlash when communicating that we could not deliver all of the various views of demand (such as anticipated market share performance) that the rest of the business wanted from us. But we communicated that news anyway.

The building of trust did not stop at transparent communications. We followed through on our commitments rigorously. Using the market share performance example, we initially were not providing data on market share by brand but were able to provide an aggregate view. We committed to providing that aggregate view, and then did it. We couldn't control what others would do, but we could ensure that we did everything in our power to be the most reliable and credible partners as possible.

On an individual level, I had each person on the team set monthly and quarterly goals for themselves. I focused primarily on setting goals that each person could and would achieve. The goal itself was not as important as the behavior it created. What mattered most was that the team learned the behavior of following through with their commitments. That fostered a culture of reliability that influenced all aspects of their work.

Over time, our cross-functional partners in sales, finance, and supply chain learned that they could trust us. They could rely on the plans and information that we provided. They trusted that we would do what we said we would do. This led the business toward operating with one demand plan, and consequently provided the foundation for making critical business decisions that addressed the actions needed to achieve the planned business objectives.

I share this example because it illustrates that building trust is not something for someone else to do. Everybody has a role to play, and it is best to focus first on making yourself and your deliverables trustworthy before expecting others to trust and rely on them.

The rest of this book addresses the best practices that have proven time and again to help business leaders develop trusted demand plans. It is a skill that involves developing both people and processes. The remainder of this book covers how to develop those skills and best practices—starting with understanding the customers of the demand plan.

SUMMARY

- Trust is what separates companies with exceptional planning processes from those that are regularly frustrated by their planning processes.
- For a team to work well together, there must be trust in the people, process, and tools.
- High-trust companies create an environment where people have less stress, more energy, higher productivity, and higher job satisfaction.
- Trust is not easy. It involves making the choice to be vulnerable because it will be worth it in the long run.
- When trust is lacking, time and energy is wasted second-guessing, hedging, positioning, and politicking.
- Leaders play a critical role in fostering trust by communicating its importance and positively reinforcing trustworthy behaviors.
- Establishing trust starts with making yourself trustworthy and choosing to trust others; it is not for someone else to do.

QUESTIONS TO ASK

- Do you view your company as being high-trust or low-trust?
- Are you comfortable making commitments that you can deliver? Do you feel pressure to make commitments that you are not able to keep?
- When somebody else in your organization fails to keep a commitment or lets you down, do you offer support or criticism?
- What expectations of trusting and trustworthy behavior do you set for your team?

ENDNOTES

1. Jacob Engel. *Why Does Culture 'Eat Strategy For Breakfast'?* Forbes, 2018. https://www.forbes.com/sites/forbescoachescouncil/2018/11/20/why-does-culture-eat-strategy-for-breakfast/.
2. Paul J. Zak. *The Neuroscience of Trust.* Harvard Business Review, January–February 2017, pp. 84–90.
3. *Trust Definition and Meaning. Merriam-Webster,* 2022. https://www.merriam-webster.com/dictionary/trust.
4. *How Many Cars Are There in the World?* CarsGuide. https://www.carsguide.com.au/car-advice/how-many-cars-are-there-in-the-world-70629.
5. "How Marzetti Navigates Good and Bad 'Weather' With Class A IBP." Oliver Wight Americas. www.oliverwight-americas.com.

CHAPTER **6**

CUSTOMERS OF THE DEMAND PLAN

The demand plan is not created just for the sake of creating a demand plan. A demand plan, like any other plan or piece of information, is created so that it can be followed, executed, and used for decision making.

The demand plan has a wide range of useful purposes—and value—to a business. In my experience, however, many leaders have a narrow view of the usefulness of the demand plan and the demand planning process. There is often a presumption that the demand plan is only useful for the supply chain or manufacturing organization.

Take for example a company that makes product in advance of selling it to customers, known as using a make-to-stock strategy. Before receiving customer orders, the manufacturing managers must make decisions about availability of capacity, sourcing of materials, and production of goods. The demand plan's projection of volume, timing, and product mix is a vital input for enabling manufacturing managers to make those decisions.

Enlightened business leaders see the broader value of a demand plan, however. They increasingly think about other internal customers of the demand plan as well. *Internal* customers are those who rely on the demand plan as a critical input to their functional activities, plans, and responsibilities. When business leaders appreciate the value that a demand plan can bring to other functions, they think more broadly about demand planning and Demand Management. The demand planning process and the demand plan become an essential part of the business.

I use the term *internal customers* because they should be treated as customers. Their needs should be understood and the demand planning process should aim to serve them. This is key to establishing one plan and fostering trust in the demand planning process.

Defining the internal customers of the demand plan can be accomplished in a few hours. The effort to identify internal customers of the demand plan may often reveal some surprises. One of those surprises includes overlooked internal customers who are dependent on the demand planning process. Commercial teams are an example of that.

It may be natural to think of sales, marketing, and product management teams as providing inputs into a demand plan, but they also need to understand how their actions impact sales volume, revenue, and margin. The demand plan and assumptions tell them whether their actions are positioning the company to achieve its business goals and strategies. Commercial teams also need to know when there are gaps between the current trajectory of anticipated demand and the achievement of targets, such as the annual plan or budget. With this information, they can take actions to close any gaps. It is far more productive to know as early as possible that gaps exist than to be caught in a last-month, last-quarter, or end-of-the-year surprise.

The finance team is another internal customer. Finance needs to understand the sales revenue and margin projected as a result of the anticipated demand in the demand plan. They also need to know the assumptions behind those projections. This information is critical in order to plan cash flow, make financial projections, and understand upside and downside potential. The finance organization uses the information to determine the commitments that can be made to external stakeholders, such as banking, investment firms, and other financial institutions.

Over a longer term horizon, marketing and product management teams need to understand the expected growth and market share that will be achieved with the existing portfolio of products and services. This information enables them to optimize and plan sufficient innovation to achieve long-term growth objectives.

When considering what each internal customer needs to know about the demand plan, it is important to identify the information of value over the entire planning horizon. It may seem intuitive to think that manufacturing lead times are the longest of all internal customers, but that is not necessarily so. Other long lead times in business include development of marketing promotion campaigns, commitment to buy materials, and capital investment for equipment and facilities. Some investment decisions may span months or even years.

Rather than guess or presume what demand information each internal customer needs, just ask them. To start, ask them if they are currently using the demand plan as an input to their planning and decision-making processes—then ask whether they find the information reliable.

If the current demand information is not being used, ask why. It may be that the demand plan in its current form doesn't provide the necessary detail or useful information. It may be that internal customers simply don't trust the demand plan or the supporting information. Work from the premise that they are customers and that you won't be successful by *forcing* them to use the demand plan. You must make the demand plan information relevant and trustworthy before it will be relied upon.

Here are some basic questions to ask that will lead to a better understanding of each internal customer's needs:

- What level of detail is needed over different future time horizons?
- What dimensions or groupings are needed? For example, groupings by product, customer, region, or brand?
- What quantitative information is needed? For example, volume, value, and/or gross margin? In the case of volume, what unit of measure—units, pounds, cases, etc.?
- What qualitative information is needed? Which type of assumptions are most important?

Having discussions with internal customers about required demand information has another benefit: Internal customers educate each other along with the demand planning organization about their business focus and planning needs. In the end, everyone develops more savvy about the business and cross-functional needs for information and coordination.

Figure 6.1 shows an example of the output from documenting the different needs of internal customers of the demand plan. For some internal customers, plans may need to be represented in volume and value, by customer, and by product family and the product item. Other internal customers may need to see projected market share and inventory as a result of the demand projections. As you can see from the example shown in Figure 6.1, information is needed in various levels of detail and units of measure, depending on the internal customer.

Once the information needed is defined, the next question is: How will each piece of information be provided? This is an important question to answer—and it is up to the demand planning team to answer it. For example, manufacturing might have their needs met by publishing the volume output of the demand plan in a planning tool or system. Sales, by contrast, might need qualitative information, such as promotional activities, published in a way that a broad group of sales leaders can easily access it. A common practice for defining and documenting both the inputs and the outputs of the demand planning process is through a SIPOC diagram, where the suppliers, inputs, processes, outputs, and customers are defined. For output of the demand planning process, the customers are identified and the format and mechanism by which their needs will be met is documented. Figure 6.2 provides an example of a SIPOC.

Needs	Sales	Marketing	Manufacturing	Logistics	Finance
Product	Promoted Group	Brand	Product Family		Brand
Geography & Customer	Customer	Country	Region	Distribution Center	Country
Unit of Measure	Revenue	Revenue, Margin	Cases, Units	Cases	Units, Revenue, Margin
Horizon	8 Months	24 Months	18 Months	6 Months	Current Year
Time Bucket	Months	Months	Months	Months	Quarters
Other Needs	Promotional Activities Product Launches Product Exits	Market Share Promotional Activities Product Launches Product Exits	New Products by Item New Markets New Regions Product Exits	New Customers Change in Warehousing with Existing Customers	Pricing Strategies

Figure 6.1 Example of Demand Information Needs by Business Function. © Oliver Wight International, Inc. Used with permission.

Suppliers	Inputs	Process	Outputs	Customers
Demand Planners	• Statistical forecast • Holidays • Weather	1. Data collection and analysis	Demand Plan Volume	• Manufacturing • Logistics • Finance
Sales	• Promotions • Change of Distribution • Customer Contracts (New/Lost)	2. Prepare and review statistical forecast 3. Gather updates on open action items 4. Quantify assumption changes	Demand Plan Revenue, Gross Margin	• Sales • Marketing • Finance
Marketing	• New products • Discontinuations • Competitive intelligence • Market and industry trends	5. Update assumption journal 6. Update Risks & Opportunities list 7. Conduct Demand Review	Market Share	• Marketing
			Promotional Activities	• Sales • Marketing
Executive team	• Business Plans • Pricing adjustments	8. Publish final Demand Plan, minutes, action items	Product Launches & Exits	• Sales • Marketing • Manufacturing

Figure 6.2   Example of a SIPOC Exercise. © Oliver Wight International, Inc. Used with permission.

The process of understanding the internal customers of the demand plan also requires understanding the business model that a company operates within. Business models are choices, usually made by executive leadership and the board of directors. The business model often dictates how integration of plans needs to occur and how information is shared within the organization.

One of my client's business models was particularly complex. They were part of a large group of affiliated companies. One entity manufactured and distributed products to all the affiliates. Each affiliate was responsible for marketing and selling the products to end customers.

The incentive model for the entire group company, including the product managers in the manufacturing entity, rewarded sales by the affiliates to end customers. The corporate group recognized revenue when sales to end customers were booked by each affiliate. Transfer of product from the manufacturing entity to the affiliates were treated as intercompany transactions. While these transactions were documented and executed, they were not reported in the group company's financial results as revenue. Most of the functions in both the affiliates and the manufacturing entity (sales, marketing, and finance) naturally focused on planning sales to end customers. After all, that was their primary responsibility.

The incentive structure for the manufacturing organization was different. The top priority for manufacturing was to deliver replenishment orders to the affiliates. Even though the rest of the organization was focused on end customer sales, each entity still operated as a stand-alone company. The timing and fulfillment of replenishment orders had cash flow and tax implications. Accordingly, they developed a process to create a demand plan for each affiliate that represented the expected intercompany replenishment orders. The tools and processes that were developed had no connection with end customer sales. They were singularly focused on the needs of the manufacturing organization. Nobody else in the organization saw any value in or paid attention to that demand plan because it wasn't relevant to their needs.

While working to improve the demand planning process, we identified the two different types of demand—intercompany and end customer—and expanded the scope of the demand planning process to include both. It is important to note that had the group company been fully integrated, the solution would likely have been to define demand *only* as sales to end customers. One company's demand is another company's supply, after all. That would have left planning the movement of inventory up to the supply chain organization. In this case, however, the manufacturing entity had no authority to direct the buying behavior or change the planning processes of the affiliates. A fully integrated solution was not an option.

By expanding the scope of their demand planning process, the manufacturing entity made the resulting demand plan relevant to a much broader group of internal stakeholders. Product managers, finance, and manufacturing could all get what they needed from one demand plan, anchored in one set of assumptions.

The time spent thinking through the two different types of demand was well spent. By identifying where the two types of demand did not correlate, the business leaders were able to resolve many long-standing disconnects. These disconnects had caused chronic struggles for both the commercial teams in the affiliate organizations and the manufacturing team in the group company organizations. There had been in the past forecasts of end-user demand that would not be realized due to insufficient inventory at the affiliate. The inventory may have been sitting with the manufacturing entity, but not shipped to the affiliate due to a misalignment with the replenishment plan.

Another benefit was realized. Working together to communicate plans and solve misalignments to those plans created trust among the teams. The affiliate and manufacturing leaders begin to think about the well-being of each function. The pitting of functions against each other and the affiliates against the group company became the exception rather than the rule.

Identifying the demand information that internal customers needed in order to more efficiently do their jobs was a time-saving activity in the long run. The manufacturing organization no longer had to create a replenishment forecast from scratch, which had always involved a lot of guesswork. The finance team did not need to create a separate revenue and margin forecast for their financial reports and projections. When multiple forecasts are eliminated, time does not have to be spent reconciling the differences between them or answering questions when performance expectations are not realized.

For the demand planning organization, serving the needs of many internal customers of the demand plan usually requires more effort than serving the needs of oneself. My client needed better software tools, planning skills, and capabilities. They hired a full-time demand manager to orchestrate the process. They also had to gain access to information that previously had not been made available to them.

I frequently encounter similar challenges when working with consumer goods companies. Marketers routinely need projections of market share and consumer sales, while supply chain needs a projection of sales orders to customers or distributors. A demand planning team, reporting into the supply chain organization, often does not have access to the syndicated point-of-sale data that would be needed to create a projection of market share. They often consider market share projections superfluous and fail to invest any time or energy into understanding them. This leads marketers to take things into their own hands and create their own, independent views.

In my experience, this type of situation exists in companies across all industries. If a demand planning organization has only one customer, the table depicted in Figure 6.1 would be much less complex. The focus would most likely be on communicating information that the supply organization needs in order to produce product and ship orders. This information typically would be demand volume for product in weekly time buckets in the near term and in monthly time buckets beyond the next few weeks.

It becomes more complicated when addressing demand information that is of value for the sales, marketing, and finance functions. These teams work in the dimension of revenue and margins as well as volume. Accurate financial projections are essential to making good decisions on investment priorities and tactics. Without a view of revenue projections based on the demand plan and accurate pricing information, the various functions all too often develop their own financial projections independently of one another. These various plans often create confusion about performance expectations and accountability for that performance.

Converting the volume demand plan into revenue projections may not be a simple task for a demand planning team. Investment in people and tools is almost always needed to develop the demand information needed by a broader group of internal customers. The exercise in defining a SIPOC for demand planning will naturally uncover the process steps (the *P* in SIPOC) needed to serve internal customer needs. In my experience, these investments are worthwhile. It is best to focus the resources of an organization on creating *one* demand plan that serves all customers and stakeholders. Creating multiple different demand plans and then reconciling them is confusing and inefficient. More important, it dilutes ownership of the plan. To minimize effort and eliminate duplicative work, investments in planning tools and capability are best made in support of one process for developing, communicating, and updating the demand plan for all internal customers.

While considering the best ways to develop and communicate the demand information to internal customers, some pitfalls should be avoided. One pitfall is trying to rely on systems alone. Too many demand planning organizations decide to drive demand data to the lowest common denominator.

Planning software frequently has this capability, such as disaggregating information down to the item level by distribution location. With this approach, pivot tables are used to reaggregate the data in the various ways needed to satisfy each internal customer.

The problem with reaggregation of data is that people may challenge who owns the data and the plan. Having the capability to structure data using pivot tables will not stop people from saying, "That's not my number." And all too often the people are correct.

For example, let's say that a salesperson commits to selling 20 cars next year. The demand planning software is structured to break down this demand volume by historical sales proportions. It converts the 20 cars to this product mix: five sedans, five convertibles, and 10 sport utility vehicles. The converted demand data is then communicated to three different product managers, each responsible for a different type of vehicle.

The product manager for convertibles sees the demand number and questions why the salesperson is planning to sell only five convertibles next year. She had previously discussed selling 10. The salesperson is understandably confused. She had communicated only the total number of cars, not the mix.

There's another pitfall to the approach of disaggregating and reaggregating the demand plan volume. Usually, the assumptions are not considered or communicated. The internal customers of the demand plan miss the critical activity of aligning on the assumptions pertaining to mix over the relevant time horizons. In this example, the demand planner should have confirmed with the salesperson that the mix would be according to historical proportions. That way the salesperson could let the demand planner know if that was a valid assumption.

Another issue to watch out for is the frequency with which demand plan information is updated and communicated. When collecting the various needs of different internal customers of the demand plan, they should be asked how quickly they can digest and respond to the demand information.

For example, I find that companies are often able to make commercial changes much more quickly than their supply chain can respond. Making those changes *intentionally* without consulting the supply organization can be a fruitless exercise that creates frustration and lack of trust. There is little sense choosing to add a promotion next week for a product that is low on inventory and has a lead time of longer than a week to produce.

When this sort of decision is made, the supply organization often responds by pressuring for a mandate to freeze the demand plan and not allow any changes at all. The motivation is a desire to create stability in the supply planning and production processes.

Freezing the demand plan is not the right way to approach the problem, however. It causes all sorts of other business problems. Freezing a demand plan is akin to pretending that known changes aren't going to happen. It limits visibility, which limits what flexibility might exist.

Change is a norm in business. Inputs to the demand plan that are outside of a company's control will continue to change within time horizons in which the supply chain is unable to respond. Customers will not buy as planned. Some customers may, without warning, choose to take their business elsewhere. Internal customers of the demand plan may still need to see these near-term changes in demand. For example, the finance team may need to assess the risk to financial commitments caused by a sudden reduction of demand in the near term, even when there is no way for manufacturing to make a corresponding change to the production plan. In fact, that may be a reason why it is even *more* important for finance to see that change.

It is always best to focus on that which you can control. Accordingly, commercial *actions* should certainly consider the time horizon and capability of the supply chain to respond. Keep in mind that the supply chain may not always have the longest lead times. Portfolio actions, such as shifting the timing of a new product launch, may need to consider the lead time that the sales team needs to secure customer commitments.

The exercise of identifying the customers of the demand plan inevitably creates a new understanding of what it takes to respond to change. Commercial leaders learn why it may not be wise to launch a promotion or shift the timing of a product launch at the last minute. This knowledge leads commercial leaders to resist making near-term changes to the plan. And that discipline helps stabilize and reduce churn across the business.

When working with client companies to identify the internal customer of the demand plan, functional leaders often find the experience educational. In one instance, many were surprised to learn that the marketing organization was spending significantly more than expected on advertising because they were unable to give their ad agency enough lead time to produce the content. The marketing team had made the choice to coordinate advertising activities with their retail customers' promotional activities. The retail customers had a much shorter lead time for making commitments to support promotional activities. When the cost implications of these short lead times came to light, the sales team discussed the issue with their retail customers. The retail customers agreed to provide more lead time when making sales commitments than in the past. The result was significant reductions in advertising costs.

Once the information needs of the internal customers of the demand plan are defined, the next step is to focus on how best to develop assumptions. Assumptions are based on information shared about demand and are considered to be more important than the demand numbers. The next chapter explains why.

SUMMARY

- Internal customers are those who rely on the demand plan as a critical input to their functional activities, plans, and responsibilities.
- Rather than guess what demand information each internal customer needs, simply ask them. If the current demand information is not being used, ask why.
- For the demand planning organization, serving the needs of many internal customers of the demand plan usually requires more effort than serving the needs of oneself.
- Investment in people and tools is almost always necessary in order to develop the demand information that is needed by a broader group of internal customers—but these investments are usually worthwhile.
- It is best to focus the resources of an organization on creating one demand plan that serves all customers and stakeholders.
- Relying on tools and systems alone to serve the needs of different internal customers is problematic and leads to problems of ownership and unclear assumptions.
- A demand plan should not be frozen, but commercial functions should take care to try not to change the demand plan more quickly than the organization can react.
- Identifying the customers of the demand plan inevitably creates a new understanding of lead times and what it takes to respond to change.

QUESTIONS TO ASK

- Who are the internal customers of your demand plan?
- What information do they need from the demand plan to make decisions?

- Are they using existing demand plan information today? If not, why?
- Is the demand planning team adequately equipped to support the needs of the different internal customers?
- What investments in capability might be needed to create one demand planning process that serves all internal customers?
- With one process, what other redundant plans or planning processes could be eliminated?

CHAPTER 7

ASSUMPTIONS

Years ago I worked for a company that was a client of Oliver Wight. I was asked to share a copy of our demand plan so that they could become more familiar with our business. I happily obliged and sent a copy of the spreadsheet by email. I remember being confused by the response that I received: *That's not a demand plan.*

At that point in my career, I hadn't yet understood the difference between expressing outcomes and plans. The Oliver Wight principal put it simply: *The demand plan is made up of words, not just numbers.*

Making the demand plan relevant to internal customers in the desired level of detail and how it is expressed numerically does not, on its own, make it reliable. There are no *facts* in the future, and therefore, the demand plan can only reflect beliefs or *assumptions* of what will happen along with the associated consequences to demand.

Many people jump straight to the consequences and evaluate the demand plan based on what the plan foretells about the result. This is an exercise in futility. To create a reliable plan, it is far more important to focus on the assumptions upon which the result is based.

When I was responsible for leading a Demand Review (DR), I always found the exercise of briefing my manager to be valuable. It tested my ability to step back and synthesize the result of complex analytics into digestible commercial terms. I understood that the story surrounding the demand plan and its implications to the business, and not necessarily the most robust analytics, was far more important. Executive business leaders are focused on running the business, not on understanding the nitty-gritty of statistics.

This is a truth that frustrates many demand planners. They may come armed to talk to their manager with data that shows how accurate their models are, as if business leaders thought this type of conversation was relevant. It isn't. It is far more important to understand the actions being taken to generate demand, what customers say about their buying intentions, the issues that could cause demand to be less than planned, and the opportunities to increase sales over the volume projected in the plan. Incorporating these aspects of the business into the plan strengthens trust in the plan.

Assumptions are the key to creating a business-driven rather than a statistical plan. Used well, assumptions drive clear communications and fact-based discussions. By debating the assumptions rather than the numbers, accountability is strengthened. For example, a demand plan may have stated assumptions for promotions, marketing campaigns, and new products. Clearly outlining those assumptions and reaching consensus on them (which we will cover in the next chapter) creates accountability for executing the plan. The teams that are responsible for executing promotions and campaigns, launching new products, and making the sales to customers know what is expected and can be clearly held responsible.

Assumptions describe the very things that make a demand plan a *plan*— namely the sales and marketing activities that will be undertaken to generate and influence demand. Assumptions describe strategic activities that may go above and beyond day-to-day sales and marketing activities, such as mergers and acquisitions or divestitures. They also describe the anticipated market conditions, competitive activities, and customer behaviors. These aspects of the marketplace are things that a company may not have direct control or influence over but are important to consider when creating the demand plan. The considerations are made explicit in the assumptions.

The key word here is *describe*. Meaningful assumptions are more words than numbers. They explain the *how* and the *why* of the demand plan, whereas the numbers cover the *what* and *how much*. Articulating assumptions and doing what is described in the assumptions are necessary to make the demand plan trustworthy.

For example, if I ask you to invest $10,000 in my new startup company and I tell you that you will get $20,000 back in three years, you might be hesitant to make the investment. You might be wondering how I plan to generate those returns. You might want some comfort that I'm not running a Ponzi scheme or planning to do something illegal or unethical. You will be much more inclined to trust my plan if I explain to you how and why I expect to do what I'm promising. It's standard practice for a bank to ask for a business plan before granting a loan. It is best practice for executives to expect assumptions to be documented and communicated before approving a demand plan.

* * *

Let's catch up with SmartCorp and see how they are doing with their Demand Management process. It turns out that they are wrestling with how to achieve consensus on the demand plan. SmartCorp's demand planning process involves a preparatory meeting on what to present in the DR, followed by the DR itself with the senior commercial business leaders.

Jeff, the Director of Demand Planning, facilitates the preparatory meeting with participation from the sales, marketing, and finance functions. The decisions made in this meeting establish the proposed demand plan that is presented to John, the Chief Marketing Officer, and Jacob, the Vice President of Sales, in the DR meeting. The senior commercial business leaders also participate in the DR.

Henry joins the preparatory meeting for the first time. Jacob recently hired Henry to lead sales planning and represent the sales organization in the Integrated Business Planning (IBP) process. Jacob felt that it would be more efficient to have a central sales planning function represent the growing field sales organization.

In the preparatory meeting, Breanne, a marketing director, explains the expected results of media investments in advertising and promotion. "With the additional media investment that has been approved, we're expecting to see demand in the fourth quarter increase by approximately 10 percent. Aside from that, there are no other material changes to the plan this month," she tells the group.

"I'm glad to see that we have established visibility to the media investment plans. We used to find out about changes in media spend after they had already happened," comments Jeff.

"I completely agree," responds Henry. "While it's nice to be looking out that far ahead, I'm more worried about the misalignment that we have in the first quarter. We collected projections from our sales account managers last week, and it looks like the proposed demand plan is $40 million higher than what the account managers are projecting customers will buy."

"Do you have a sense of what might be causing the difference?" asks Breanne.

"It's tough to say," replied Henry. "I've spoken with both Felix and Eva, and they're fully committed to delivering their sales plan. Can we agree to use the sales projection for the first quarter, and then use your plan for the rest of the planning horizon?"

"You mean our plan, right?" Jeff interjects. "We have to reach a consensus to the whole horizon."

"That's fine," Henry replies, "but I still think that we should use the sales projections for the near term. We can't bring a recommendation to Jacob that has this much of a difference between what his team is telling him and the current number in the demand plan. The sales team is closest to the customers and knows best what customers are going to order."

"But if we can't explain it, how am I supposed to agree to it?" asks Breanne.

"I think the bigger issue is that if the gap is real, we may be missing something else in the longer term horizon. Our performance has been hurt in the past when we didn't fully understand the assumptions," says Jeff.

"What do you suggest, Jeff?" asks Breanne.

"First, are we all in agreement that we should increase demand in the fourth quarter as a result of the new media investment?" asks Jeff.

Breanne and Henry nod their heads in agreement.

"Good. Second, we have proposed a $40 million decrease to the plan in the first quarter, but we're not quite sure what the assumptions are behind the decrease. I suggest we put that on the list of risks and bring it to the DR with John and Jacob. In the meantime, I'll work with you, Henry, to better understand the assumptions. It is best to understand those before we discuss the implications in the DR. Does that work?" asks Jeff.

"I can live with that," says Breanne.

"Sounds good," agrees Henry. "I appreciate the help."

* * *

Several things can be learned from this SmartCorp example. First, the use of assumptions helped the team to find areas of agreement and consensus. Increasing demand volume and revenue in the fourth quarter based on new media plans were clear and straightforward. Conversely, the gap that Henry identified was not explained with assumptions. Breanne rightfully pushed back, not on the number, but on the inability to explain the proposed decrease in demand. Finding and resolving areas of agreement inevitably comes down to discussing and clarifying the assumptions.

Second, let's look at how the disagreement about the first quarter of the next year was handled. Jeff recognized that without the needed detail behind the sales projection, any debate would just be conjecture. When the team couldn't come to agreement on a change, they agreed to document it as a risk and agreed on the action to revisit the underlying assumptions. They left the preparatory meeting with a clear understanding of the demand plan assumptions and story to tell in the DR. That story included describing what they agreed to change and the follow-up actions to be taken to address areas where consensus was not reached.

Achieving an assumption-oriented discussion of demand isn't always easy. Most demand planning tools cannot combine or organize commentary. These software tools also cannot write an executive summary for us.

In the SmartCorp example, Henry's view was likely the output of a sales planning tool that captured numerical projections but lacked the ability to summarize the assumptions. It was easy to see that there was a difference between the current and past numerical projection of demand. It was not easy to see *why* there was a difference.

Planning software and tools tend to contribute to the problem of focusing on numbers instead of how demand is being influenced and generated. Demand planning tools are fundamentally anchored in numbers. They help to create statistical models. They can aggregate and disaggregate numerical data. They are used to create pivot tables to show numbers in different views, such as translating between different units of measure and isolating specific data by categories. Planning software also can consolidate multiple forecasts from different source systems into a form for identifying any significant differences in the numbers.

Utilizing tools to crunch, slice, and dice numbers is essential, especially for companies that have hundreds or thousands of product items or stock-keeping units (SKUs). However, the problem with demand planning software is that it does not typically provide the functionality for documenting qualitative information. Namely, it does not offer a place for words to live.

When demand planning processes are numbers centric, it stymies the ability to plan with a focus *on* the business. The numbers alone are insufficient for understanding actions that will be taken to influence demand. It's also insufficient for making credible decisions on where to invest and how the market and customers may be shifting in their attitudes and needs. Demand planning software also does not express the level of certainty and uncertainty—and degrees of uncertainty exist in all plans. Uncertainty must be considered in the context of upsides and downsides to the plan, which also must be documented in words, not just numbers.

Mathematician Blaise Pascal is quoted as saying, "If I had more time, I would have written you a shorter letter." This sentiment certainly applies to demand planning. Capability, business understanding, effort, and judgment are required to effectively summarize and highlight the most critical assumptions.

Demand planning is a regular, routine process, with expectations to produce an updated plan and assumptions typically every month. Time is of the essence, and it always feels like there is never enough time to produce the assumptions, numbers, and story that explain the latest view of demand for the executive team.

Adapting the demand planning process to focus *on* the business and consider qualitative information requires a robust assumption management process. Given the level of effort required, anticipated time constraints, and the criticality of proper documentation, assumptions shouldn't be left to chance or simply be considered nice to have. A best practice assumption management process has the following characteristics:

- Ownership of different assumptions, at different levels of detail, over different time horizons, is assigned.
- How and when assumptions are captured, documented, and by whom is agreed upon.
- A mechanism is in place to ensure that qualitative assumptions are consistent with the quantitative demand plan numbers recorded in the demand planning tools.
- A process exists for evaluating and challenging the quality and accuracy of assumptions. This process is used to improve judgment and the understanding of the business.
- Demand plan presentations in the DR include assumptions that are easy to read and digest.

The following is a description of each of these characteristics with an explanation of how they help create a trusted, credible demand plan.

The first step in moving toward an assumption-based approach is to think about the key levers or drivers that influence demand in your business. There may be dozens of different assumptions about the future, but only some of them will be impactful. For example, demand for medical devices might be primarily driven by hospital admissions. Other assumptions, such as clinical marketing efforts, may matter, but to a lesser degree.

One way to distinguish the most important demand drivers is to ask the following questions:

- When the demand does not materialize as planned, what are the most common reasons?
- Did we shift a promotion?
- Did we bring on a new customer?
- Was a new product delayed?
- Are customers not buying at the rate we anticipated, and why?

The drivers of demand will be different across business and industries, but they very often come back to the fundamental four Ps of marketing—product, price, place, and promotion. Assumptions about these four Ps typically come from the commercial side of the business. These same people provide input into the demand plan, as first outlined in *Demand Management Best Practices*,[1] and illustrated in Figure 7.1. The use of these inputs and perspectives remains highly relevant today and is considered a best practice.

As you identify the key drivers of demand in your company, think about which function in the commercial organization is most aware of or is in control of each driver as they develop their plans. For example, pricing is often controlled by sales management or marketing management. There may be situations where the responsibility for pricing decisions is handed off at different points in the planning time horizon. A product management team may initially establish price guidelines for a new product. As the time nears to introduce the product, responsibility may transition to sales management for firming up customer contracts and exact pricing.

Some drivers are generated and controlled by the company's commercial organization—for example, sales development efforts, promotions and branding, and product innovation. Those commercial functions are responsible for communicating assumptions about the drivers under their control.

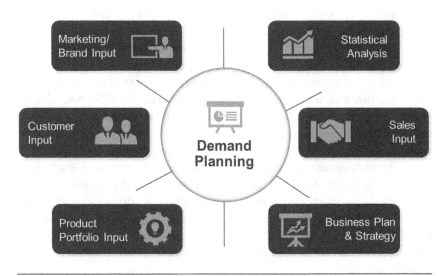

Figure 7.1   Inputs into the Demand Plan in a Best Practice Process.
© Oliver Wight International, Inc. Used with permission.

Some drivers are external in the marketplace and are largely outside the control of a company. Some examples would be market trends, tariffs, regulatory frameworks, and competitive activities. It may take some work to generate market intelligence on these drivers and understand how they impact a company's demand. Different groups in the company may have valuable perspectives on these drivers for different time horizons and in different levels of detail. For example, sales organizations tend to have better insight on the trends being seen with individual customers and sales channels. The marketing organization typically has greater knowledge of longer term market trends, market share, and competitors. Since these are generalizations that may not reflect your organization, it's worth taking the time to explore this topic openly with the different commercial groups in your company.

Wisdom and judgment play a role in consolidating and reconciling the different perspectives reflected in assumptions. Remember, though, nobody has a monopoly on wisdom. It is critically important to have clarity and consistency as to how assumptions are communicated so that the wisdom of the collective commercial organization can be leveraged. As external assumptions are collected and subsequently discussed and debated in the DR, the owner of the demand plan will ultimately have to decide which assumption to base the demand plan numbers on. Unlike an assumption for something within the commercial team's control, the demand plan owner can't simply assign a task and then hold someone accountable for execution. They will be best served by hearing different perspectives. This is made possible by having the right people present and the right balance of discussion in the DR. We will cover how to conduct the DR in more detail in the next chapter.

It helps to have a standard way to document and communicate assumptions—whether business is relatively stable or volatile. The following table illustrates an example framework for establishing the responsibility and inputs for assumptions (see Figure 7.2).

Utilizing assumptions includes agreeing on how the assumptions will be captured and documented. Assumptions often are communicated in a variety of forms, and it is best to leverage the information that already exists within the organization. Examples include portfolio plans, reports or extracts from a promotion planning tool, data received directly from customers, or external briefs from market research firms or trade magazines. This information might come in the form of presentations, spreadsheets, documents, emails, or databases.

For one of my clients, Salesforce Chatter, a social collaboration tool tied to the Salesforce.com platform, was a highly valuable source of inputs from the field sales organization. I pondered at the time that it might not be long until

Assumption	Functional Responsibility	Required Inputs
Market Trends	Marketing Insights	Review of market trends and macroeconomic perspectives
New Products	Marketing	Latest product portfolio plan and in-market performance of newly launched products
New Products	Sales	Updates on customer acceptance of new products
Distribution	Sales	Changes to planned customer acquisitions or geographic expansion
Advertising	Marketing	Changes to planned investment in advertising and latest view of advertising effectiveness
Promotions	Sales	Changes or new approvals on promotional spending or activity
Pricing	Marketing	Impact of pricing in market, pricing vs. competition, price protection, commodities outlook
Customer Inventories	Demand Planning	Changes in expected customer or channel inventory levels
Competition	Marketing Insights	Competitive intelligence and key assumptions of future competitive behavior
Trends	Demand Planning	Statistical trend

Figure 7.2   Responsibility for Assumptions. © Oliver Wight International, Inc. Used with permission.

people were using Twitter to tweet or SnapChat to snap their opportunities and assumptions. The point of these examples is to express the need to communicate assumptions, not via an additional process, but as an extension of existing processes and communication channels, whatever they may be.

Capturing and time-stamping assumptions is critical. I like to think of it as having a virtual shoebox of sorts that I use to collect the various inputs. By keeping and dating the source documents, I can always point back to the source of the assumption. I can better explain the rationale behind a planning assumption as well. I also can call upon the person who communicated the information in order to get more detail if needed.

Demand planning tools tend to fall short, as previously noted, when it comes to recording assumptions and other qualitative information. That being the case, demand planning software can be augmented with what I call an assumption journal. This journal should be structured to easily document, track, sort, and update demand plan assumptions. Some assumption journals take the form of a simple table in a presentation. Other journals are managed with a more sophisticated tool, like a database. An example of a more sophisticated assumption management tool is illustrated in Figure 7.3.

If you're not sure how assumptions are being documented or tracked in your organization, do some digging. An assumption journal often already exists in some form as a bridge document that a demand planner, brand manager, or finance manager is maintaining.

The assumption journal makes it efficient to determine how demand projections changed between planning cycles. It can also be used to highlight gaps between the demand plan and the annual budget as the demand plan changes and evolves through the course of the year.

An assumption journal helps tell the story of the latest demand projections along with the market conditions and customer trends. It ties the assumptions and their quantitative impacts to the volume, revenue, and profit numbers.

Figure 7.4 provides an example of an assumption journal.

Key elements of an assumption journal include:

- The planning cycle or month when the assumption was added or changed
- The assumption itself—written descriptively in a way that is intuitive and easily understood
- The time-phased volume and revenue impact of that assumption

An assumption journal is generally managed at an aggregate level of detail. This keeps the journal from becoming unwieldy, particularly when a business has many items or customers. In that case, maintaining assumptions at

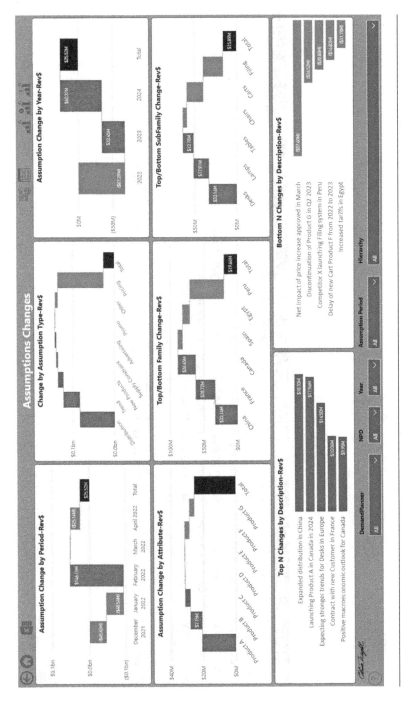

Figure 7.3   Example of a Tool for Tracking Assumptions. © Oliver Wight International, Inc. Used with permission.

Plan Version	Driver	Assumption	M0	...	M12	...	M24
January Cycle	Innovation	Launching new High Definition Satellite Radio			200	300	400
January Cycle	Distribution	Expanding sales of Industrial into 3 new States	150		100	100	75
January Cycle	Promotion	Coupons on portables for the Summer period			75		
February Cycle	Advertising	Advertising spend cut in March to hit Q1 margin objective				(200)	
February Cycle	Cannibalization	Aligned that HD Radio will only be 75% Incremental			(30)	(30)	(30)
February Cycle	Inventory	Key customer is reducing their level of inventory		(75)			
March Cycle	Distribution	Expanding into online sales channel			150	150	150

Figure 7.4   Template for Assumption Journal. © Oliver Wight International, Inc. Used with permission.

the lowest level of detail would be too time-consuming and cumbersome to review and manage. If your planning tools only operate at a detail level, consider it another indicator that the tools are not well suited for managing assumptions. Other means for documenting and managing assumptions, such as a journal, are necessary.

Deciding the level of detail at which to document assumptions must be well thought-out. Different assumptions will apply at different detail levels in the planning hierarchy. Chapter 10 discusses everything from aggregate on up to detail planning and highlights the importance of aligning planning hierarchies with key inputs and assumptions.

Assumption capture and documentation is just like any other process—garbage in will lead to garbage out. The quality of the inputs and assumptions that are captured directly drives the quality of the resulting plan. When assumptions about the plan are either missing or are too general, it is difficult to commit to and then execute the plan with confidence. Without the information provided by the assumptions, business leaders often end up debating the numbers, which is usually a waste of time and energy. It is difficult, if not impossible, to confidently make decisions when the numbers are in question and salient information is lacking.

If you look through your DR materials and see comments like the following, you might have a problem with assumption quality:

- Product X increased from +4% to +10%
- Miss in January rolled forward into February
- Call-down due to lack of momentum
- Increase in Brand X driven by increase in item ABC
- Taking down November due to underselling
- Forecast increase due to strong consumption

Each one of those examples is vague, lacks needed specificity, and does not address the *how* or *why* behind the assumption. It is not clear what needs to be done for the demand to be realized. Understanding what caused the changes in demand increases the usability of the assumptions and provides more credible information to the business leaders.

For example, if the comment "Miss in January rolled forward into February" was restated as "January order from Customer ABC delayed to February due to a pricing discrepancy that has been resolved," it would be clear that no action is needed. By contrast, if "Increase in Brand X driven by increase in item ABC" was restated as "Increase in Brand X driven by new promotional activity planned for item ABC," it would be clear that a promotion needs to be executed.

Sometimes general assumptions, as shown in the previous examples, result from not asking questions about the changes in demand projections. Demand planners and managers cannot be expected to know everything about customers, marketing plans, and the business itself. They must ask questions.

Asking the right questions often takes courage. The good news is that there is no such thing as a stupid question, so asking questions is usually a relatively safe endeavor.

Let me share my experience. I ask questions all the time. I often find myself in a DR with a new client where I don't know the history or nuances of the plan nearly as well as the other people in the room. Asking a few simple questions can uncover gaping holes or misalignments in the assumptions about the demand plan and performance of the business.

Questions need to be asked in a constructive spirit. The purpose of the questions is not to criticize or throw anyone under the bus. Figure 7.5 illustrates a simple, straightforward conversation for better understanding assumptions.

Asking questions in a constructive manner to better understand assumptions is an application of the Socratic Method. The Socratic Method, developed by the Greek philosopher Socrates, is a cooperative dialogue where a group explores the underlying beliefs, or assumptions, that shape their views and opinions. By exploring and better understanding those underlying beliefs, contradictions can be eliminated. You can help the team to draw out presuppositions and strengthen their collective understanding by asking probing questions such as:

- How do we know this?
- What would this imply?
- What would be an appropriate alternative?

As assumptions are captured and documented in the Demand Management process, handoffs of the information will take place. For example, a sales leader who is accountable for a demand plan may receive marketing inputs pertaining to new products. The sales leader shouldn't blindly add volume for new products to the demand plan. The sales leader should ask enough questions to understand the assumptions for those new products. The litmus test is whether the sales leader can subsequently, and on his or her own, explain and defend the assumptions and volume changes, if necessary.

Figure 7.6 shows an example of the flow of an assumption management process. The various inputs about future demand are communicated to the demand manager, as shown on the left of the process flow. The demand manager is responsible for reviewing and consolidating the different inputs.

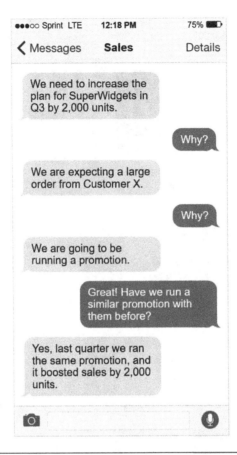

Figure 7.5   A Conversation to Clarify an Assumption.

As the inputs are consolidated, asking pointed questions to validate them is critical. Doing so filters out weak or questionable assumptions early in the process. Identifying a weak or questionable assumption is not always straightforward, however. There may still be questionable judgment behind well-formed assumptions.

For example, an eager salesperson might communicate the assumption that he or she expects to win a large contract with a new customer. The assumption might be correctly formed, but the probability could be highly unlikely. Asking pointed questions to validate inputs should also take into consideration past performance. Sound judgment by the demand manager is also required. The final decision to incorporate an assumption into the demand

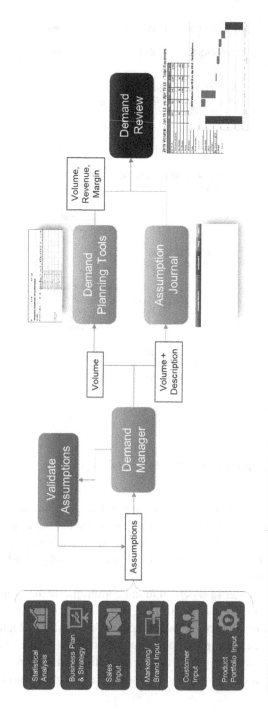

Figure 7.6   Assumption Management Process Flow.

plan, however, occurs in the DR. It is not solely up to the demand manager to decide what is discussed in the DR. Nevertheless, demand managers must ensure that the assumptions brought to the DR are explainable and understandable. Demand managers are also responsible for highlighting issues and requesting that decisions be made in the DR.

The demand manager is usually accountable for creating and maintaining the assumption journal. This accountability helps ensure that the documented assumptions are aligned with the demand plan numbers—and vice versa.

* * *

Let's see how things have progressed at SmartCorp since the preparatory meeting was held. While they endeavor to reach a consensus on the demand plan, it emerges that some of the assumptions lack clarity and continue to pose some challenges in reaching a consensus on the demand projections.

"I'm feeling pretty good about next quarter," says Jacob, the Vice President of Sales. "Our forecast is coming in at $210 million, and Project Alpha is really taking off. Despite the rocky start with RetailMart, Project Alpha products are selling at a much higher velocity than the old version."

Jacob expresses this enthusiasm in the SmartCorp DR meeting. The meeting is being facilitated by Jeff, the Director of Demand Planning. John, the Chief Marketing Officer, is also in attendance.

John has a different assessment than Jacob. "I'm always glad to hear that you're feeling good, Jacob. The thing is, based on our view of those admittedly strong velocities, we think that revenue in the next quarter should be much higher. It should be $250 million," John says. "Breanne walked me through her projections, and the math is solid." Breanne is one of John's Marketing Directors and is always very methodical in her approach to planning.

"This leads us to a topic that I want to address with the team," says Jeff. "We identified a disagreement between sales and marketing on the demand projections for the first quarter during our preparatory meeting last week. I took the action to work with Henry in sales planning to try to understand the difference between the two numbers. Unfortunately, we haven't been able to come to a resolution."

"Henry told me that you were working on it," says Jacob. "I trust my sales team and their projections, but we probably need to come to some sort of compromise here. What if we split the difference and agree on $230 million?"

"I'm fine with that," agrees John, "so long as we keep an opportunity in front of Supply for the additional $20 million. I don't want us to give up on it completely."

"Great, we have a consensus," Jeff says. "Let's wrap up with a process critique and then we're done for the day."

Jeff appears visibly relieved. He has been worried that by not completing the follow-up with Henry, that they wouldn't be able to reach a consensus in the DR.

A few weeks later, the SmartCorp leadership team discusses their latest predicament.

"We just can't keep up with all these orders," says Colin, the Vice President of Supply. "We're going to have to go into allocation. Wasn't this new consensus process supposed to improve the accuracy of the demand plan?"

"It's supposed to," says Jeff. "We had agreement from both Jacob and John. We even kept a buffer for demand volume that would result in an additional $20 million in revenue, but even that wasn't enough."

Jacob jumps into the discussion. "The problem is that my team has no line of sight to the ad campaign for the Alpha products that Breanne was planning in the first quarter," he said. "If we would have known about that, then we wouldn't have approved promotional pricing. We could have managed the volume and held higher margins."

"What promotional pricing?" asks John. "Since when are we authorized to discount new products?"

"Good question," adds Mike, the Chief Financial Officer. "We didn't include price discounts in the P&L model."

"Everybody calm down," says Katia, as she takes a deep breath. "This is a problem, make no mistake, but at least it's a good problem. Jeff, given what we know now, how high could the demand be?"

"Well," says Jeff, "my team has done some modeling. Our statistical baseline suggests $180 million. We layered on top of that projection the impact of the price discounts in increasing demand volume. That boosts revenue another $40 million and then the ad campaign which gives us another $80 million. We are looking at $300 million this quarter."

"Thanks Jeff," says Katia. "First, we need to make sure that the consensus process is getting ahead of these sorts of issues. Second, and more important, I want to understand why, regardless of our ability to supply, we have ended up promoting and discounting a new product at the same time. That doesn't make any sense," said Katia.

* * *

Katia is correct. This was the learning for the commercial side of the business: the plan assumptions need to include all efforts to influence the volume, mix, price, and timing of demand. While some marketing information was communicated, the focus was more on numbers than actions being taken to spur demand, like price discounts and the ad campaign.

In this SmartCorp example, the team took an approach that might be familiar to you. They took two forecasts and decided to split the difference. They could have chosen to lean more heavily in favor of the sales team's input under the presumption that the sales organization, by virtue of their connection with customers, is more directly able to recognize and influence near-term demand. They could have chosen to rely on a statistical forecast, as it has no bias and has been developed to mathematically deliver the lowest statistical error. Either of those options, however, would have led to an even worse outcome.

Both approaches would be focused on the wrong thing. All too often, people are preoccupied with the demand plan numbers and fail to spend adequate time truly understanding what is driving demand and what they're signing up to do to achieve the plan. By shifting the thinking toward understanding market conditions, competitors, and customer needs, and then discussing and aligning appropriate actions, business leaders start to make better business decisions.

Had the pricing plan and new ad campaign plan been communicated properly, the discussion would have shifted to the wisdom of those decisions. In the DR, the business leaders could have questioned whether it made sense to run an ad campaign and implement promotional pricing at the same time. Synergies, trade-offs, and negative consequences could have been considered.

Aligning on the assumptions would also have established clear accountability for the sales organization to implement the promotional pricing and the marketing team to run the ad campaign. In essence, ownership of the various components of the plan would have been established. If either of those activities failed to occur as planned, it is relatively easy to explain the results and assign accountability for improvement. No matter who caused the gap between the demand plan and actual sales, the commercial side of the business is accountable for taking actions to create a more credible and trustworthy demand plan.

When the debate about the demand plan centers on a number, confusion and misunderstandings are common. It is not clear whether there is a disconnection between the activities, the quantification of the activities, or both. In the SmartCorp example, it was not evident during the DR that there was misalignment between John and Jacob in terms of what pricing and promotion activities were expected. In doing a postmortem discussion at the end of the quarter, however, it was clear that John did not know about the price discounts and Jacob did not know about the ad campaign. Lack of clarity leads to frustration in the consensus process. Worse yet, it leads to reaching consensus on a number without agreement to or understanding of the underlying commercial activities, as happened with SmartCorp. Always remember, commitment without understanding is a liability.

Better understanding of assumptions also helps when projections of demand are already acceptably accurate. Take, for example, a manufacturer with a product line that had a very predictable demand pattern. The pattern was seasonal, and there were periods of ups and downs that were consistent year over year. The statistical forecasting models considered the level (average), trend, and seasonality of demand for each planning period. The statistical projections provided a degree of accuracy that was acceptable to the business. In response to the demand plan, the supply chain organization, for example, was able to create a cost-effective production plan that provided high service levels with a relatively low level of safety stock.

At one point a key raw material for the product became constrained. Through the IBP process, the supply chain team recognized that there would be shortages and that service levels would be negatively impacted. They started working to resolve the gap between demand and supply that would result from the shortage of raw material. It was a straightforward exercise. Everybody trusted the demand plan, and therefore worked to find a substitute raw material to maximize production output and have product available to fulfill the product requested in the demand plan. The substitute raw material was more costly, however.

The team failed to appreciate that quite a few of those seasonal high points in demand were driven by promotional activities. Nobody had done the homework to investigate and understand the assumptions that were implicit in the demand plan. In fact, assumptions were not reviewed in the DR or in the Management Business Review (MBR).

Had the underlying demand plan assumptions been more obvious, other less costly options could have been considered. An option that could have been considered was delaying or canceling promotional activities until the raw material shortage with the original supplier was resolved. The money invested in promotional spending could also have been shifted to a different project. The finance organization could have been consulted for help with quantifying the financial impacts of the various options on revenue and profit projections. Consideration of these types of options is referred to as *demand shaping*, and it depends entirely on understanding the assumptions and levers of demand.

In this case example, the supply chain team trusted the demand plan without truly understanding it. The Integrated Reconciliation process did not trigger functional managers to consider the assumptions that drove demand projections either—nor did the executive team in the MBR.

When situations like this case example occur, it often leads to trust being eroded or lost. The supply chain team may have relied on the demand plan for years because it was acceptably accurate. More important, they relied on the demand because there were no negative consequences to doing so. If the supply chain planning team had been reprimanded for having made the wrong decision to expedite the substitute raw material, their willingness to trust the demand plan in the future would be diminished.

The documentation and the understanding of assumptions are often critical inflection points for companies. The discussion about the assumptions behind the demand plan demonstrates that better business decisions are made when business leaders know what is driving the plan. Rather than just creating a more accurate projection of demand, business leaders reach a new level of maturity that allows them to be more planful, and consequently, to create a more agile organization. Agility comes from being able to identify issues and create scenarios that consider different options. These scenarios are driven by different sets of assumptions as to what might occur on both the demand and supply sides of the business. Scenario planning will be covered in more detail in the following chapters.

SUMMARY

- Assumptions are the key to creating a business-driven demand plan.
- Assumptions drive clear communication and fact-based discussions, thereby strengthening accountability.
- Assumptions describe:
  - Sales and marketing activities that will be undertaken to generate and influence demand.
  - Strategic activities, such as mergers and acquisitions or divestitures.
  - Anticipated market conditions, competitive activities, and customer behaviors.
  - Any other relevant expected actions or conditions that would impact demand.
- Assumptions explain the *how* and the *why* of the demand plan, whereas the numbers cover the *what* and *how much*.

- Assumptions are managed as part of the demand planning process, with clear ownership and an agreed-upon process to collect, document, evaluate, and track them.
- Assumptions are included in the DR in a way that is easy to read and digest.
- Some assumptions are better than others. Constructively asking questions to clarify assumptions is a great way to avoid vague or nonspecific assumptions that lack the *how* or *why*.

QUESTIONS TO ASK

- What assumptions are most impactful to the demand plan and the business in general?
- Where are assumptions being documented and tracked today?
- Who is ensuring that communicated assumptions are consistent with the numbers (volume and value) being entered into the demand planning tools?
- What tools are best suited for documenting and managing assumptions?
- Are the most important assumptions easily visible to the internal customers of the demand plan?

ENDNOTE

1. Colleen Crum and George Palmatier. *Demand Management Best Practices: Process, Principles and Collaboration.* J. Ross Publishing, Inc., 2003.

CHAPTER 8

REACHING CONSENSUS IN THE DEMAND REVIEW

For many sales and marketing executives, the Demand Review (DR) meeting itself is the only way that they engage in the demand planning process. They are rarely involved in the many preparatory meetings or the significant work done in advance of the DR to collect, quantify, and document assumptions. Through that preparatory work, gaps in expected revenue and margin as well as in performance are identified, and recommendations are prepared to present at the DR. These elements of the plan and performance measures must therefore come together in a way that is appropriately summarized for the executive participants of the DR.

The DR is not simply an information-sharing session, and it is about more than just the demand plan. It is a decision-making forum that is used to determine how best to achieve business goals and strategic objectives.

Critically, the DR is a forum for commercial leaders to work *on* the business and set the plans that their teams are empowered to execute. Recall from Chapter 2 that for leaders to do work on the business, they must:

1. Have confidence that their teams will follow the demand plan, and will escalate up the decision chain of command when deviations to the plan are anticipated or occur
2. Be confident that the plan they helped develop and approve can be executed
3. Along with their teams, understand how the plans are connected across functions and how the plans will enable achievement of the company's business objectives

The DR, therefore, is a place where the commercial team shares their different perspectives, makes decisions, and importantly, encourages and strengthens teamwork. When a demand plan is agreed to in the DR, the different players—sales, marketing, and product management—must play their positions and trust each other to do the same. In this chapter, we will discuss the DR meeting itself, what to expect, and what behaviors to watch for. We will also identify best practices to ensure that the DR is time well spent.

The primary purpose of the DR is to reach consensus on the demand plan and align on the activities, actions, and investment required to execute the plan and achieve business goals and strategies. One way to simplify the required points of alignment and agreement in a DR is to consider the following four questions:

- How have we been performing in executing the demand plan and achieving our goals and strategies?
- What new information have we learned that should cause the demand plan to change (since last month's DR meeting)?
- How does the demand plan measure up against our business goals and strategic objectives?
- What decisions do we need to make at this DR and in future DRs to achieve those goals and objectives?

Posing and answering those four questions will lead to the right outcomes for the business.

First of all, the demand plan must be executable. Being executable means that it can be followed by the commercial organization and used by other internal customers and stakeholders without ambiguity. Leaders need to have confidence that when a plan is approved, it can and will be followed and will deliver the expected results (within a reasonable tolerance). It is important, therefore, to evaluate how well the business has been performing with existing plans and adjust as necessary. For example, if the demand plan is consistently too optimistic or pessimistic, recommendations need to be presented in the DR to eliminate that bias.

Second, the demand plan must be responsive to changes in the business and marketplace. New information must be captured, considered, and contemplated in the plans being put forward for approval. Responding to that new information isn't enough on its own, however. The implications of those changes must be evaluated to ensure that business goals and objectives will still be met. If they aren't, then decisions are needed on how to meet goals and objectives. The topic of business goals and objectives will be covered in more detail in the next chapter.

One of the decisions that will be made each month is whether there is consensus on the demand plan itself. Many other types of commercial decisions are commonly made in the DR as well, such as:

- Adding or removing investment in sales, marketing, and other activities (promotions, incentives, discounts, media, sampling, consumer spending initiatives, etc.)
- Prioritizing resources, such as salespeople, sales support, marketing investments, or promotional budgets between customers, markets, brands, and categories
- Approving changes to prices and pricing strategy
- Responding to competitive activities, market trends, and economic conditions

Decisions pertaining to any of the four Ps of marketing (product, place, price, and promotion) are relevant in a DR. After all, a DR is all about the commercial side of the business. Decisions are typically brought forward in response to gaps between the current demand plan outlook and business objectives. They may also be triggered by cross-functional issues identified through the Integrated Business Planning (IBP) process.

Recall the example from Chapter 4 where a company made the decision to delay a significant new product launch. The decision to delay was not due to a gap or issue in either the portfolio or demand plans, but instead was determined the best way to achieve a company level profit objective. The delay would naturally lead to decisions having to be made in the DR to shift demand to existing products and adjust the timing of customer communications for the new product.

Consider where significant commercial decisions are being made in your own company that impact demand volume, revenue, and margin. Each of these types of decisions should be either made in, or properly connected to, the DR. This commercial focus might seem foreign or uncomfortable at first to people who have a supply-chain-centric view of demand. As the demand plan assumptions become the focus of discussion in the DR, it becomes naturally evident that the forum to make commercial decisions and the forum to decide on demand plan assumptions should be the same.

For example, a client company was in the early stages of implementing IBP. The sales, marketing, and finance teams had historically made commercial decisions in a monthly leadership meeting. Separately, representatives from the sales and marketing teams met with the demand planning team to share their inputs to the demand plan. The discussions in the two forums were very different.

Some of the differences in the two meetings was intentional. There was a behavior of making conservative commitments in the leadership meeting, and then providing aggressive projections in the meeting with demand planning. Most of the difference, however, was simply because the sales and marketing leaders participated in the leadership meeting but did not participate in the demand planning meeting. Their teams, therefore, put more effort into explaining their assumptions and articulating their plans in the leadership forum.

As part of designing the IBP process, the two meetings were consolidated. The feedback from the demand planning team was immediate and positive. They were amazed by the amount of information that they were now privy to, simply from being included in the commercial decision-making discussions. Similarly, the feedback from the commercial leaders was also positive. They were impressed with the supporting information and context that the demand planning team was able to provide.

Companies with a supply-centric view of demand planning all too often do not consider commercial issues in a DR. Decision making has a distinct orientation around impact on supply capabilities instead. A supply-centric orientation fails to address:

- Strategies and tactics for influencing and generating demand
- Actions and changes needed to attain commercial goals and strategies
- Ways to grow demand volume and revenue to help achieve business goals and strategies

With this context and the objective of the DR in mind, let's take a moment to consider the participants of the DR. Participants can be categorized into three groups: the *executive owner*, the *process leader*, and the *consulted attendees*.

The *executive owner* is the sales or marketing leader who is ultimately responsible for execution of the plan and accountable for performance. The executive owner chairs the meeting and facilitates reaching consensus on a plan that is realistic and trustworthy. The executive owner also facilitates making decisions on how best to achieve business goals and objectives. When the executive participants cannot reach consensus on the plan and decisions, the executive owner will approve the plan and make the decisions.

We can see from the examples of commercial decisions addressed in a DR that the executive owner would typically hold decision authority over the profit and loss statement (P&L). It is therefore up to the executive owner of the DR to set the expectation that the DR is where P&L related decisions will be made. That means making decisions as they are brought forward and not *taking them offline* or addressing them in another forum.

The adage "with great power comes great responsibility" is true for the executive owners. They must take their ownership role seriously.

The difference between an executive owner who takes the role seriously and one who abdicates or misuses the responsibility can be dramatic. I observed this difference firsthand when the Senior Vice President (SVP) of Sales to whom I reported changed roles. The former SVP had significant leadership experience in a manufacturing company and understood the importance of a trustworthy demand plan in running the business. The new SVP had nearly all of his experience working in software companies. While he brought great commercial experience to his SVP role, he had limited understanding, or concern, for demand planning. I was instructed to make the demand plan equal to their budget and be done with it.

When situations like this one exist, some would suggest that this is a good reason why the executive owner of the demand plan should not be a commercial leader. The right solution, however, isn't to take demand plan accountability away from the commercial side of the business. That only creates other problems that surface when the executive team becomes misaligned. Instead, in companies with a best practice IBP process, the President or Chief Executive Officer holds the DR executive owner accountable for taking the role seriously and for:

- Delivering a consensus demand plan that is trustworthy and unbiased
- Delivering a consensus plan that all commercial leaders are committed to execute
- Using the DR for commercial decision making, and not relying on separate, disconnected processes for decision making

The owner of the DR also sets the model of behavior both in the DR and during the day-to-day operation of a Demand Management process. Some of the key behaviors include:

- Upholding demand planning best practices
- Ensuring that the plan is not arbitrarily overridden or adjusted
- Ensuring that all significant changes to the volume and revenue projections in the demand plan are tied to the assumptions
- Communicating the latest assumptions along with the volume and revenue projections in the demand plan

The DR owner is assisted by a *process leader* who is responsible for orchestrating the demand planning process. The process leader is typically, but not always, a demand planning leader. As noted in Chapter 2, demand planning leaders do not necessarily have to report to the executive owner, but they must be trusted by the executive owner. They also must be able to advise the executive owner and provide honest counsel. That requires mutual respect.

The process leader synthesizes inputs, prepares for, and facilitates the DR meeting. This person must feel comfortable elevating the tough conversations and decisions that need to take place in the DR, while ensuring that appropriate meeting norms are followed. The most effective process leaders do not shy away from conflict. They are skillful at facilitating when there are disagreements and helping people with diverse viewpoints to resolve issues.

My colleague Timm Reiher recounts how his skills grew when he was a DR process leader:

> "I facilitated what I believed to be very good DRs. Everyone got along well. People were happy, even joking some. We stayed on agenda, the numbers were good, and we had confidence in the plans.
>
> "I would feel great after a meeting, quietly congratulating myself on how good I had become at my role. I would crack a smile as I gave myself a well-deserved mental pat on the back while returning to my office. My company was very lucky to have me!
>
> "Occasionally I would facilitate a DR that I would describe as a trainwreck. New information and supporting assumptions were unclear and in dispute. People did not agree, and tempers would flare. We were not making our numbers and had a hard time finding a way to close the gaps between the demand projections and annual goals.
>
> "Several times I had to intervene to calm the group down. After one such meeting, I felt terrible, almost as if I had failed. No one was happy, and I was the one who facilitated the trainwreck.
>
> "Rather than patting myself on the back, I began to ponder what changes I would have to make because I never wanted to go through that again. And then the phone calls and emails started to roll in. Here are some examples:
>
> - 'Finally, we addressed it.'
> - 'I know that was not fun, but we had to tackle those problems.'
> - 'I feel so much better now.'
> - 'Thank you!'
>
> "This feedback made me realize that sometimes when we are in the position of facilitating a meeting or a process in general, we get too wrapped up in the mechanics. Our personal idea of success is a meeting or process that runs smoothly with no challenges and people who participate generally feel good about it.
>
> "With Demand Management and IBP in general, that is not always the case. The participants know when problems are not being

addressed and are grateful for the opportunity to manage through them. Their perception of a successful meeting can be very different than the facilitator's.

"It is important to recognize this dynamic and not avoid confrontation. A good demand manager should facilitate confrontation while maintaining professionalism, which is sometimes not easy!"

I have worked with clients in a wide range of cultures. One culture could be described as overly *nice*. Another common culture was *no-holds-barred*—very direct and abrupt in discussions. Even though it is emotionally challenging, the *no-holds-barred* culture can often get to the heart of an issue and resolve it far more quickly than the *nice* one.

In companies with a *nice* culture, I find people are willing to sit in DR meetings and politely debate superficial issues with one another for hours. Then they leave in a stalemate. The rooms were full of so-called *elephants*. Controversial issues were obvious, but no one wanted to discuss them. It was too uncomfortable and perceived to be culturally unacceptable to do so.

In situations where conflict is likely, process leaders have the task of facilitating in such a way that people feel safe in participating in the discussion and decision making. Creating this safe environment doesn't just involve good facilitating during the DR; it requires advance preparation and engagement of key players prior to the review.

First, the process leader should identify in advance the contentious topics that need to be discussed. Then the process leader should plan how the discussions will be facilitated so that they are productive and constructive.

This preparation may involve having a discussion with the executive owner beforehand. The facilitator and owner should discuss how to respond and react when controversial information is shared. The discussion may have a wide range as facts and feelings surface. The process leader may feel more like a therapist than a demand manager at times, but it's all part of developing a trusted relationship with the business leader. Various details about these conversations should be kept confidential, unless the owner is comfortable in the details being shared with others.

The third category of DR participants are the *consulted attendees*. Identifying the right consulted attendees is a balancing act. The term *consulted* is important. This group of people should, for the most part, have something to contribute to the discussions in the DR.

I often come across DR meetings (or frankly meetings in general) where dozens of people are invited to attend. It's not uncommon in large organizations to see meetings with 80 to 100 people on the invitation list.

Meetings with many participants are almost always ineffective. Leaders shy away from having the truly tough discussions when too many people cram into a meeting room. In the article *Why Your Meetings Stink—and What to Do About It*, author Steven G. Rogelberg writes:

> *"Once you know why you're meeting, decide who needs to be there to help you. Too many attendees can lead to a cacophony of voices or social loafing (whereby individuals scale back their efforts under the protection of a crowd), not to mention logistical challenges. That said, you don't want to pare the invite list down so much that necessary people aren't there or others end up feeling slighted. To find the right balance, think carefully about key decision makers, influencers, and stakeholders. Make sure that those outside the circle feel included, by asking for their input before the meeting and promising to share it and keep them in the loop."*[1]

Smaller groups almost always lead to better discussions, tougher decisions being made, and fewer discussions being taken offline. That being said, once consensus is reached, the distribution list for sharing the agreed plan should be broad. The approved demand plan should not be a secret.

I worked with a rapidly growing company that struggled with meetings. The hiring of employees had far outpaced the maturity of the company's governance processes. As a result, the number of people in meetings had grown out of control. There was initial concern that by uninviting people from meetings, they would feel disempowered and wouldn't get face time with the executives. What business leaders found, however, was that the real decision making was taking place outside of the formal meetings. The executives would have the tough conversations in private, ad hoc discussions. The face time that invited meeting participants were getting with the executives was superficial.

When the DR attendee list was pared back, the process leader was asked to extend the invitation to others as needed, based on the issues being discussed. This approach ensured the opportunity for exposure with the executive team when appropriate. It also ensured that discussions during the DR were far more impactful with a smaller number of participants.

As noted earlier, identifying the right number of consulted attendees is a balancing act. Having multiple inputs and perspectives into the demand plan is also critical. In the book *The Wisdom of Crowds*,[2] author James Surowiecki shares how consensus decisions are regularly better than decisions made by any one individual. The example he uses is a country fair contest to guess the weight of an ox. No one's guess, regardless of their level of expertise, was more accurate than the collective average guess of the entire crowd. Even in situations where there are experts involved, the addition of multiple perspectives, over time and over many iterations, tend to drive the group to better decisions.

The number of different perspectives on demand and in the marketplace will depend on the size and complexity of the organization. In a complex business, there may be commercial perspectives from account-level salespeople, product managers, category or market insights leaders, shopper marketing leaders, brand directors, and more. Each will bring a different perspective to the information being discussed in a DR.

One way to identify the right list of consulted attendees is to look at the list of most impactful assumptions that help create a trusted demand plan. Which functions or groups within an organization are responsible for the demand-generating activities? Which functions or groups are accountable for delivering the projected results? Who generated the information upon which the assumptions are based?

If you have completed the exercise from Chapter 7 of defining the most critical assumptions for your business, identifying the right consulted attendees should be straightforward. Referring to the example framework for assumption and input ownership (see Figure 8.1), the consulted attendees should reflect the different assumption owners.

For multiple perspectives to be heard in the DR, there must be a balanced discussion without any one individual or function dominating the conversation. When one person or group takes over the discussion, others become reluctant to contribute.

Having balanced discussions is not only important to ensure that the best decisions are being made. In my experience, balanced discussions give everyone a voice in the process. Without full participation in planning, consensus, and decision making, it is unreasonable to expect full alignment in execution. When someone is not able to contribute to the discussion but is expected to abide by the decisions made, it becomes difficult to enforce the execution of the decision. It offers the excuse to say, "That's not my plan," and shirk accountability.

The success or failure of reaching a consensus on the demand plan and other decisions in the DR is not measured based on how well the discussion goes during the meeting. If it were, my client with the *nice* culture would have had a perfect score. It is measured, instead, by how well everyone adheres to the plan that is approved and the decisions that are made.

Reaching consensus on the demand plan doesn't mean that everyone loves the decisions made during the DR. It means that everyone agrees to execute the plan. In the context of a monthly planning process, it means

Assumption	Functional Responsibility	Required Inputs
Market Trends	Marketing Insights	Review of market trends and macroeconomic perspectives
New Products	Marketing	Latest product portfolio plan and in-market performance of newly launched products
New Products	Sales	Updates on customer acceptance of new products
Distribution	Sales	Changes to planned customer acquisitions or geographic expansion
Advertising	Marketing	Changes to planned investment in advertising and latest view of advertising effectiveness
Promotions	Sales	Changes or new approvals on promotional spending or activity
Pricing	Marketing	Impact of pricing in market, pricing vs. competition, price protection, commodities outlook
Customer Inventories	Demand Planning	Changes in expected customer or channel inventory levels
Competition	Marketing Insights	Competitive intelligence and key assumptions of future competitive behavior
Trends	Demand Planning	Statistical trend

Figure 8.1   Responsibility for Assumptions. © Oliver Wight International, Inc. Used with permission.

everyone will support the plan—at least until the next month when new information, assumptions, or performance results justify making changes to the demand plan.

When participants leave the DR meeting and choose to operate a different plan than the one approved, consensus has not truly been achieved. For my *nice* client, the stalemates in the DR led to confusion and misalignment. There was no consensus, and as a result, different functions operated different plans. Without consensus or agreement to execute the plan, leaders are inevitably dragged down into the details of execution. That leaves them little time to spend working *on* the business.

Note that in Figure 8.1, the finance and supply chain functions are not shown as inputs into the demand planning process. They commonly have representation in the DR, however.

The finance team may sometimes provide input such as marketing or promotional budgets that they have helped commercial teams to develop. The finance team is also responsible for ensuring that the financial projection that was developed through the IBP process is consistent and aligned with the assumptions in the demand plan.

Finance representatives in the DR may pose questions to better understand assumptions, but their role is not to override the plan. Disagreements on the financial aspects of the demand plan may be addressed in the Integrated Reconciliation process as part of the IBP process. Disagreements may also be brought to the President or CEO, if they are significant, in the Management Business Review. These actions do not shift ownership of the demand plan to the finance team. Ownership and accountability for the demand plan rests with the executive owner of the DR.

The supply chain organization may also have representation in the DR meeting, but it is important to be cautious when this is the case. Having a supply chain leader present at the DR can lead to discussions about the ability to produce product, which is the objective of a Supply Review, not a DR.

It is helpful, however, for a supply chain representative to hear the discussions about the demand plan firsthand. The supply chain representative can better understand the nuances of the demand plan that may not be readily apparent through the numbers in a planning system or report.

Etiquette and protocol for the supply chain representative's participation in the DR meetings should be well understood by all participants in these meetings. For example, the supply chain representative should not be expected to answer supply-related questions, nor should the supply chain representative bring up supply-related issues.

Publishing an agenda for each DR helps remind participants of their roles and accountabilities. It also helps to keep the review properly focused. Figure 8.2 shows an example of a typical agenda for a DR meeting.

As noted earlier, the DR is a decision-making forum. Therefore, it is best practice to outline the required decisions up front. First, this challenges the process leader to think through the required decisions and ensure that the request for a decision is clear and well-articulated.

One executive whom I worked with would start each meeting by asking what decisions were needed of the participants. If the process leader who was facilitating the meeting couldn't answer succinctly, the executive would leave. That executive is now the CEO of a very successful multi-billion-dollar company.

I coach process leaders to put the executive owner to work. The process leader should think through and make clear what is expected of the executive owner. Similarly, executives should expect to be put to work. Executive owners can and should provide guidance as to what topics they would like to address in each DR.

Determining decisions that need to be made in the DR is a two-way street. Any participant should feel free to request a decision to be made and should work through the process leader to do so. The process leader also may identify decisions to be made and should work through the appropriate participants to be ready to explain the request for a decision.

This discussion about decision making highlights the importance of the process leaders in the DR and their level of influence. The process leaders are accountable for setting the agenda for the discussions in the DR. They also facilitate the discussions about decisions in the DR and, in doing so, influence the decisions that are made.

The decisions outlined in the agenda should be communicated prior to the DR. This discipline means that the executive business leaders must then come prepared to make those decisions. The materials for the DR should be communicated between 24 to 48 hours in advance of the meeting. This timeline gives the participants sufficient time to read and understand the materials and come prepared to contribute to discussions in the meeting.

One of the decisions made each month is reaching consensus on the demand plan itself. The approach to consensus is anchored in the principle that *we have a plan until we decide to change it.* The focus of the DR is to agree to the proposed changes to the demand plan. Done well, those proposed changes are expressed in assumptions that explain the conditions that caused the proposed changes. The assumptions may be questioned or debated to validate consensus on the resulting changes in volume, mix, pricing, and revenue. For

	Description	Owner	Comments
1	Opening Comments and Focus of the Demand Review	VP Sales or Marketing	Set focus of meeting and comment on current situation
2	Key Decisions Required	Process Leader (Demand Manager)	Need to be made today Need to be made in the future
3	Review Outstanding Action Items	Process Leader (Demand Manager)	Completed action items are listed in Appendix
4	Performance Review	Consulted Attendee Owners	Key performance indicators. Actions being taken to improve.
5	Business Trends	VP Marketing	Key market trends being monitored that may trigger change of tactics and other actions
6	Strategic Initiatives Review	VP's / Consulted Attendees	Review of progress toward achieving strategic initiatives
7	Demand Plan Review by Family • Significant Assumption Changes Since Last Month and Impact • Risks & Opportunities • Required Decisions	Sales or Marketing Directors	Issues addressed as needed by appropriate Sales or Marketing Leaders
8	Summary of Risks & Opportunities	Process Leader (Demand Manager)	Recap and summarize key Risks & Opportunities Identify potential scenarios for Supply Review to evaluate
9	Input to Next Cycle, Review Action Items, and Meeting Critique	Process Leader (Demand Manager)	What to address next month. Validate agreement on action items. What needs to be improved with the IBP process.

Figure 8.2 Demand Review Agenda. © Oliver Wight International, Inc. Used with permission.

those parts of the demand plan that are unchanged, it is a waste of time to revisit the plan and assumptions during the DR.

In a best practice DR process, there is trust that due diligence has been performed in reviewing and updating the assumptions—which results in trust that the changes recommended and decisions requested in the DR are the proper focus for the executive owner and consulted attendees. This is an area where I often coach leaders to step out of the details and empower their teams to tell them where they should focus. Trust isn't automatic—it is two-way, and it is earned. Leaders need to give their teams the opportunity to earn their trust and guide their focus in the DR.

When trust and empowerment do not exist, a certain pattern of behavior is evident. Dozens of slides and an enormous amount of supporting detail are typically prepared for the DR. When asked *why*, the answer typically is that while they don't want to, they *have* to, because they never know what questions the executives will ask. They need to be prepared for all possibilities.

When I question the executives as to why they ask such detailed questions about the plan, they tell me they don't want to, but feel they *have* to because they keep finding mistakes. They believe they need to pressure test the demand plan to make sure it is accurate.

This behavior becomes a vicious cycle. The planning team is relegated to preparing reams of supporting detail, and the executives are expected to sift through it and find the important nuggets of relevance. Nobody is happy with the effort required, and often are not satisfied with the resulting plan.

The solution is to set the right expectations. I coach leaders to stop expecting perfection. No demand plan is 100 percent accurate, and their teams may not be as capable as the executive business leaders in finding and resolving every issue. I advise business leaders to become comfortable with being approximately right instead of precisely wrong. Doing so requires a change in behavior. Business leaders must step out of the detail, and instead, coach and develop their teams to be able to identify needed decisions and bring credible recommendations to the DR. This isn't a demand planning skill that is lacking; this is a leadership skill that needs to be developed.

Discussions in the DR should always be anchored in assumptions and other pertinent information rather than feelings, hunches, or aspirations. Assumptions and information should not live only on a notepad of someone responsible for providing input into the demand plan or in a demand manager's head. They must be presented clearly in the DR.

Most organizations do a good job of getting the demand volume and revenue numbers on the page. Quite often I encounter what I call the *wall of numbers* in a DR. What the wall of numbers lacks, however, is a distillation of the key assumptions that have the most significant impact on the plan numbers. It is insufficient to simply show a set of numbers and expect the commercial leaders to figure out what the numbers represent in terms of the actions they and their teams will need to take for those numbers to be realized.

I have over the years seen many different formats and approaches for presenting assumptions in a DR. The following are a few examples for how demand plan information and assumptions can be presented in a way that best tells the story of the demand plan. Good storytellers know their audience and adapt their approach accordingly.

The first example leverages an assumption journal to help tell the story of the demand plan in the DR. The assumption journal in this example is adapted to succinctly explain changes that have occurred since the last DR, and possibly prior DRs as appropriate (see Figure 8.3). Some people call this chart a change journal or bridge report.

Use of a change journal or bridge report is often an ideal place to start a review of the latest demand projections because it focuses on new information and changes to the demand plan. Reaching a consensus on the demand plan can be as simple as agreeing to each of the items listed in the change journal or bridge report.

This approach may also be used to connect the proposed demand plan with a prior financial commitment or annual budget. Doing so helps preserve the integrity of the story and key assumptions. It also is helpful in overcoming *demand plan amnesia*, where changes that were agreed upon during a prior month are forgotten—sometimes by the people who proposed them in the first place.

An effective change journal or bridge report requires careful thought about how to summarize what may be dozens of discrete changes to the demand plan. The information shown should reflect the most impactful and/or controversial changes to the plan. These changes should be easily understood by the participants in the DR. The wording should not be ambiguous and the unit of measure used (which is not explicitly stated in Figure 8.3) should be easily understood by all participants. While it is best practice to present the demand plan in both volume and value, it may be ideal to present certain views in volume and others in value to illustrate the impact of the changes to the plan more concisely.

Figure 8.4 shows a useful way to summarize demand information for presentation in the DR. This presentation is sometimes referred to as a plan on a page. It combines a graphical presentation of demand information with what is commonly called a *six-box summary* (due to the six boxes at the bottom of the page). The plan on a page summarizes the key elements of a demand plan. It can be presented for a brand, product family, channel, or total business.

	Q2	Q3	Q4	FY	Q1	
March Demand Review	77,153	77,266	78,363	304,906	78,800	...
New promotion with Customer ABC in August		7,000		7,000		
Cancellation of advertising campaign tied to budget reduction	(1,000)	(1,000)		(2,000)		
New product launch delayed by 2 months to incorporate additional feature			(7,000)	(7,000)		
Additional volume expected from new product as a result of additional feature					4,000	
Revised base trend given macroeconomic outlook	(2,500)	(2,500)	(2,500)	(7,500)	(2,500)	
April Demand Review	73,653	80,766	68,863	295,406	80,300	...

Figure 8.3 Change Journal or Bridge Chart. © Oliver Wight International, Inc. Used with permission.

Time Phased Volumetric Plans

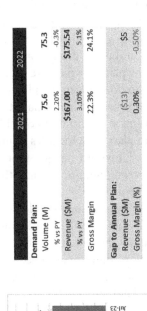

Legend: Annual Plan · Actual Sales · Demand Plan · ····· Prior Year

Financial Rollups

	2021	2022
Demand Plan:		
Volume (M)	75.6	75.3
% vs PY	2.20%	-0.3%
Revenue ($M)	$167.00	$175.54
% vs PY	3.10%	5.1%
Gross Margin	22.3%	24.1%
Gap to Annual Plan:		
Revenue ($M)	($13)	$5
Gross Margin (%)	0.30%	-0.50%

Decisions Made
- Price reduction will stay in-plan despite changes in customer inventory holding level.

Decisions Required
- Approve competitive response contingency plan

Key Planning Assumptions
- Category growth will continue at 4% CAGR
- New Product X will receive full distribution by August
- 10% Temporary Price Reduction in February

Assumption Changes
- Inventory holding for distributors is set at 25 days of inventory, except for Central at 19 days of inventory

Risks/Emerging Issues
- New Product X may be delayed ($2.3M Impact)
- Competitor Z may enter the market in April

Opportunities
- Pipeline for Langkawi sales from Labuan
- May: New 40g Tri Pack/Banded Pack

Figure 8.4 Demand Review Plan on a Page. © Oliver Wight International, Inc. Used with permission.

This page combines a graphical, time-phased representation of the demand plan with qualitative commentary outlining the assumptions, risks, opportunities, and required decisions. A graphical presentation of demand enables the executive business leaders to quickly grasp the state of the business and changes to demand volume, revenue, and profit projections.

The assumptions summarized in the plan on a page are usually not exhaustive. In fact, it is typically impossible to do so given the physical limitation of space on the page. That limitation, however, is beneficial. It forces the preparer to think critically about what is most important to consider in reaching consensus and approving the demand plan. That includes assumptions where there is likely disagreement. I like to ask myself what questions the executives will either most likely ask or have a strong opinion on, and then outline the answers in the appropriate areas on the page.

In my experience, the summary of assumptions should consider the lens of the commercial team. Think about what the sales, marketing, and product management leaders need to know about the demand plan. Consider any key assumption changes that relate to actions they are expected to take or results they are expected to produce. It is best to make it easy for the executives to quickly be able to see what is expected of them and their teams.

Another approach to telling the story during the DR is the use of a table that outlines key assumptions over the planning horizon (see Figure 8.5). This table is different from a more detailed assumption journal in that it summarizes assumptions by time periods. This type of table works well when there are well-defined types of assumptions that can be quantified or described briefly.

Note that the assumptions in Figure 8.5 also include notations of the degree of control that the company has over that variable. (Recall the cough drop example from Chapter 2 where a company has full control over the price of cough drops, but little or no control over the severity of seasonal cold and flu illnesses.) Also note that not every assumption is numeric—some could be binary (yes/no) and others could be briefly described in the table.

The assumption table shown in Figure 8.5 has several advantages. It is easy for a sales or marketing leader to scan the list of assumptions and verify that their understanding is properly reflected in the demand plan. It allows business leaders to see what is most relevant to the business. For example, a sales executive can see that the demand plan assumes that the average number of products sold to each customer is expected to steadily increase over time. Similarly, a product management executive can see the volume that is expected to be generated from new product introductions. All business leaders

Assumption	Degree of Control	Now	3 Months	6 Months	9 Months	12 Months	15 Months	18 Months	24 Months
Market Assumptions									
Population of users	Some	20,000	22,000	22,000	22,000	22,000	22,000	23,000	24,000
Growth of economy	None	.5%	.5%	.5%	.25%	0%	0%	0%	0%
Rate of new product introduction	Full	0	2	1	1	0	0	2	2
Number of competitors	Some	20	18	16	14	10	8	8	8
Competitor activity	None	None	None	None	New products	Promotions	Promotions	Promotions	Promotions
Market price movement	Some	+5%		+10%		+10%		+5%	
Promotional activity	Some	High	High	High	Medium	Medium	Medium	Medium	Low
Market share	Some	25%	25%	25%	26%	30%	30%	35%	35%
Sales Assumptions									
Customer population – Small	None	200	200	180	150	120	120	100	100
Customer population – Large	Some	20	25	30	35	40	40	40	40
Share of customers	Some	40%	50%	50%	50%	50%	50%	50%	50%
# of products listed per customer	Some	5	5	5.5	6	6	6.5	7	7
Competitor activity	None								
Etc....									

Figure 8.5 Assumption Table. © Oliver Wight International, Inc. Used with permission.

should quickly be able to validate that the assumptions are consistent with what they expect their teams to deliver.

In the DR, it is informative to highlight with an annotation any recent changes or proposed changes to assumptions. For example, when there are changes to assumptions, a box placed around those entries serves as a flag for attention. Adding a note or call-out to the slide helps explain the change in assumption and the impact to the demand plan. An example of this type of presentation should also tie back to the changes outlined in the change journal or bridge chart (see Figure 8.3).

Where possible, it can be very advantageous to take the summary of changes to assumptions a step further. Linking the impact of the assumption changes to anticipated volume and/or revenue enables business leaders to focus on how the changes impact the business. This approach is often referred to as using building blocks. An example is shown in Figure 8.6. This figure shows the volume demand plan. The same approach can be used to show projected revenue and projected profit.

Building blocks establish a common language for categorizing and communicating planning assumptions. In the example shown in Figure 8.6, the building blocks are the labels across the horizontal axis (Price, Competition, Distribution, Advertising, etc.). They are derived or taken directly from the

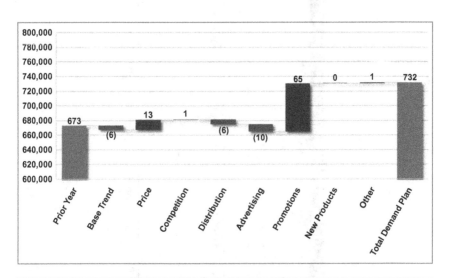

Figure 8.6 Waterfall Chart of Building Blocks Used to Create the Demand Plan. © Oliver Wight International, Inc. Used with permission.

work that was done to define assumptions and input ownership (see Figure 8.1). Building blocks are grounded in the language that the business leaders use when speaking about the business and communicating demand-driving activities. When used appropriately, building blocks make it easier to tell the story of the demand plan. Larger organizations commonly use building blocks when there are many different brands, channels, or categories. It enables consistency in language and explanations when talking about the demand plan.

Building blocks are a method of categorizing and grouping different assumptions. For example, the *Advertising* building block may contain within it multiple campaigns, tactics, and activities. Each of these discrete assumptions is documented, quantified, and categorized as being part of the *Advertising* building block. The volume and financial impacts are then summarized, making it easier for business leaders to view aggregate information in the DR.

Figure 8.7 shows how each key building block impacts demand volume over time. In this example, the full-year demand plan is 731,757 units (last column). It is expressed as the summation of the prior-year volumes and each of the different building blocks. Each building block explains a change or difference between the current-year plan and prior-year actual results.

Driver	Q1	Q2	Q3	Q4	FY
Prior Year	164,839	167,364	192,972	147,977	673,152
Base Trend	(1,465)	(1,376)	(1,509)	(1,193)	(5,542)
Price	(346)	173	4,643	8,857	13,327
Competition	0	83	215	351	650
Distribution	(3,061)	(1,690)	(979)	(670)	(6,400)
Advertising	(450)	(800)	(1,200)	(7,500)	(9,950)
Promotions	4,311	42,133	11,728	7,171	65,343
New Products	0	0	0	0	0
Other	40	62	1,039	37	1,178
Total Demand Plan	163,869	205,948	206,909	155,031	731,757
% vs Prior Year	-0.6%	23.1%	7.2%	4.8%	8.7%
Change vs Prior Year	(970)	38,584	13,938	7,054	58,605
Change vs Budget	(346)	(9,731)	1,236	3,619	(5,222)

Figure 8.7 Table of Building Blocks Used to Create the Demand Plan.
© Oliver Wight International, Inc. Used with permission.

This approach to developing a demand plan is commonly used in companies where demand is relatively stable year over year and where leaders tend to speak about commercial objectives in terms of growth-rate percentages.

A Base Trend building block is commonly used to reflect the long-range trend of the business (growth or decline). This trend is usually calculated using a statistical projection. Moving then from Prior Year and Base Trend, the various assumption categories are summarized by each building block. The impact that those assumptions have on the demand volume is shown for each quarter and the total year. In this example, Promotions contribute the most to the year-over-year increase in demand volume. Most of that increase in demand volume is expected to occur in the second quarter.

Viewing the demand information in this manner helps to validate the credibility of the demand plan. A sales or trade marketing leader can quickly assess whether the demand generated from promotions makes sense. Does that demand volume and the timing of the promotions coincide with what the leaders know is planned for promotional activity? Are the leaders still committed to delivering the demand volume that is expected from trade promotions? Do any uncertainties exist that might impede execution of the promotions?

Remember, the DR and IBP are aggregate planning processes with a focus *on* the business. Should more detailed information be needed for specific discussions, the underlying detail is available. The process leader and demand planners are accountable for preserving the details on key assumptions and drivers.

I worked with one Marketing Director who referred to areas of uncertainty as *squishy blocks*. She would review each of the demand plan building blocks and note those that were *squishy* versus those that were *solid* (solid meaning high confidence in both the assumption and the quantification). She would then spend her time clarifying the actions and expected results that were explained in the squishy blocks. That meant either removing demand volume from the plan that was represented in uncertain assumptions or focusing on validating that a squishy assumption was really going to happen. For example, a squishy promotional building block could be made solid by confirming the promotional plans and the anticipated result with the respective owner of that assumption.

As noted earlier, executives need to trust that this sort of due diligence has been done; they should not expect that all the details are brought to the DR and reanalyzed. Answering a detail question with, "I'll get back to you" should be acceptable and should not derail the DR.

Accountability is significantly strengthened by defining building blocks and grouping assumptions so that they align with the responsibilities for creating or influencing demand and, by extension, the functional owners of those activities. For example, the sales organization may be accountable for the activities that drive customer promotions. By communicating assumptions in a building block approach, it reduces ambiguity and makes it clear what each executive is accountable for delivering. It enables them to see their part of the plan more clearly.

Recall the SmartCorp example from Chapter 7 where John and Jacob decided to split the difference between their two views of demand. If that discussion had instead been supported with building blocks, Jacob would have been able to see the presence of an advertising building block and the absence of a promotional building block. The misalignment of assumptions would have been obvious, and the issue avoided.

If there is a disagreement with the assumptions or the resulting demand and revenue projections, adjustments to the plan can be made. Sometimes these adjustments are made prior to the DR through discussions with the process leader, the responsible commercial party, and the demand planner. Other times, the discussion occurs in the DR, especially when proposed changes significantly impact the plan that was approved the previous month. In either case, the adjustments are grounded in assumptions rather than arbitrary adjustments based on gut feelings, intuition, or splitting differences.

Using building blocks to tell the story of the demand plan makes it more credible. The participants of the DR validate that the plan is based on reality, rather than wishful thinking. Business leaders are better able to reinforce with their teams what they are expected to deliver. Business leaders can also look the owner of the DR in the eye and say, "I can commit to this plan."

There is one more essential aspect to a DR. Once executives understand and agree to the demand plan and the assumptions that underpin it, they will then have a basis for determining if that plan will result in achieving the intended business goals and objectives. That creates a platform for decision making. That is the focus of the upcoming chapter.

SUMMARY

- The DR is a forum for commercial leaders to work *on* the business and set the plans that their teams are empowered to execute. It is a decision-making forum that is used to determine how best to achieve business goals and strategic objectives.

- Discussions focus on points of disagreement or areas where additional clarity is needed to reach a consensus.
- The DR should answer these four questions:
  - How have we been performing in executing the demand plan and achieving our goals and strategies?
  - What new information have we learned that should cause the demand plan to change (since last month's DR meeting)?
  - How does the demand plan measure up against our business goals and strategic objectives?
  - What decisions do we need to make at this DR and in future DRs to achieve those goals and objectives?
- The participants of the DR include:
  - The *executive owner* is the sales or marketing leader who is ultimately responsible for execution of the plan and accountable for performance.
  - The DR owner is assisted by a *process leader* who is responsible for orchestrating the demand planning process.
  - The remaining participants are *consulted attendees* who contribute to the discussions in the DR.
- Reaching a consensus on the demand plan through the DR is cross-functional, involving the business leaders from sales, marketing, product management, and demand planning.
- The number of participants in the DR are kept to a minimum. It is recognized that a large crowd makes reaching a consensus and making decisions more difficult and time-consuming.
- For multiple perspectives to be heard in the DR, there must be a balanced discussion without any one individual or function dominating the conversation.
- To ensure a focus on decision making, it is a best practice for the process leader to outline the required decisions at the beginning of the DR.
- The demand plan, supporting information, and discussions are based on assumptions with a focus on the business.
- A consensus covers the entire planning horizon (ideally, at least 24 months).

QUESTIONS TO ASK

- Do you have the right cross-functional participation in your consensus process—at the right level of responsibility?

- Are the commercial leaders involved? Do they take ownership of the plan?
- Are consensus discussions grounded in assumptions and other facts about the business or do discussions focus on picking a number?
- Does the DR process leader facilitate tough, controversial discussions and help the decision makers to resolve disagreements?
    - If not, who does? And is this the appropriate person?

ENDNOTES

1. Stephen Rogelberg. "Why Your Meetings Stink—and What to Do About It." Harvard Business Review, November 25, 2020. https://hbr.org/2019/01/why-your-meetings-stink-and-what-to-do-about-it.
2. James Surowiecki. *The Wisdom of Crowds*. Anchor Books, 2005.

CHAPTER 9

ACHIEVING BUSINESS GOALS AND OBJECTIVES

My colleague Timm Reiher often tells the story of a conversation he had with an executive in a large consumer goods company. The company was working to improve its demand planning process. The executive understood the principles of demand planning, but he expressed a real concern. "I'm worried that we're just creating a process that makes us comfortable with a lower number," he told Timm.

The executive feared that the commercial teams would reach a consensus on a demand plan that was lower than the annual budget number. He was concerned that no actions would be planned or executed that would narrow the gap between the demand plan and annual budget.

It was a valid concern. It is a shallow business leader who would accept reaching a consensus on a demand plan without discussing how the annual budget, business goals, and strategies are going to be achieved.

Yes, the demand plan should reflect reality. It also should show the gap between the unbiased demand projections and the business plan and financial commitments that have been made to senior leaders, the board of directors, and shareholders. That means the Demand Review (DR) and the Management Business Review (MBR) meetings should focus on plans for achieving the business goals and strategies. Decisions should be made in these reviews that chart the path for executing the goals and strategies. Why *don't* executive teams utilize the DR and MBR to close these types of gaps? The reasons are mostly behavioral.

In my experience, it is a common characteristic of senior business leaders to be passionate about meeting or exceeding business targets, especially when a high proportion of compensation is tied to delivering on those targets. When business and performance targets are at risk, commercial leaders commonly ask these questions:

- When there is a gap between the demand plan and my objective, how do I know and trust that people are working on closing that gap? If I accept a plan that doesn't meet the target, how can I trust that my team won't give up on closing the gap?
- How can we close the gap if we don't have an adequate supply of product? How can I push the sales team to sell more if I know we're not producing enough of the product that they are focused on selling?

These are good questions to ask. It is even better to develop processes and behaviors when these types of concerns surface. It is a best practice to design the Demand Management process to regularly expose gaps between the latest demand projections and the annual budget as well as business goals and objectives. It is a best practice for executives to ensure that activities and actions have been assigned to close any gaps. It is also a best practice, as painful as it may be, to communicate when gaps cannot be closed. These leadership behaviors ensure that everyone is working toward achieving the company goals and strategies rather than seeking comfort with low demand projections.

When companies plan over a 24-month rolling planning horizon, business leaders gain the advantage of time for resolving issues that cause gaps. Gaps are visible far enough in the future that the commercial and supply organizations have time to respond in the most cost-effective way. This visibility gained is illustrated in Figure 9.1.

Making gaps visible as early as possible is fundamentally about avoiding surprises. When people make commitments—to one another, to their leaders, to boards of directors, to shareholders, and to their teams—they are expected to deliver on their promises. This is a best practice.

What should people do when something happens that threatens their ability to meet a commitment? Consider the example of your son or daughter going out with friends. Before they leave, you agree with them that they will be home by 10 P.M. When they return home an hour late, not only have they broken the agreement, but they have undermined your trust. There might be a completely legitimate and valid reason for being late—perhaps their car broke down or they were stuck in traffic. The explanation, however, rarely makes you feel any better about the situation.

In the book *Crucial Accountability*, the authors illustrate this common problem as the result of accepting the following trade-off:

$$Results = no\ result + a\ good\ story[1]$$

All too often, organizations get in the habit of avoiding the tough conversations until it is too late to take action that would enable achieving the original

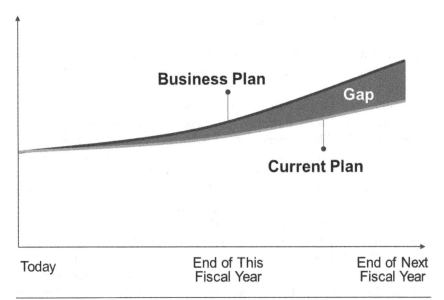

Figure 9.1   How to Visualize Gaps Between the Business Plan and Current Plan. © Oliver Wight International, Inc. Used with permission.

promise. One sales executive explained it to me like this: "I'd rather be beaten once for missing my target, than beaten every single month for showing the gap between the demand plan and annual budget." A cynical demand planner once told me his job was to predict what would happen, and then explain why it didn't. These types of behaviors hold back organizations from reaching their objectives.

A former Oliver Wight principal would regularly remind his clients: "Don't confuse effort with results." Most business objectives are not simply to *try hard* or *do our best*. A pattern of not delivering on commitments but instead providing explanations or excuses does not create trust and is rarely tolerated for long.

The better behavior is to encourage transparency and regular communication. The CEO of one of my clients said it well in an MBR: "Good news is good news, bad news is good news, but no news is bad news." The point is that news of any kind, good or bad, is better when shared early rather than late—it affords the organization time to respond to the news.

The authors of *Crucial Accountability* provide a similar solution to this problem that can be summed up in a sentence: "If something comes up, let me know as soon as you can." Communicating any risk of not fulfilling the plan as quickly as possible is critical to preserving trust.

Leaders should be grateful for being given visibility to gaps. This might sound counterintuitive at first. Why would someone be grateful to hear that there is a chance that goals will not be met? The answer is simple. It gives business leaders critical advance notice and allows them to consider alternative courses of action.

Communicating potential gaps between the latest projections and the business goals is like looking at the long-range weather forecast when planning a trip to the beach. If there is rain in the forecast, we may choose a different day or a different activity. Providing visibility to gaps is like providing visibility to the chance of rain. If business leaders don't see the weather forecast, they can't plan around it. It is a key responsibility of business leaders to reinforce a mindset of continuous gap closing in their organizations.

When the forecast is looking *iffy*, leaders need to understand what is contributing to the gap between demand projections and business goals. This is where a robust list of opportunities can be worth its weight in gold. When considering how to close the gap, the first place to go is the opportunity list. The question to ask is: Which of these opportunities should we now leverage to close the projected gap?

Trust is the foundation that ensures that gaps are visible with enough lead time to address and resolve them. Organizations that have not developed trust within teams, with leadership, and cross-functionally, would rather not acknowledge potential gaps in meeting business goals. Lack of trust results in gaps being communicated at the latest time possible, as depicted in Figure 9.2. The gap is revealed in the near term because there just isn't any hiding from it anymore, and the long-term view remains neatly aligned with the business plan.

When gaps are communicated only in the near term, it can trigger many counterproductive behaviors and decisions. Some organizations find themselves compensating for near-term misses by arbitrarily increasing the demand plan in future months or quarters to show on paper that the annual plan will be achieved. This behavior contradicts the best practice to plan based on reality.

The language when the demand plan has artificially increased is a telltale sign itself. The override may be expressed in the plan as a *go-get*, plug, whitespace, or gap filler. Use of these terms should be red flags for business leaders, especially the company President, CEO, CFO, and the heads of sales, marketing, and supply chain.

The impetus for these overrides is often twofold. First, is the desire to hide or avoid communicating the gap. Second, commercial leaders may argue that filling the gap in demand with sales that have not yet been developed is a

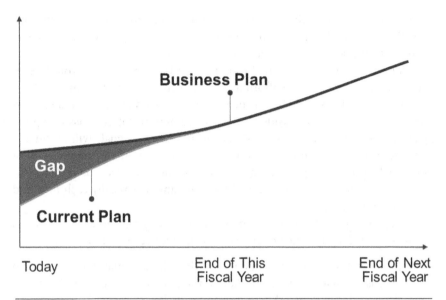

Figure 9.2 When Trust Is Lacking, Potential Gaps in Meeting Business Goals Are Identified Only in the Near Term. © Oliver Wight International, Inc. Used with permission.

necessity. Otherwise, the supply organization will never be able to produce product that materializes at the last minute to close the business gap. The thinking is that they *don't want to take themselves out of the game prematurely.*

This type of behavior can result in problematic hockey-stick-shaped plans where demand at the end of a quarter or the end of a year becomes extremely exaggerated. These time periods are when performance results are usually reported and compared to targets and goals. The impacts of this behavior go well beyond demand planning. Commercial and supply activities are often undertaken that are costly and unsustainable.

I have on many occasions found businesses stuck in a vicious cycle of end-of-quarter or end-of-year pushes to achieve targets. These end-of-period activities often involve giving incentives to customers to buy more than they would otherwise need at that time. All too often these push activities do little to create incremental demand, and only shift demand from one period to another. Worse yet, it trains customers to expect to receive incentives or discounts by simply holding back orders until the end of the period. This cycle can be extremely difficult to break.

Ideally, decisions on how to resolve gaps between the latest demand projections and the business goals should be made well in advance of critical lead times. These lead times include the time it takes to develop new customers, the lead time for developing and executing market promotions, and lead times for production and the purchase of raw materials.

Not wanting to give up on closing the gap is normal, and I would never suggest that a company not afford itself that decision. The problem is that it is not a decision that should be executed via the demand plan. This is a *business* decision that needs to consider the risks and opportunities of assuming the gap between the demand projections and the business goals will eventually be closed. The decision directly impacts the supply plan and supply costs of potentially producing product that will not be sold. The decision directly impacts the financial circumstances of the company, specifically cash flow and potential revenue and profit.

Being transparent about gaps between demand projections and business goals—and the sooner the better—is important for several reasons:

1. It reinforces the accountability of the sales and marketing leaders to ensure that the demand plan is based on assumptions and is unbiased. If the demand plan is chronically low or high when compared to actual sales, commercial leaders must ensure that behavior is corrected at the source and not masked with overlays.

2. It makes the implications on inventory and financial results transparent. Plugging the demand plan with artificial volume creates an optimistic view of revenue, inventory, and margins. It degrades trust in the company's business plans, especially among the company board of directors. Adjusting the company supply plan and financial plan based on the most likely demand retains the integrity of the supply and financial plans. It makes transparent the most likely projection of inventory and cash investment to support the plans.

3. It affords supply leaders the flexibility to consider and recommend different strategies that put the company in the best position to respond to increased demand as gap-closing activities are achieved. Some of the supply strategies often include flexible labor and postponement of production. Decisions on the best strategy must take into consideration the acceptable risks from customer service and financial points of view.

Supply chain planners may ask the demand organization for detailed information to consider when recommending how to best minimize supply risks. This detailed information often can be readily gathered from the opportunities list. When the demand opportunity list is updated every month, there should be no need to artificially force opportunities into the demand plan.

The decision on actions to take in order to close the gap between projected demand and the business plan is not solely made by the commercial organization. The decision to invest in having product ready in case the gap is filled is not solely made by the supply organization. These decisions need to be made by the cross-functional executive team. That's one purpose of an MBR as part of the Integrated Business Planning (IBP) process.

The basis of these decisions needs to be what is best for the business and what is best for the customers. Collaboration among the executive team to decide the best way to approach the gap in demand is far preferable to requiring the commercial organization to artificially include demand in the plan just to trigger production. The cross-functional business leaders need to understand how likely it is that the actions being taken by the commercial organization will close the gap. They need to review a financial assessment of the implications of not achieving the business revenue target versus investing in inventory to fulfill unprojected demand. Leaders also need to understand the impact of gap-closing actions on future performance, such as the period-end pushes that were described earlier. They may realize that solving a near-term gap is just buying time and not helping to address why customers are buying less than what is needed to achieve business goals.

This is why gap closure is a key topic that is addressed in the DR and throughout the IBP process. Discussing options and alternatives to close gaps creates confidence and trust with cross-functional leadership. They see that the commercial organization is aggressively turning over every stone to create demand that will meet the business goals, both in the short term and long term.

When the commercial organization has a proven record of proposing options and alternatives to ensure achievement of the business plan, their recommendations are taken more seriously by the cross-functional business leaders. That even includes when they find themselves in a situation where the gap simply cannot be closed. The conversation in delivering this bad news can be less stressful when trust is a hallmark of executive leadership. The executive team is already aware of everything that has been done to increase demand. The cross-functional business leaders are less likely to shoot the messenger when they believe the commercial organization has done everything in their power to close the gap.

Business leaders are responsible for thinking more broadly about what could happen that is different than what is currently being assumed, even if those possibilities have a lower likelihood of occurring. These possibilities are commonly labeled as identifying risks and opportunities. A best practice Demand Management process considers significant risks and opportunities that could materialize.

One way to stay focused on closing the gaps is to review risks and opportunities in the DR and throughout the IBP process. Figure 9.3 illustrates some example assumptions and the variations of those assumptions that would make them either risks or opportunities. Risks, by definition, are things that if they happened, would cause demand to be lower than currently planned. Opportunities are things that if they happened, would cause demand to be higher than currently planned. A common convention for demand planning is that product volume associated with opportunities *is not* in the demand plan, and product volume associated with risks *is* in the demand plan.

One reason for reviewing risks and opportunities is to keep everyone's eyes on the business. The review provides business leaders information on the likelihood of the demand plan materializing as planned. It also arms commercial leaders with a better understanding of the market potential and how the business might assertively realize that potential—and even exceed it.

Deciding whether a risk or opportunity should be incorporated into the demand plan requires experience and judgment. It also requires a process with inclusion criteria that is well-respected by the organization. The process for managing risks and opportunities also helps ensure that there is no double counting in the demand numbers.

I have not found a perfectly objective method for determining the likelihood of a risk or opportunity to materialize, although I have seen people try. Care must be taken to ensure that the process does not become an over-engineered exercise in false precision. For example, if your inclusion process creates a distinction between an opportunity that has a 67 percent probability and one that has a 72 percent probability of occurring, I would question the time and energy being spent assessing those probabilities. The effort will not create a more trustworthy demand plan. A better approach is to use simple categories of high, medium, and low probability and then focus on what actions could be taken to improve the likelihood of opportunities and reduce the likelihood of risks. In some cases, a sales funnel, with criteria linked to the stages of the selling process, can be leveraged to determine whether demand should be included in the plan or remain an opportunity.

I also caution against consolidating the total volume of risks and total volume of opportunities and then creating a risk-adjusted number or view. Demand does not always materialize in averages. Each risk and each opportunity will either materialize or it won't. Judgment must be made to exclude risks and opportunities from the demand plan because they are not likely to occur. In the case of opportunities, a judgment must also be made as to whether that demand is worth expending resources to generate. For example, a chemical client had an opportunity for additional business outside the

Risk	In the Demand Plan	Opportunity
New tariff comes into force in Q3 which would increase the shelf price of our product by 15%.	No new tariffs come into force over the next 24 months.	Existing tariffs are lifted starting in Q3.
Key customer delays expansion of their retail footprint by 10 months.	Key customer is expanding their retail footprint from 250 to 300 stores over the next 8 months.	Key customer expands their retail footprint to 400 stores over the next 6 months.
	No lift assumed.	We secure placement in a key customer promotion in Q4 of next year which will drive a 30% lift to velocities through that period.
	Product reformulation assumed to launch in September.	Product reformulation can be accelerated by 6 months.
Customer de-lists our product in favor of a competitor.	No de-list assumed.	
Customer demands slotting fees for additional items to be listed across their banners.	No slotting fees assumed.	

Figure 9.3 Example of How to Communicate the Impact of Risks and Opportunities. © Oliver Wight International, Inc. Used with permission.

United States, but it would yield a lower margin. During the DR, business leaders decided not to include the demand in the plan and to only develop that business if other higher margin demand failed to materialize.

The management of risks and opportunities should be a routine part of the demand planning process. It is unfortunately common for business leaders to canvass the commercial organization for opportunities only when the demand plan is falling short of objectives. The downside to this approach is that people respond by communicating everything they are doing to try to generate demand, whether these efforts are likely to come to fruition or not. They brainstorm demand-generation ideas. Such opportunities are all too frequently documented without understanding if the assumptions behind those opportunities are truly being acted upon and whether the opportunities are already included in the demand plan.

Even when the demand plan projections are meeting or exceeding targets, a culture of continuously driving for more is best. Targets should not be downward limiting. I can remember a Vice President of Sales in the biotech industry barking at her sales managers, "You are not order takers! You're responsible for developing new business and growing revenue!"

Leaders that consistently deliver on their commitments don't do so by chance. They do so by having a wide range of options and alternatives that they can leverage in response to the things that they can't control. If one customer goes bankrupt, they should have been working to develop another customer to compensate. The key is to be working on these contingencies in advance—not to start from scratch when an issue or gap arises.

As organizations mature their demand planning process, there is a clear shift in how time is spent in the DR and MBR. Discussion shifts away from debating, or *pressure testing* the plan numbers and assumptions. Discussion shifts to strategies and tactics for achieving the business goals for revenue, margin, and market share. Greater time is also spent on considering risks and opportunities and their impact on the business. In the most mature processes, most of the time is spent discussing opportunities and what it would take to realize them. This not only creates options for leaders, but it also sets the expectation that teams aggressively pursue growth opportunities.

Identification of gaps and management of risks and opportunities leads to better decision making in the DR and MBR. Good decision making is often aided by using a template. Figure 9.4 shows the structure of a decision template. It also illustrates an example through which a decision to increase promotional spending is presented.

In the example in Figure 9.4, several best practices come together:

Decision – Increase promotional spending to deliver incremental revenue, market share, and avoid inventory liquidation exposure.	
Situation Assessment	Customer X has delisted product ABC, leaving us with a significant amount of inventory that is nearing expiration. Originally Customer X offered to help deplete inventory, but at such a low price that we refused the offer due to the high risk of disrupting price stability in the market. The team has worked to identify additional potential retail opportunities to sell the product.
Decision Needed & Timing	Customer Z is the most likely buyer. Sales account manager is confident that a deal can be reached with an incremental 30% promotional investment. Securing this deal would expose some price-matching risk at Customer A, estimated at $50K but could be as low as zero, based on volume and price point. Payment of price-matching penalty is contingent on a request from Customer A and is very unlikely. Important to note that we have NOT had any price-matching to date on any of the pricing activity for this product, despite Customer X currently selling at $7.99 (down from the target price of $9.99). Given the unique nature of these items the liquidation team feels that they would be very challenged to sell through traditional liquidation channels. The cost of the finished goods + semi finished goods is approximately $150K. Additionally, packaging write-offs could be expected if the current semi-finished goods are not completed. (The value is not yet available, but is estimated to be $50K.)
Options / Alternatives	1. Provide promotional funding to Customer Z sales team, plus accrue for possible Customer A price-matching to sell through the remaining inventory ($85–136K). Realize $250K revenue and drive market share. Approximate ROI of 2.3 to 3.7. 2. Attempt to liquidate. Realize up to $300K revenue, but at a 5% profit margin, and through channels where market share is not measured. Approximate ROI of 0 to 1.7. 3. Status Quo. Write off excess materials (estimate $200K). Realize no revenue.
Recommendation & Next Steps	Recommend proceeding with Option 1 immediately.
Owner	Proposal: Demand Planning Manager / Decision: Demand Review Executive Owner

Figure 9.4 Example Decision Template. © Oliver Wight International, Inc. Used with permission.

- The new information of customer X delisting a product is clearly communicated. This news would also be reflected in the DR materials that outline changes in assumptions (for example, a change in the distribution building block).
- The implications of this change in demand are thought through from multiple perspectives (for example, revenue, market share, profit).
- Different alternatives are considered and a recommendation is made.
- The information is summarized concisely and would be communicated as part of the DR materials 24–48 hours in advance of the meeting.

Decision templates are a best practice for driving decisions not only in the DR, but in any business forum. They establish clear expectations for both the individuals bringing the decision forward and the executive decision makers.

Using a decision template reinforces that *telling the story* about the decision is required to facilitate sound decision making. It also trains executives to pause and read decision templates in more detail, knowing that they will be expected to make a decision. In my experience, organizations that adopt decision templates become significantly more efficient and effective at decision making. Business leaders are more confident with the decisions they make because they have enough information to make an informed decision.

Decision making involves understanding options, alternatives, and contingencies, which usually leads to scenario planning. Scenario planning is a powerful, but often underleveraged tool for managing uncertainty. Use of scenario planning significantly increases the chances of achieving goals and objectives.

As Peter Metcalfe, a Partner with Oliver Wight, noted in his whitepaper *Navigating Uncertainty:* "Our research uncovered the startling statistic that only 7% of companies develop and review scenarios on a monthly basis."[2]

Risks and opportunities form the foundation for scenario planning. Scenarios can be created by selecting different sets of assumptions as well as including or excluding risks and opportunities from the current plan. This approach makes it possible to anticipate the impact should the scenario materialize. Scenarios are intended to be shared cross-functionally. That way the supply and finance teams can consider the impact and tactics, even though the scenario is not reflected in the current demand plan.

When people consider the value of scenarios, they usually find that the potential benefits of preparing for a scenario far outweighs the costs. The following story is a personal example that illustrates the value of scenarios.

Several Oliver Wight colleagues and I were together teaching our public Demand Management course. At the end of each day, we would reconvene for dinner. The timing of dinner would vary since we would spend time after class answering questions from the participants.

One of my colleagues always seemed to have dinner reservations that coincided perfectly with when we would regroup and where we wanted to go. At first, I thought it was coincidence or luck. After having this happen regularly, I asked her how she always managed to have dinner reservations at the right place and time. Her answer was simple: she would make multiple dinner reservations at different times and places. The cost to cancel a dinner reservation was zero. The opportunity cost of not having a dinner reservation was high. All it took was some thinking ahead, and she had prepared backup plans on top of backup plans.

Scenario planning creates preparedness. Being prepared isn't only about planning for what we think will *likely* happen, but also planning for what *might* happen. Being prepared builds credibility with business leaders. Leaders understand that plans never materialize exactly as anticipated. When the commercial side of the business demonstrates they are thinking about what might happen and have examined the what-if situation in a scenario, it demonstrates that they are focused *on* the business. It shows they are prepared to respond if the scenario materializes. Creating scenarios develops commercial managers to be better business thinkers.

Using risks and opportunities as a foundation for scenario planning will help to avoid becoming paralyzed by evaluating an infinite number of future possibilities. It makes visible a manageable range of possible demand outcomes. It is also incredibly helpful for understanding the implications even if only a few different scenarios materialize. It gives the supply and finance teams the opportunity to plan their responses should the demand materialize.

Scenario planning leads to greater leadership and planning competence. It helps the organization understand which assumptions truly matter and need to be managed and when actions and decisions need to be taken. In leveraging risks and opportunities to create scenarios, a clear set of assumptions is defined. With this understanding, business leaders can challenge whether the assumptions supporting the scenario are plausible.

Leveraging the documented assumptions, risks, and opportunities as a starting point (see Figure 9.3), different scenarios can be crafted. Figure 9.5 shows how a selection of opportunities can be included in a scenario labeled Scenario A. Similarly, a selection of risks could be used to develop Scenario B. Those two scenarios form an optimistic and pessimistic view of demand that define a range of possible outcomes.

Near the end of the COVID pandemic, one of my clients struggled with planning demand for a key brand. There had been significant inflationary

	Risk	In the Demand Plan	Opportunity
	New tariff comes into force in Q3 which would increase the shelf price of our product by 15%.	No new tariffs come into force over the next 24 months.	Existing tariffs are lifted starting in Q3.
	Key customer delays expansion of their retail footprint by 10 months.	Key customer is expanding their retail footprint from 250 to 300 stores over the next 8 months.	Key customer expands their retail footprint to 400 stores over the next 6 months.
		No lift assumed.	We secure placement in a key customer promotion in Q4 of next year which will drive a 30% lift to velocities through that period.
		Product reformulation assumed to launch in September.	Product reformulation can be accelerated by 6 months.
	Customer de-lists our product in favor of a competitor.	No de-list assumed.	
	Customer demands slotting fees for additional items to be listed across their banners.	No slotting fees assumed.	

	Volume	Gross Sales	Net Sales	Margin	
Optimistic Scenario	150,000	$1,800,000	$1,500,000	$525,000	Includes A's
Demand Plan	100,000	$1,200,000	$1,000,000	$300,000	50/50 Plan
Pessimistic Scenario	80,000	$960,000	$640,000	$192,000	Includes B's

Figure 9.5 Example of How to Use Risks and Opportunities to Create Scenarios. © Oliver Wight International, Inc. Used with permission.

pressure on not only their business, but for competitors as well. My client was surprised that after making significant increases in price, sales continued to increase. That was counterintuitive to what one would expect. The marketing team hypothesized their competitors were increasing prices more aggressively than they were, resulting in their products being priced lower relative to competition. The continued growth in demand volume created concerns, given my client's manufacturing capacity limitations.

The market response to my client's pricing decisions left them with significant uncertainty. That led the demand, supply, and finance organizations to consider some additional scenarios. The capacity constraints were not straightforward. There were interdependencies in the supply chain network, and the mix of product formats mattered. The commercial organization put forward two demand scenarios that represented increased volume but with different price points and competitive assumptions for the different product formats.

Creating and then simulating the two scenarios with the supply planning team revealed which assumptions would likely lead to supply constraints. For those specific assumptions, the team identified how to plan around them and minimize the constraint.

This experience also highlighted the value of teamwork. Neither party (marketing nor supply chain) would have been able to reach this conclusion on their own. They created much more credible plans by working together than they would have otherwise.

Scenarios help answer the question: When does a decision need to be made to trigger the scenario? A best practice is not to commit company resources until they are needed. A premature decision can create handcuffs that cannot be shed when business conditions change and the scenario fails to materialize.

A scenario planning process should be standard practice. It creates agility within the organization, including agile decision making. All of the assumptions won't be correct, but business leaders gain an understanding as to which assumptions, along with the conditions framed in those assumptions, would cause them to decide to change course or lead to a significant decision. With this knowledge, those key assumptions can be monitored in order to be prepared to decide whether or not it is best to change course.

This ability helps business leaders to separate the things that they don't need to worry about (things that don't influence the outcome of a decision) from things that warrant their attention. It focuses them *on* the business, where their time and energy are better spent.

Identifying and evaluating risks, opportunities, and scenarios causes planning managers and business leaders to think differently about the demand planning process. Their thinking shifts from *what's the right number* to *what should we be concerned about and what actions should we be taking to achieve the business goals and objectives.*

These tools help create a trustworthy, unbiased plan. They also help business leaders to better execute the plan by identifying how to close gaps between the latest projections and business goals. In my experience, business leaders who routinely evaluate risks, opportunities, and scenarios are the ones who have the best track records in satisfying their boards and shareholders.

SUMMARY

- Encourage clear visibility of gaps between the latest demand volume and revenue projections and the business goals and objectives.
- Don't shoot the messenger—early visibility to issues gives you more time to find solutions. Thank the team for revealing gaps and other issues that could prevent the achievement of business goals and objectives.
- Lead by example—insist on making gaps visible and lead in the development of gap closing activities.
- Gap closure often leads to business decisions that go beyond the commercial team. Collaboration among the executive team to decide the best way to approach the gap in demand is far preferable to requiring the commercial organization to artificially include demand in the plan just to trigger production.
- Lead discussions and actions about risks and opportunities to generate the demand needed to accomplish business goals and objectives.
- Focus Demand Management process decisions on how to achieve—and even exceed—business goals and objectives.
- Good decision making is often aided by using a template. Using a decision template reinforces *telling the story* and trains executives to pause and read decision templates in more detail, knowing that they will be expected to make a decision.
- Use scenario planning to think more broadly about the future and what might happen—along with the impact on the business.

QUESTIONS TO ASK

- Are gaps between your business objectives, such as the annual budget and your current demand plan, clearly visible?

- Do the gaps tend to be in the long term or short term?
- Are risks and opportunities part of the routine demand planning process and IBP process?
- Are the supply chain and finance organizations able to see and respond to risks, opportunities, or scenarios?
- How well do you trust your team and others in your organization to bring forward solutions to close gaps?

ENDNOTES

1. K. Patterson et al. *Crucial Accountability*. McGraw-Hill, 2013.
2. Peter Metcalfe. *Navigating Uncertainty: Is Your IBP Process Fit for the Future*. Oliver Wight Asia/Pacific. www.oliverwightasiapacific.com.

CHAPTER 10

AGGREGATE AND DETAIL PLANNING

By this point it should be apparent that demand planning is no small feat. We will now move beyond the why and the what, and shift into some of the best practices for constructing a trustworthy demand plan. We will focus on practices that strengthen cross-functional trust in the plan at all levels in the organization. These practices include leadership alignment on the aggregate, long-term demand plan as well as the detail demand information that is needed in the near term for execution.

Collecting assumptions from multiple sources in the commercial organization about what the company is going to do in order to create demand and evaluate the condition of the marketplace—called a *multiple-input planning process*—is a best practice. Different assumptions and inputs will naturally exist at different levels of detail. For example, investments in advertising might apply to a brand or market. Promotions might apply to a subset of products within a brand or family. Discontinuation of a product might apply to a single item.

Information at various levels of detail is needed by the commercial organization to manage and influence demand—or in other words, to do their jobs. It is therefore necessary to have a way to view and adjust the demand plan at different levels of detail. A sales or marketing executive should not need to review the demand plan item by item to make sense of it. They do need to see whether their planned activities are reflected in the demand plan. Attempting to review the demand plan item by item often creates confusion, frustration, or both.

On the flip side of that coin, however, a demand planner is accountable for making sure that the appropriate level of detail exists and is as accurate as possible. This diligence is needed in order to execute the plan and to support the needs of the different internal customers, such as the finance and supply teams.

Use of a planning hierarchy is an effective way to ensure that the various views of demand are accessible and considered when developing the demand projections. A demand planning hierarchy creates relevant groups of demand, for example, by products, brands, customers, and markets. The hierarchy facilitates capturing and applying different assumptions effectively. It enables communicating the demand plan at the level of detail that makes sense for any given stakeholder or customer of the plan.

With a hierarchy in place and assumptions documented and considered at different levels in that hierarchy, it is a best practice to reconcile the demand plan up and down the hierarchy. Reconciliation creates a demand plan that is aligned at the aggregate and detail levels.

For example, a chemical company may group products based on having a common active ingredient. The active ingredient might dictate how customers use the products. In this case, it is important to ensure that the total demand for products with the same active ingredient is consistent with the assumptions on how that active ingredient will be used by customers or end users.

At the same time, there may be dozens of different ways that products are formulated, blended, and packaged. The same ingredient may be found in products sold in liquid or powder form, in single-use or bulk packaging, or other variations. This additional detail will be relevant at some point in the planning horizon, usually in the near term. At that time, the item-by-item plan will need to be reconciled so that the total of all item-level demand is equal to the total demand at the active-ingredient level.

Execution of the approved aggregate demand plan is difficult, if not impossible, when it is not properly aligned or is inconsistent with the item-level plan. It should not be up to finance or supply chain to have to guess the demand at the item level. The demand planning team, working with the appropriate sales and marketing people, is responsible to make sure the item-level and aggregate plans are aligned.

* * *

Jeff, the Director of Demand Planning at SmartCorp, is learning the value of the best practice of aligning the aggregate and detail plans the hard way. He has brought a small team together to review the accuracy of the most recent demand, which is disappointing.

Jeff starts the meeting by stating, "We unfortunately had a significant miss on forecast accuracy last month. It looks like when we captured the upside on the economy-size latex glove promotion at RetailMart, we did not consider that the promotion would diminish demand for the regular-sized packs."

"Where do you think the breakdown is?" asks Breanne, the Director of Marketing. "I'm hearing from Max that these errors are causing real challenges for his team in managing inventory."

Max, Director of Supply Planning, has been escalating issues to Breanne lately. He is frustrated with the process. Max is of the opinion that he could do a better job forecasting the business himself. Given the forecast error, Breanne doesn't really blame him for thinking that way.

"We can't say the process is completely broken. Our collaboration with Felix provided advance visibility of the expected increase in demand for the economy-size packs," answers Jeff. "We just need to keep working at it. Maybe we need to spend more time with Felix going over the plan item by item."

"I can tell you right now that the last thing Felix and Eva want is to have to spend more time going over item-level plans. They're already complaining that they spend too much time planning, and not enough time in front of the customer," says Henry, Director of Sales Planning.

"Hold on," Breanne says in a forceful voice. "Before we go there, did anybody look at the total demand? Did we really think that we would see growth on both economy-size and regular-sized packages of gloves at the same time? I'm looking at the plan, and we would have had to grow the total demand for latex gloves by more than 20 percent. We've never experienced growth anywhere close to that in the past."

Breanne's observation caused the group to pause the discussion. They realized that perhaps the issue wasn't a lack of focus on the detail, but a lack of focus on the total.

* * *

In my experience, when companies come to this same realization, it is a breakthrough event. They think differently about how to improve the accuracy and credibility of the plan. They realize that greater focus is needed at the aggregate level, as Breanne pointed out.

Planning in aggregate is often referred to as top-down planning. Planning at the detail level is referred to as bottom-up. Most people are familiar with bottom-up approaches for several reasons:

1. Demand planning often has its origins in the supply chain organization, where there is a need for very granular information in order to procure material, manufacture, and deliver product.
2. There is an inherent logic to planning at a granular level. The detail adds up to the total. The sum of every item sold will equal total sales.

It is logical for people to assume that if they plan every single item, all they need to do is add up the volume of each item to achieve the correct total.

3. Planning systems are often built on top of databases that are structured at the very lowest level of detail (such as, ship-to / item number / week).

Relying solely on bottom-up planning has its limitations for planning most accurately and communicating the way internal customers need to see demand projections. When planning at a detail level item by item, it is difficult to accurately account for the interaction between items. It's the old expression that you can't see the forest for the trees.

Cannibalization is one form of interaction and a term that is frequently used in demand planning. It is a term that describes the impact that demand for one item has on another. Cannibalization is often top of mind during new product launches, where sales of existing products decrease when a new, similar product is introduced to the market.

Take for example the introduction of a new video game console. When the latest and greatest new model is released, sales of the older model are greatly diminished. The new item is said to cannibalize sales of the existing items.

While it may not be as obvious, cannibalization occurs in many other situations. For a given portfolio of products, if one product is promoted, it is likely that the increased sales for the promoted item will reduce demand, to some degree, for products not being promoted. That is what occurred in the SmartCorp example.

Some companies find themselves competing within the same category of products with one or more of their own products or brands. This situation creates the need to consider total demand for the category, which requires a top-down planning approach.

Take cookie producers, for example. It is common for the producer to market several brands of cookies. For example, Oreo and Chips Ahoy! cookies are produced and sold by the same company. In these cases, it may be a common practice to plan each distinct brand separately, but very often there is a need to coordinate and account for the interaction between them. A consumer buying more Oreos that are on sale at a reduced price would likely buy fewer Chips Ahoy! cookies.

That principle doesn't only apply when considering the interaction of similar types of products. It is also worthwhile to consider the interaction of distribution points or sales channels. Adding a third or fourth retailer to sell the product may not result in an increase in demand that is above and beyond the sales at the first and second retailers.

Products sold online illustrate this point. Customers commonly buy certain products from Amazon instead of buying them from traditional brick-and-mortar retail stores. There may be some degree of incremental increase in sales at the online channel over sales at a retail store, but it is not 100 percent. The size of total demand, sometimes called the *total pie*, needs to be considered when planning demand.

Similarly, in many markets, a manufacturer's customers may compete with one another. Take the mobile phone industry, for example. The phone maker typically assigns separate sales teams for each retail carrier, such as Verizon, T-Mobile, AT&T, and Sprint. Each sales team gathers inputs and builds their individual sales plans—often collaboratively with the wireless carrier.

The challenge is that each carrier has plans to gain market share from their competitors. It is common for the phone maker to find that each carrier's plans are intrinsically valid. When the phone maker adds the plans of all carriers together, however, the total far exceeds what would be reasonable to expect for the total market. This dynamic isn't unique and exists in many other markets. Consumers purchase food from competing grocery stores. Farmers choose to purchase equipment and chemicals from competing dealers. Even manufacturers themselves will purchase capital equipment from competing distributors.

In theory, the commercial teams and demand planners could try to model all of the interactions discretely to predict which carrier would gain the most sales. This approach is common with new products where a cannibalization rate is calculated and applied to impacted products.

In practice though, when retail sellers are competing for the same business, it is impractical to model every interaction. The better solution is to plan in a hierarchy, at different levels, and then reconcile those levels to identify and resolve the impact of the interactions. Using the previous mobile phone example, the best course of action is to develop an assumption for total demand in the market. Then, reconcile the demand proportionally for each carrier with the total market demand. The reconciliation is based on internal intelligence and assumptions about the carriers and market.

Planning in a hierarchy and starting with an aggregate, top-down view, as noted earlier, might not be intuitive at first. I have frequently observed executives who were frustrated with surprises stemming from poor demand plan accuracy direct their teams to spend more time in the detail. Similarly, leaders will boast about the robustness of plans that have been laboriously built item by item, bottom-up. This behavior is a natural tendency. The instinct that the problem lies in the detail is correct, but it is rarely solved by focusing only on the details.

In the SmartCorp example, Breanne realized that by looking at the total demand, and not just the detail at the item level, it became readily evident that the plan was unrealistic. Had there been an independent view of the total demand projection for RetailMart, the demand picture would have been obvious. It was unreasonable to expect a change in demand for economy-size latex gloves to have no impact on the regular-size packs.

Let's take a moment to recall the best practice of making the demand plan relevant to the different customers of the plan. This is a prerequisite for creating a credible plan. Imagine in the SmartCorp example that Mike, their Chief Financial Officer, looked at the demand plan through a different lens than Jeff or Breanne. Let's say he evaluated the total promotional spending budget for RetailMart and benchmarked it against the total revenue projection. Through that lens, he would have likely noticed that a growth of over 20 percent was an unreasonable expectation. This situation illustrates how focusing only on the detail can quickly erode trust in the plan.

By enabling Mike and others, as appropriate, to see the total demand at RetailMart and the promotional plans, the flaws in the plan would be quickly exposed. The spotlight would reveal that the demand plan did not consider the impact of the promotion for the economy-size product on the regular-size product.

Neglecting to develop demand assumptions and projections at the aggregate level has another consequence. When total demand routinely does not align with demand at the detail level, internal customers may be motivated to create their own independent projections. Giving in to this temptation is counterproductive, however. The Demand Review (DR), Integrated Reconciliation (IR), and Management Business Review (MBR) steps of an Integrated Business Planning process provide the opportunities to evaluate and challenge interactions of planned marketing activities on total demand and item-level demand. Using these forums to ensure that aggregate and item-level demand are reconciled is a far better approach than each function creating its own demand plan.

Top-down and bottom-up perspectives must be embedded in the planning process, not just the output. Reconciliation of the two perspectives is also needed. It is common for the aggregate-level projections to produce a different total demand number than the summation of individual item-level projections. When this happens, a demand planner needs to dig in and identify the causes of the discrepancies. That's where the assumptions about activities to generate demand—such as promotions and new product launches—are invaluable.

For different views at different levels of detail to make sense, a demand planning hierarchy should group together products into families that tend to share similarities. The groupings should also align with the way that the commercial organization makes sales and marketing decisions.

Figure 10.1 illustrates an example of a demand planning hierarchy for a medical devices company. The business may have different product platforms (e.g., hypodermic needles and catheters). For each platform, demand may be generated in different regions around the world (e.g., North America, Asia, Europe). Within each region, different relevant product families might be sold, and within each family, there may be several individual items or SKUs (stock-keeping units).

There are many ways that this hierarchy could be structured. For example, regions could be moved to the top, with platforms and product families subordinate to them. Deciding how to best structure the hierarchy requires careful thought about how commercial leaders think about the business and manage demand. Thus, the design of the demand planning hierarchy should not be treated as a trivial exercise. Too often it is an afterthought or something that is adopted from a system implementation or financial reporting structure.

For a demand hierarchy to enable effective demand planning, it must be easy to organize the demand plan assumptions and apply them to the appropriate hierarchy levels. The demand hierarchy should reflect the commercial decision-making structure of the business. Products grouped together within the hierarchy should have important commonality. For example, a product

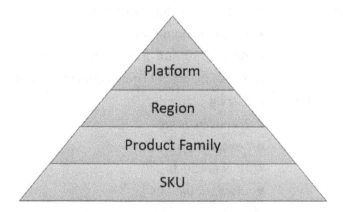

Figure 10.1   Example of Product Hierarchy in a Consumer Goods Business. © Oliver Wight International, Inc. Used with permission.

grouping might share a similar pattern of seasonality, be commonly promoted together, or serve the same market segment.

Figure 10.2 shows, for example, how planning assumptions can be easily captured and incorporated because the hierarchy is aligned with the way sales and marketing inputs are formed and decisions are made.

The structure shown in Figure 10.2 should be designed to avoid having to awkwardly split up assumptions. In this case, advertising activities would naturally apply to all product families in a region. Therefore, by having region as a level in the hierarchy, the assumptions pertaining to advertising can be applied and documented at that level. If that level didn't exist, one would have to collect all the regional advertising assumptions, add them together, and then apply them individually to every product family.

With an effective hierarchy, the story of the demand plan can be preserved. To every extent possible, it is best that the demand plan easily and accurately reflects key assumptions without distorting or diluting them. Capturing, reflecting, and debating aggregate assumptions almost always leads to making more informed decisions about the impact of those assumptions on demand. Ultimately, it leads to a more reliable aggregate plan.

The demand planning hierarchy should be oriented to the way in which demand is managed to influence customers to buy the company's products and services. It is inefficient and ineffective to base the demand planning hierarchy on the way in which manufacturing is organized to procure, produce,

Level	Assumptions
Platform	■ Long-term category trends
	■ Macroeconomic inputs
Region	■ Advertising and promotional activity
	■ Sales and channel development activities
Product Family	■ Pricing
	■ Trends in usage
	■ Seasonality
SKU	■ New products
	■ Discontinuations

Figure 10.2 Defining the Inputs at Each Level in the Planning Hierarchy.
© Oliver Wight International, Inc. Used with permission.

and deliver. In a supply-centric business model, planning hierarchies often reflect asset groups or production processes. This structure is common in organizations where demand planning is viewed as a supply chain necessity. It certainly is not optimal for producing reliable, trustworthy demand plans. It also limits the usefulness of the demand plan for driving commercial discussions and decision making.

Consider the SmartCorp example where demand for economy-size and regular-size packs are interrelated. While the latex gloves themselves would be the same, the packaging process for those two products would likely be different. A manufacturing centric hierarchy would make it difficult to determine total demand based on lower sales of the unpromoted regular item and increased sales for the economy packaged item. Validating whether the total demand for the brand and demand for each package size makes sense is essential. The answer becomes apparent only when the demand for the two different package sizes is combined.

One of my clients is a manufacturer of medical devices where there can be a high degree of substitution between product items. The company supplies syringes, needles, and catheters, which come in a variety of sizes and configurations. Each type of product has a different manufacturing process.

In a hospital setting, patient care comes first. There may be little hesitation, and even an obligation, on the part of the doctor or nurse to make substitutions if the ideal syringe, needle, or catheter is unavailable. When planning demand for these products, it is critical to step back and determine the overall pattern of total demand. It is a waste of time to get caught up in trying to determine how substitutions resulted in significant distortions of demand for each item without first understanding the total.

Planners found it more effective to create assumptions and metrics on hospital admissions and illness rates. This approach provided a much more stable foundation for projecting total demand. From there, assumptions of product mix were made to create and communicate a detail-level demand plan to support manufacturing.

It is important to note that the demand planning hierarchy is rarely static. It should evolve to reflect changes in the business strategies, markets, and decision-making structure. When establishing demand planning hierarchies, I tell clients that they most certainly won't get it right the first time. This reality can be particularly difficult in organizations where planning hierarchies are codified in master data and adjustments require significant effort.

When the hierarchies fail to stay synchronized with the way demand is influenced and managed, avoidable errors tend to crop up. I see situations like this all the time: the demand plan on 24-ounce containers of pickles was overstated because of a promotion on 32-ounce containers. Or the demand plan for one product was overstated because it did not account for the marketing campaign being run for another product. Or the demand at one phone carrier did not account for the *buy one, get one free* promotion being run by another phone carrier. These examples are not solely the fault of a flawed hierarchy. Lack of communication and diligent consideration of planning inputs are a factor. A properly designed hierarchy does, however, help planners to identify and avoid these situations.

Another warning when structuring demand planning hierarchies: avoid grouping things together indiscriminately, sometimes referred to as lumping. For example, consumer goods companies may be tempted to lump different retail channels together. The thinking is that the demand patterns in each channel are very similar. Or maybe there's an urgency to create the hierarchy, and time is not taken to consult with the commercial side of the business. Decisions to lump things together when structuring hierarchies are also frequently spurred by a preference for manufacturing-centric hierarchies.

The pitfall is that lumping channels together negates differentiation between grocery chains, department stores, discount stores, and warehouse club stores. Each of these channels are typically managed differently. In fact, different people are typically responsible for managing each channel. In many cases, the demand patterns, product assortment, promotion activities, and pricing between these channels are very different. Lumping channels together commonly results in chronically inaccurate demand projections for product mix and channel mix.

Instead, evaluate each hierarchy grouping and determine what can be appropriately combined because of similar demand patterns, strategies, and tactics to influence demand. Consider also whether the products proposed to be included in the grouping typically interact with each other and share common planning assumptions.

Avoid the temptation to consider hierarchies to be inflexible and, thus, expect to resort to *scrubbing the detail* to improve demand plan accuracy. A focus at the minute-detail level usually does not result in getting at the root cause of demand plan errors. Unacceptable levels of demand plan error become chronic, causing frustration for both planners and executives.

In one organization, an award for *crushing complexity* was (erroneously, in my view) given to a group of individuals in the finance organization for eliminating what was believed to be an onerous task. The company decided to reject all requests for changes to the planning hierarchy. The rationale was that the proposed changes would result in the finance organization having to restate prior financial statements, which took a lot of time and energy.

That time and energy, however, was minimal compared to the time wasted by demand planning and commercial teams when they could not leverage the planning hierarchies effectively. The appropriate solution was to separate the financial reporting hierarchy from the demand planning hierarchy and give control of the demand planning hierarchy to the commercial organization.

It is important to note that while top-down planning helps to identify and resolve potential inaccuracies that can't be easily seen from the detail, the opposite is true as well. There are insights to be gained by looking at the bottom-up views.

For example, sales of a specific brand of chewing gum had been declining for several years. A top-down projection concluded that the trend would continue. This judgment was validated by supporting assumptions that included the declining number of cigarette smokers, a shift in consumer preferences toward larger pack types where competition was stronger, and a loss of shelf space at grocery store checkouts as they converted more lanes to self-service.

A deeper look into the detail, however, shed a different light on the decline in sales. Demand was decreasing at the assumed trajectory for only a subset of the items, dragging down the total sales for that brand. Furthermore, an inflection point would be reached where sales of those items would not be expected to decline any further because it would reach zero in certain channels. (Demand can't be negative at any level in the hierarchy.)

This analysis caused business leaders to make a different decision about the demand plan. They made sure that the aggregate plan for the brand and detail-level plan for the declining items reflected the point in time where the decrease in demand volume would stabilize.

Who should be responsible for the analysis that was just described in reconciling aggregate and detail projections of demand? In practice, it may be the responsibility of different people working independently and then reconciling the differences in the two demand projections. For example, a brand or product manager might be responsible for an aggregate view, and a demand planner might be responsible for a detailed view. The mechanics of top-down/bottom-up reconciliation can vary—sometimes supported by a planning tool, sometimes performed manually by a demand planner.

In all cases, however, reconciliation involves dialogue and discussion of assumptions. In the earlier chewing gum example, it wasn't the demand planning tool that made the decision to adjust the aggregate plan. It was a commercial leader who, after understanding the assumptions gleaned from the bottom-up exercise, made the decision. Most important is that both views are considered, and then ultimately reconciled to one view. If the bottom-up approach indicates an issue in the top-down projections, that issue must be resolved and adjusted to bring the two views into alignment.

Leaving a gap between the top-down and bottom-up views is simply not finishing the job. When the detail plan and the aggregate plan are not aligned, a less accurate plan is the result. The reason is that inconsistent sets of assumptions are being used, and expectations for managing and influencing demand often are not aligned. Lack of credibility in the eyes of business leaders is the inevitable consequence.

The executive owner of the demand plan is accountable for ensuring that the demand plan is fully reconciled top-down and bottom-up. A sales or marketing executive certainly won't be responsible for doing the work, but they must ensure that it is happening. One way to check is to compare the detailed output of the demand planning process—in other words, what is being provided to supply chain—with what is being approved in the DR. The totals should be aligned. Knowing the top-down and bottom-up views are reconciled creates confidence. The commercial leaders know that the aggregate plans approved in the DR and MBR are the best reflection of reality and can be well executed.

Planning in a hierarchy also enables companies to effectively extend their planning horizon, and consequently identify and address issues and gaps sooner. The most impactful decisions driven by demand planning affect the future—months if not years in advance. Decisions, such as expanding into new territories, adding new product lines, building new factories, even acquiring new businesses, have long execution lead times. The actions that are taken to create significant competitive advantage, drive growth, and win in the marketplace are also not contemplated a month or two in advance.

Time and time again, I come across businesses where the planning horizon of demand plans barely looks out ahead to the next few months. There can be many reasons for this short-term focus, including the perception that it is not possible to plan further ahead in time. It can take a change in mindset and some skill building to develop longer term plans. One of the key enablers to long-term planning is to consider future demand at different levels of aggregation.

When demand planners and commercial teams are asked to help facilitate planning over a longer term horizon, they often turn to their planning software and spreadsheets. They use these tools to extrapolate demand over the longer planning horizon. The mathematical calculations may be based on decisions to simply extend the current trend over 24 months. Or they may replicate the demand that occurred at the same time the previous year. What's missing is basing the numbers on the business strategies and goals as well as the anticipated condition of the marketplace.

When I'm asked where to start in adding a second or third year to a demand plan horizon, I recommend starting without any numbers at all. A high-level discussion of what people expect to happen in that time horizon—positive or negative for the business—is a worthwhile first step. Through these discussions, the key planning assumptions for that longer term horizon are developed. Armed with these assumptions, a planner can start to quantify their impacts in volume, revenue, and margin. They will realize, however, that it is often difficult, if not impossible, to apply these longer term assumptions to a detailed plan.

Take, for example, something seemingly simple like master data. Master data in most planning systems is comprised of specific information on components and materials required to produce a specific product. Within the near-term horizon, it is reasonable to expect to know what specific products are going to be sold and which customers will purchase those products. Information two or three years into the future at that level of specificity is probably not available. Relying strictly on extrapolations of historical data also does not consider new products that will be introduced or new markets that will be penetrated in the longer term future. Companies typically have a new product pipeline out of which some items will make it to market, along with others that won't. Opportunities with new customers or demand channels also may not currently be contemplated in specific product detail.

Planning demand over the longer term is best achieved by planning at an aggregate level according to the agreed upon planning hierarchy. Over longer term horizons, decision makers typically don't need very granular detail to identify significant gaps between operating assumptions and strategic objectives.

In my experience, most executives working *on* the business will naturally be thinking in aggregate about channels, markets, brand, and product lines as opposed to product items or shipping locations. Plans at the aggregate level are much more relatable to the strategic objectives of the organization over the mid- and long-term horizon. Similarly, the internal customers of the demand plan will likely be satisfied with more aggregate views. Supply, for example, can typically identify significant bottlenecks and capacity constraints with an aggregate view of demand over the longer horizon.

Confidence that being roughly right is okay can make a huge difference in how time and energy is spent planning. The level of detail and precision that is put into developing a piece of information is only relevant to the degree to which it would influence a decision to be made differently. In other words, let's say that demand exceeding 10 million tons of product per year would require an additional factory to be built. Business leaders and planners don't need to know the specific mix of items or customers in the demand plan to make the decision to invest in building a new factory. They just need to know the total demand volume and revenue that the new factory would produce.

Similarly, take a minute to think about the planning assumptions for your business that apply to the long-term time horizon. Very few of those assumptions are likely to be at a very granular level of detail. The fact is that *we don't know what we don't know*. Trying to create detail out in the longer term horizon is false precision and a waste of time. It can even be misleading since the false precision can lead internal customers of the demand plan to believe that something is known when it really isn't.

For example, a company sold seasonal products, but the sales volumes for those products changed from year to year. The demand planning tools had been configured to extrapolate the demand plan detail long into the future based on recent actual sales. The demand planners believed that no one would look at the detail in the longer term horizon because decisions were not being made that far in advance. That was true—until it wasn't. A raw material buyer was notified by a supplier that they were discontinuing a unique raw material that was used in some seasonal products. The planner took the opportunity to buy as much of that material as he thought would be needed to cover all the demand in the system. Unfortunately, that material was only needed for one seasonal product, and that product was going to be discontinued the following year. Demand volume in the demand plan had not been shifted to a new item. The demand planner was waiting for a decision on the replacement product and when it would be released to the market.

This example illustrates how important it is to be clear when communicating to the internal customers of the demand plan. What is known, what is not known, and at what level of detail are all important assumptions to be shared.

The next chapter continues with the theme of stepping back and evaluating the demand plan from a broader perspective. We will add another level to the planning hierarchy that goes beyond the company to the broader market and value chain in which it operates.

SUMMARY

- Information at various levels of detail is needed by the commercial organization to manage and influence demand. A sales or marketing executive should not need to review the demand plan item by item to make sense of it.

- Use of a planning hierarchy is an effective way to ensure that the various views of demand are accessible and considered when developing the demand projections.
- It is a best practice to reconcile the demand plan up and down the hierarchy to create a demand plan that is aligned at the aggregate and detail levels.
- Planning in aggregate is referred to as top-down planning. Planning at the detail level is referred to as bottom-up. Both are needed to ensure that interactions between items are appropriately accounted for and to ensure that planning assumptions have been captured and accounted for properly.
- For a demand hierarchy to enable effective demand planning, it must be easy to organize the demand plan assumptions and apply them to the appropriate hierarchy levels.
- Groupings in the demand hierarchy should be defined by what can be appropriately combined because of similar demand patterns, strategies, and tactics to influence demand.
- The executive owner of the demand plan is accountable for ensuring that the demand plan is fully reconciled top-down and bottom-up.
- Planning in a hierarchy enables companies to effectively extend their planning horizon, and consequently to identify and address issues and gaps sooner.

QUESTIONS TO ASK

- Does your demand planning process operate bottom-up, top-down, or both?
- Are you frequently having to *scrub the detail* in response to finding avoidable errors in the demand plan?
- Is the aggregate demand plan that is signed off on or approved by leadership aligned with the detailed demand plan recorded in planning tools?
- Are you able to adapt the way you consolidate and view demand to the commercial structure of the business or is it tied to a financial or manufacturing hierarchy?
- Are the same tools and approaches being used to plan short-term (e.g., 0–3 month) and long-term (e.g., 4–24 month) demand?

CHAPTER **11**

STAYING FOCUSED ON END USERS

When a business is formed, the founders have a clear view of the problem that they are trying to solve or benefit that they aim to deliver to a target market. Entrepreneurs are attuned to the wants and needs of the users of their products or services. There is an inherent focus on the consumer or end user.

As companies grow and markets mature, however, complications arise that can take the focus away from the consumer or end user. What starts out as a simple business model with transactions between buyers and sellers may evolve to include many different trading partners—manufacturers, assemblers, distributors, wholesalers, and retailers.

With growth, the internal processes and organizational structures of companies evolve and become more complex as well. Roles become more specialized and grouped into functions. In a small start-up company one person might be responsible for calling on customers, creating marketing plans, and managing production schedules. In a large company these activities are handled by different departments, each with their own reporting structures and protocols. To the one person in the start-up, it would be natural to pay attention to how and where their products and services are ultimately being used. It is relatively straightforward to connect end-user information and trends back to the actions for influencing future demand. In larger organizations, those connections often require a conscious effort to make an explicit connection.

I often find that the people involved in demand planning tend to focus solely on the customers that the company transacts with directly. This narrow focus is not surprising. Those immediate transactions (orders, shipments, invoices, and payments) are what must be executed. They also are what generate revenue and profit for the company. The narrow focus that excludes end-user information goes beyond demand planning. Salespeople are typically measured based on transactions with customers, and the supply chain is tasked with and measured by how well they fulfill orders. While demand is defined as what immediate customers want or need, there is more to that definition alone when planning and managing demand. From a marketing point of view, it is shortsighted to think only of immediate customers if those who purchase a company's products and services are not the end users of those offerings.

Executive leaders tend not to be as shortsighted. In my experience, executives across the organization frequently have a better understanding of how and where the end consumer uses their companies' products. At the executive level, end-to-end business discussions are more common, and data on consumers, end users, competitors, and overall market trends are typically shared and discussed.

A shortfall that I have observed is that many executive leaders do not ensure that this same understanding of consumer, end-user, and market behavior flows down to lower levels in the organization. The flow of this information is not automatic. Let's examine a couple of reasons why.

First and foremost, demand planners and salespeople often lack an understanding as to *why* paying attention to consumer or end-user demand is relevant. Their view is frequently limited to understanding future customer orders rather than the wants and needs of end users. The challenge for executive leaders is ensuring that a more comprehensive view of the business extends to people who are lower in the organization.

I often help organizations improve their demand planning process by incorporating consumer or point-of-sale data and assumptions. In most cases, the starting point is the same. Point-of-sale or end-user data are available and being reviewed somewhere in the company. The data frequently are not linked or connected to the demand planning process, however. People leading the process also often dismiss this type of data. Understanding what end consumers are buying is not a top priority. Their job is to forecast orders from their immediate customers.

The second reason is the difficulty in predicting the impacts of end consumer demand on the demand plan. Planners who understand *why* paying attention to end users is important may struggle with *how* to connect consumer or end-user data to the generation of demand. They also, more importantly, may not know the best way to present relevant consumer or end-user data to an executive audience. Savvy use of consumer and end-user information is not always a straightforward exercise.

One of my clients is a manufacturer of nylon. Nylon has a wide range of uses in different markets, such as automotive (air bags), consumer (carpet), electrical (terminal blocks), and textiles (clothing and apparel). My client's customers in the automotive industry are not the end users of the product. The nylon is turned into car parts. The car parts are turned into cars. The cars sit in inventory on a car dealership lot until purchased by consumers.

Knowing the number of cars that are predicted to be sold each year and how much nylon goes into the making of each car model becomes valuable knowledge for the producer of nylon.

The executive team naturally pays close attention to the automotive market. What happens in the automotive market is a key leading indicator for their business. This knowledge, documented as assumptions, can be parlayed into a demand plan that more accurately reflects reality.

Applying this knowledge in the demand planning process, however, requires that planners understand the makeup of various car models. They must pay attention to market share and market trends. They need to make assumptions with respect to inventory levels at car manufacturers and dealerships. This information may not be readily available or straightforward to acquire. The planners and salespeople also may not have the skills to interpret this type of information and then incorporate it into the demand plan.

Paying attention to consumers and end users can pay big dividends. It frequently leads to better planning, better decision making, and more credible and trustworthy demand plans. It is therefore the responsibility of executive leaders to establish the expectation that the demand planning process considers this information. It is also their responsibility to ensure that people at all levels of the organization understand *why* it is vital to consider this type of information. When people understand *why*, executive leaders must then ensure the investment is made to provide the appropriate tools and information. They also must allot the time needed to educate planners and the commercial organization on *how* to interpret and use the information. This is a best practice.

To understand why paying attention to consumers or end users is important, start with the bullwhip effect. The bullwhip effect is aptly named for describing responses to demand along the supply chain. Think how cracking a whip transfers a relatively small movement from the handle of the whip into a sort of sonic boom at the tail end.

Figure 11.1 illustrates the bullwhip effect in a retail supply chain. When information is lacking as to the root causes of changes in demand, it is not unusual for businesses operating in the supply chain to overreact. Figure 11.1 shows dramatic swings in demand at each point in the value chain in response to small changes in demand by consumers or end users.

The bullwhip effect occurs when each trading partner along the value chain places orders while the drivers of demand are uncertain or unknown. The volume of the orders is typically amplified at each trading partner point along the value chain. The largest distortion of demand usually occurs with trading partners that are the farthest removed from the end user or consumer.

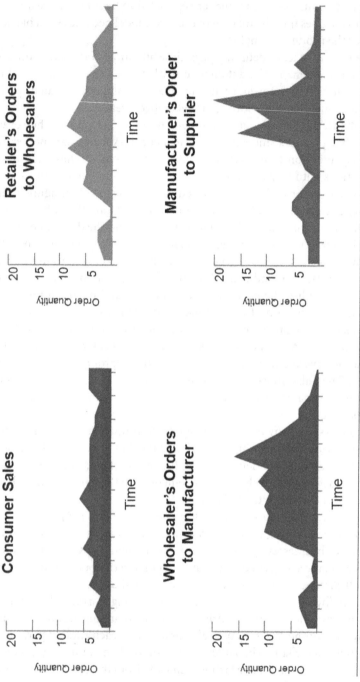

Figure 11.1   Example of the Bullwhip Effect. © Oliver Wight International, Inc. Used with permission.

These trading partners typically have the least visibility to true demand; that is consumer or end-user demand.[1]

The irony of the bullwhip effect is that all too often, consumer or end-user demand is stable and occurs in a predictable pattern. Consumer sales in the retail industry are typically the result of thousands or millions of individuals deciding to buy a product. No single person's decision will dramatically alter the pattern of demand in total.

Without information on consumer demand, distortions in the amount of inventory to carry can be introduced when retailers and wholesalers make decisions to replenish their inventory. A retail buyer, seeing an increase in consumer sales, might place a larger order with their distributor *just in case* sales increase above the norm. The distributor, not knowing that the order was placed to hedge against a potential spike in demand, might interpret the retail buyer's order as a concrete signal of future demand. The distributor would therefore decide to further increase the volume of product ordered from the manufacturer.

The risk here is that the increase in consumer sales may have been temporary. In the following period, the retail buyer might opt not to place an order at all. The extra inventory that they bought as a hedge is sufficient to cover their requirements. The over corrections to the initial increase in consumer sales continue, however, and are amplified as they move up the chain.

The farther away each value point is from the end user or consumer, the fewer order transactions occur, and the fewer people involved in those transactions. Millions of consumer transactions turn into thousands of retailer orders and then perhaps only a few wholesaler orders. A single consumer buying some extra product *just in case* wouldn't cause much of a disruption in the value chain. But, it only takes one or two buyers at large distributors to make buying decisions that are very different from consumer demand to create a costly bullwhip effect.

These types of issues aren't always the result of mistakes or over corrections. A manufacturer may, for reasons of efficiency, choose to manufacture product in batches, for example. They might therefore place orders from their raw materials suppliers in batches as well. Raw material suppliers would have a difficult time understanding the true downstream patterns of demand if they only paid attention to the orders from the manufacturer. Both partners might make more accurate plans by sharing information about their orders.

The bullwhip effect reminds me of the first time I piloted my father-in-law's boat. When driving a car, which I was very familiar with, the car responds very quickly when the steering wheel is turned to change direction. In a boat, and particularly a larger one, there is a delay when changing the direction of the helm. A small over correction in one direction often leads to a larger over correction the other way. I found myself frantically changing directions back and forth to keep the boat going straight ahead. My father-in-law taught me that the key to maintaining a stable direction is to anticipate and look further ahead.

The same goes for planning as part of a value chain. Paying attention only to the next link in the chain runs the risk of steering the business the same way that I piloted the boat. When planners pay attention to consumer or end-user demand, they can avoid overreacting to customer orders. They ask better questions and establish and validate assumptions more readily. This diligence leads to a more accurate demand plan.

As mentioned earlier, the bullwhip effect occurs when trading partners operate while drivers of demand are uncertain or unknown. One way to address this uncertainty is to build stronger relationships with trading partners. There is a principle: *When you know what the demand is going to be, communicate that information. Don't forecast it.* This applies not only within an organization, but between trading partners as well. When trading partners collaborate and share plans and assumptions with one another, they create win-win relationships. Using another boating analogy, white-water rafting is an exciting, but potentially dangerous activity. The person at the front of the raft is responsible for spotting obstacles such as rocks or logs in the river. The person at the back of the raft is responsible for steering the raft. The people in the raft must therefore communicate effectively to avoid catastrophe. It would make little sense for the person at the back of the raft to try to guess or forecast where the obstacles are.

While collaboration is the best option, it is not always possible or feasible. There may be too many trading partners, or the trading partners might not be capable or willing to collaborate. It may not be possible to prevent downstream overreactions from reaching a manufacturer in the form of unexpectedly large orders. It is still possible, however, to make an informed decision on how to respond to the orders. Paying attention to end-user demand can help to anticipate whether unexpected orders are incremental to the normal demand pattern or not. It helps determine whether trading partners are simply pulling forward orders that were planned for a later time.

In my experience, demand planners who lack the visibility to end-user data will often feel helpless to predict demand patterns. Their frustration turns to blaming the sales team for not better controlling or managing their customers. Salespeople may also feel helpless. They may struggle to meet short-term sales objectives as fluctuating order patterns make it difficult to understand the underlying trends in the business.

As I said earlier, my initial experience with planners is that they often don't care about end-user or consumer behavior. It reminds me of a cartoon that is often circulated on social media where two cavemen struggle to pull a wagon that has square wheels. A third caveman is offering them round wheels, but they are too busy pulling the wagon to stop and listen to him. They don't have time to consider the better way.

Understanding the bullwhip effect naturally leads to the realization that everything between the point of manufacture and the point of consumption or use is inventory. Whether that inventory resides in an intermediate product, a warehouse, on a shelf at a supermarket, in a supplies room in an office, or in your cupboard at home, it is inventory. Paying attention to end users provides insights and can be used to make assumptions about inventory. These assumptions should be monitored and updated regularly. Beyond mitigating the bullwhip effect, better assumptions about inventory help make better commercial decisions. Inventory isn't only influenced by downstream behavior—it can also be influenced by the behavior of a company's own tactics in the market.

* * *

As an example, let's see what SmartCorp is doing with consumer information. John, the Chief Marketing Officer; Jacob, the Senior Vice President of Sales; Mike, the Chief Financial Officer; and Breanne, a Marketing Director; are participating in the monthly Demand Review meeting. Breanne has walked the team through the latest demand volume and revenue changes and assumptions, but John has some concerns.

"We're getting into dangerous territory here, Jacob," says John. "The latest inventory report from Scott in Customer Service shows that many of our customers have higher inventory than they typically carry. I heard from Felix in Sales that RetailMart has expressed similar concerns to him directly. Is there a chance that sales could decrease because of the amount of inventory that our customers are currently carrying?"

John worried that the proposed demand plan for the first quarter could be problematic. He knew that there was pressure to show strong revenue growth. He had also been monitoring market performance. He was concerned that the revenue growth projected in the demand plan would exceed the growth in end-user sales. The consequence could be that the sales team would end up loading the channel with inventory to achieve the revenue plan. They were certainly capable of offering price discounts and calling in favors to incentivize customers to consume that inventory. These decisions needed to be well-thought-out. John did not think the longer term implications of loading the channel with inventory were being considered.

Mike, who had been quietly observing the discussion, decided to add to John's comment. "Jacob, are you sure we're not going to get a call at the last minute from RetailMart looking for incentives to consume the channel inventory?" said Mike.

"Mike, you know that I can't control RetailMart. I've got a target to hit, and we're committed to delivering it. We won't hit the revenue projections if inventory is not available in the channel. I'm not sure what more I need to say," responds Jacob.

"But this isn't just any time," says John. "With the planned price increase coming next quarter, we could put ourselves in a risky position if we're not careful. If RetailMart has too much inventory, they will look to us for price protection. RetailMart has to be committed to selling through the stock that they buy, without concessions."

"We always figure it out. That's what we get paid to do," says Jacob. "Besides, Breanne said she has plenty of media budget set aside in the second quarter to help increase end-user sales in conjunction with the price increase."

John is conflicted. On the one hand, this plan would deliver exactly what they needed in terms of revenue growth. In the back of his mind, however, he worries that it might be too good to be true. He doesn't want to be held hostage by a key customer. Or worse, he doesn't want to be in a position where the integrity of SmartCorp's revenue projections could be challenged or appear to be inflated.

* * *

John's concerns are not unwarranted. Executives often pay close attention to consumer data for reasons that go beyond avoiding the bullwhip effect. Knowledge of inventory levels in a sales channel helps avoid problems with revenue recognition. If a company finds itself aggressively selling product into a distribution channel, inventories can start to build. This is sometimes referred to as *trade loading* or *channel stuffing* and can have serious accounting and regulatory consequences. Customers may ask for incentives or support to help them sell excess inventories.

This is precisely Mike's concern. If SmartCorp recognizes revenue on the sale of product, but later provides discounts or incentives for it to be sold through the channel, the validity of the recognized revenue can come into question. The price at which the product was sold may be found not to be fixed and determinable at the time of sale.

This type of situation illustrates why end-user data and assumptions about channel inventory are important. These data and assumptions need to be integrated into the demand planning process, where concerns like the one John raised can be addressed earlier in the process.

John should not have had to triangulate consumer data with the demand plan. That assessment should have been done as part of creating the demand plan itself. Plans that would expose the organization to risks of customers demanding price protection could be discussed before loading the channel with inventory. The discussion should include the risk of being accused of trade loading. Focusing the spotlight on these risks may be uncomfortable, but inevitably results in commercial teams being challenged to come up with better solutions for achieving revenue growth. In the end, this diligence makes the demand plan more credible. It also guides the business leaders toward making better commercial decisions that don't create excessive risks to the business.

Beyond revenue recognition, there are many other scenarios where having an assumption about channel inventory is helpful. These scenarios include:

- Tracking new product launches and assessing whether on-shelf availability and consumer uptake are materializing as planned.
- Estimating the impacts of price protection or the impacts of customers temporarily increasing their inventory levels in advance of list-price changes.
- Understanding the risk related to remaining inventory of an existing product during the launch of a new replacement product.
- Measuring the potential exposure for a recall or legal liability of a product quality issue.
- Understanding the impact of a supply constraint and determining what demand is perishable or will not be consumed for other reasons, along with the impact of pent-up or unfulfilled demand pending restocking of channel inventory.

In addition to establishing assumptions for channel inventory, monitoring end-user demand patterns and behavior has other advantages. It is often the best way to determine if actions that are being taken to influence demand are having the intended effect.

For example, if a company advertises or promotes a brand or product, monitoring end-user behavior during or shortly after the promotion will show whether that promotion led to an increase in demand. When a company only monitors customer orders, it may not be possible to discern the impact of the promotion. Wholesalers or retailers could have placed orders in anticipation of the promotion to ensure that the product would be on-shelf.

This response can create a bullwhip effect. Stable end-user or consumer demand patterns are distorted through trading-partner buying practices when products are promoted or when buying incentives are offered.

Monitoring consumer data is particularly relevant for consumer goods companies where point-of-sale data is enriched with additional attributes that describe the conditions of the sale. For example, the data might indicate whether an item was sold on discount or in conjunction with a promotional tactic. Other assumptions, such as the breadth of distribution of a product, can also be measured this way. Visibility to these additional attributes is useful to track the impact of specific sales and marketing activities.

Let's use distribution as an example. In consumer goods terminology, distribution is a measure of how many retail stores carry a given product. Expanding the distribution of a product typically leads to an increase in sales. Salespeople work to secure listings for their products with retailers in order to increase distribution. Given that most physical retail stores have a finite amount of shelf space, distribution is highly competitive. Adding one item to the shelf typically means another (ideally a competitor's) item must be removed. Retailers are always trying to maximize the productivity of that finite shelf space.

A salesperson may plan to secure additional distribution for a handful of existing products with one of their customers. Without visibility to distribution through the point-of-sale data, that salesperson might have to physically go to various retail stores to see whether the product is on the shelf of that retailer's stores. When a retailer has thousands of stores, this effort might be impractical. Having access to consumer data is preferable and more efficient. If the point-of-sale data indicates that a retail customer has increased distribution in only half of their stores, the salesperson can then follow up with the retailer's buyer and find out why. The salesperson learns more about the customers' behaviors and how changes in distribution tend to materialize. This knowledge, in turn, enables the salesperson to create and execute more reliable plans in the future.

Another reason to pay attention to end users was noted earlier in the chapter. Executives tend to view the business in a broader context that includes considering competitors, end users, and the broader market conditions. They are inclined to evaluate the demand plan through that lens. When this view is presented to business leaders, they are more apt to engage in reviewing the demand plan.

Consider the saying: "That which interests my boss, fascinates me." I learned early in my career that I needed to stop and look at a demand plan through the lens of my executive team before presenting it to them. That meant understanding the context by which they are viewing the business. I found this context is often at a much higher level and with more external perspective than the management team's lens.

I have worked with many companies to help them leverage point-of-sale data in their planning process. In almost every case, this work was at the request of a frustrated executive. Executives can lose confidence with the commercial organization and planners when they can't reconcile demand plans with consumer or broader market perspectives.

When coaching demand planners, I often pose this question: "Would it be reasonable to expect your CEO to know what the demand plan is for a particular item at a particular customer four months from now?" The answer is clearly, "No." Then I ask, "Would your CEO have an expectation to see projected market share or consumer trends over the next four quarters?" The answer is far more likely to be, "Yes." If the CEO is expected to trust the demand plan, it only makes sense to articulate how the demand plan relates to expectations of market share and consumer behavior. This means taking a broader view of the business, including considering end-user buying behavior, competitor actions, market share, and macroeconomic conditions. This information may not help to predict next week's orders for a given item, but it will certainly help define the broader assumptions that underpin the demand plan, particularly over a longer term horizon.

Consider the following example. Leaders at a consumer products client were presented with a projection of revenue based on their demand plan. They also were shown projections of point-of-sale, end-user consumption, and market share data. In their industry, market share is calculated based on point-of-sale data, and accordingly, doesn't always correlate with revenue. Increases or decreases in channel inventory can distort the relationship between market share and revenue. The business leaders were routinely surprised and frustrated when the company achieved or exceeded the planned point-of-sale and market share projections, but not the revenue projection.

To complicate the situation, business leaders often did not align on the projected revenue growth. For example, the VP of Marketing would be shown a revenue plan that projected five percent growth. The strategy team projected the total market would grow by seven percent. The Brand Director indicated a gain in market share without providing a specific number. At face value, none of it added up. The VP of Marketing usually asked the Brand Directors how market share would increase when the demand plan showed growth that was slower than the total market. The Brand Directors struggled to provide a good answer, and then they would rework their numbers.

Initially, commercial leaders blamed channel inventory distortions for not achieving revenue projections. As they continued to press their teams to provide better explanations, a different story emerged. Leaders learned that the revenue plan and the market share plans were not connected at all. The projections were distinct, being influenced by different parts of their organization. The plans and projections were based on different underlying assumptions and methodologies.

When this realization came to light, the decision was made to change the planning process and methodology. Information and assumptions on total market, point-of-sale, and revenue data were integrated into the demand planning process. As assumptions were collected and incorporated into the demand plan, the demand planners routinely asked, "What implications does this assumption have on customer orders, revenue, end-user demand, and market share?" The answers to their questions were used to established one set of planning assumptions. These assumptions were used to generate projections of revenue and market share.

By viewing the assumptions and resulting projections earlier on, and throughout the process, demand planners better anticipated the questions that the leadership team would inevitably ask. The expectation to present information from the executive team's perspective had an additional benefit. It motivated the brand managers, product managers, and demand planners to better understand how revenue, market share, and point-of-sale buyer behaviors interacted. They learned and better understood how their markets operated. This, in turn, led them to become better marketers and product managers. In the end, better decisions were made on how and where to invest in order to grow the businesses.

A candy manufacturer had a similar outcome. The seasonal ordering pattern for manufacturers of seasonal products, like Easter candy, is very different than point-of-sale purchases. Easter candy is often purchased and shipped to retailers immediately following Valentine's Day as retailers change over their seasonal section or aisle in stores. Consumer buying patterns, however, differ from year to year depending on the actual timing of Easter and the effectiveness of seasonal marketing campaigns. Sales of some products are higher in a longer season. There is more opportunity for people to buy, consume, and then buy again. Other products, such as the ones the Easter Bunny delivers, may not be impacted as much by the length of the season. In any case, the day after Easter, retailers aggressively reduce the price of any leftover inventory to make room for the next seasonal product. Manufacturers are often at least partially liable for the cost of price reductions.

In this case, a new seasonal marketing campaign had been developed the year before and was expected to significantly increase demand. Accordingly, retailers agreed to buy and put more product on the shelf than they had in prior years. The retailers were not too concerned—they knew that the manufacturer would cover the cost of reducing the price for product that was not purchased by consumers. Unfortunately, the marketing campaign didn't prove to be as effective as hoped. A significant proportion of the product had to be marked down and sold at a loss.

Historically the sales and demand planning teams would plan for an upcoming season by starting with what they had *shipped* the prior season. The problem with this approach, as you might guess, is not being able to distinguish between full price and discounted purchases in their historical shipping data. The markdowns were transacted separately from the shipments. For years, the company lived with high levels of seasonal markdowns and accepted it as a cost of doing business.

When point-of-sale data was brought into the demand planning process, the demand planner used the prior year's point-of-sale results as the starting point for the next year's demand plan. This approach yielded a more accurate demand plan, and the quantity of discounted sales after the season was significantly reduced. Planning based on point of sales rather than shipments also allowed planners to account for the changing duration of the Easter season more accurately. It also led to a better mix of products being sold and, in turn, resulted in higher overall revenue and profit.

Knowing where to obtain consumer or end-user sales data may not be straightforward. Depending on your industry and where your company sits in the value chain, there may be different options. As mentioned earlier, one approach is to ask your customers to share their knowledge of the end users or consumers. This could include information about their demand plans, inventory holding strategies, and their customers' buying patterns. You may be surprised by the amount of information your customers are willing to share—particularly in the interest of a collaborative relationship.

If you are part of a consumer goods value chain, consumer data might be available, at a cost, through a syndicator such as Nielsen or IRI. In regulated markets, such as alcoholic beverages, consumer data (often referred to as depletions) might be available through a control board or regulator. In other industries, financial institutions, research firms, or other entities may be the most appropriate source of consumer or end-user data.

Today, more and more products are connected to the internet. Twenty years ago, a lightbulb manufacturer had limited visibility to consumer behavior. At best, the manufacturer could receive point-of-sale data if they were willing to pay for it. Today, a Wi-Fi-enabled smart bulb can *phone home* to the manufacturer each time it is turned on. Smart refrigerators can *see* the contents of the appliance and share that information with their owners. (It would not be a stretch for that information to be collected and sold to food companies.) A connected car could send information back to consumables suppliers (oil, filters, windshield washer fluid, etc.). There is no shortage of possibilities. Industries that have historically had little access to consumer or end-user data are now able to benefit from this type of information being readily available.

Once a source for consumer or end-user data has been identified, it is then up to leadership to establish the expectation that the data will be reviewed and considered in the demand planning process. Once leaders set the expectation, their management teams can then be empowered to establish access to the data and invest in the required training and education.

In my earlier consumer goods company examples, point-of-sale data became tightly integrated into the planning process. There are certainly benefits to creating that linkage, but it does take time and resources to accomplish. The good news is that end-user or consumer data does not have to be rigidly connected with the demand plan for it to add value and make the plan more trustworthy.

In the example of the nylon manufacturer, it might be difficult to develop a mathematical model that connects the automotive market trends with the demand plan. That doesn't have to be a barrier, however. At a minimum, all that is needed is to bring the assumptions and discussions together. When consumer or end-user data and assumptions are discussed together, in the same forum as the demand plan, planners will start to identify and resolve differences in assumptions. Being able to demonstrate the fact that consumer or end-user data was considered in the demand planning process is often enough to build executive confidence.

Having a common set of assumptions and making better business decisions typically generates far more value for a company than the improvements in demand plan accuracy alone. It leads to the demand planners themselves becoming more business savvy and trustworthy, which is the focus of the following chapters.

SUMMARY

- It is common to find people involved in demand planning focused solely on the customers that a company transacts with directly. It is shortsighted to think only of immediate customers if those who purchase a company's products and services are not the end users of those offerings.

- Many executive leaders do not ensure that an understanding of consumer, end-user, and market behavior flows down to lower levels in the organization.
- When trading partners along a value chain operate without a clear view to drivers of end-user demand, they risk falling victim to the bullwhip effect. This creates distortions in demand that are difficult and costly to manage.
- The bullwhip effect can be minimized by paying attention to demand information as close to the end user as possible. This can be done through collaboration with trading partners and by incorporating end-user data in the demand planning process.
- Monitoring end-user demand can provide insights into downstream inventory levels, which can be important in avoiding situations of *channel stuffing* and consequences to revenue recognition.
- End-user demand data can also help to track and monitor the execution and effectiveness of demand-generating activities, such as promotions.
- Executives tend to view the business in a broader context. When the demand plan is presented in the context of end users, executives are more apt to engage. This, in turn, motivates the organization to better understand how their markets operate, which leads to better decision making.

QUESTIONS TO ASK

- Is consumer or end-user data available? If not, have customers or trading partners been asked for it?
- Do salespeople, marketers, and demand planners have access to and consider consumer or end-user data when developing their plans?
- Have demand planners been given the necessary training to be able to interpret and understand consumer or end-user data?
- Is available end-user or consumer data being used in the demand planning process?
- Conversely, is point-of-sale data that is shared between customers and the supply chain organization also shared with sales and marketing? If so, does the commercial organization use the data when developing their plans for influencing and generating demand?

ENDNOTE

1. Colleen Crum and George Palmatier. *Demand Management Best Practices: Process, Principles, and Collaboration.* J. Ross Publishing, Inc., 2003, pp. 198–199.

CHAPTER 12

MEASURING PERFORMANCE

To establish the right perspective for measuring and managing performance, let's revisit a few points that were made back in Chapter 2. Planning is a means to an end, and not an end itself. The purpose of a business is not to create demand plans, but by now readers should appreciate that creating a trustworthy demand plan is an enabler to achieving a company's business goals and objectives. Philip Kotler's definition of Demand Management is precisely that—influencing the level, timing, and composition of demand in order *to accomplish a company's business objectives and goals.*[1]

George Palmatier is a retired Oliver Wight principal and respected thought leader on the practices of Demand Management and Integrated Business Planning (IBP). He distilled many business management principles throughout his career. Here is one that is particularly relevant to measuring the performance of demand planning:

> *"I had the good fortune to work with a company many years ago that was committed to improving its integrated management processes. The company's president demonstrated his commitment through his actions.*
>
> *"He published a list of what was not so important versus what was important. The list included:*
>
> - *"Not so important: That our forecasts be accurate with actual results.*
> - *"Important: That our forecasts be reviewed and measured against the actual results, making us more knowledgeable of our markets and our products."*[2]

This book has reiterated the best practice principle that the demand plan reflects the sales and marketing actions that are being taken to achieve business goals. We have also established that a demand plan is more words, in the form of assumptions, than numbers. With that in mind, the measurement of demand plan performance must also be framed so that leaders can understand—in words—the key learnings from current business performance. Measurement of demand plan performance is not a number, it's a story. Stating that the demand plan was 78 percent accurate tells us very little that will help us understand the challenges in execution and how to make better decisions. Measuring actual performance against that plan should provide crucial information, including:

- Did we do what we said we would do?
  - Were the promotions executed as planned?
  - Were new products launched on time?
  - Were customer contracts and sales completed as planned?
- Was the *impact* of doing what we said we would do consistent with what we expected?
  - Did the promotions generate the expected lift?
  - Are the new products generating as much incremental demand as expected?
  - Are new customers buying as much of our products and services as planned?
- Are our assumptions about competitors, the marketplace, and circumstances outside of our control still reasonable?
  - Have our competitors done what we thought they would do?
  - Are market trends shifting or changing unexpectedly?

By understanding the actual performance versus the plan in this way, commercial leaders become equipped to make better decisions. If the impact of promotional activity is turning out to be less positive than what was expected, knowing that should lead to changes in how promotions are planned and executed in the future. Measuring performance is not about laying blame or punishment. Measuring performance is a way to continuously learn and improve.

In order to illustrate the point, Colleen "Coco" Crum, a retired Oliver Wight principal and Demand Management and IBP expert, shared the following example from one of her clients:

> *"A pulp and paper producer was achieving its revenue goals. They did not measure demand plan accuracy by market segment. The long-term strategy was to reduce their participation in the book paper market and significantly grow their business of specialty paper products.*
>
> *"Just looking at the overall revenue goals, they should have been content. By measuring each segment, however, sales of book papers were not declining at the rate called for in the strategy and sales of specialty paper products were not growing at the rate desired. But the demand*

plan accuracy based on actual volume versus the demand plan was quite good (consistently exceeding 95 percent).

"When measuring actual performance against the business strategy highlighted, there was a problem. It turned out that the sales and marketing people did not understand the specialty products industry. Selling specialty products was very different than selling book paper. The value propositions were different, and this company was the new kid in town. The company had to focus on training. Some commercial people did not make the transition, but most did. This more than 100-year-old company continued to be in business."

This example sheds light on some of the thinking that is required when developing demand plan performance measures. In my view, business goals and objectives should be the primary measuring stick against which execution of the demand plan is evaluated. In the previous case example, the measures did not reflect the business strategy to shift from one segment to another. This example is not unique.

I have encountered a similar situation at several client companies as they venture into selling their products online. One client had a strategy to aggressively expand their ecommerce offerings through Amazon and the like. This strategy involved developing new products, new marketing tactics, and new selling capabilities. Operationally, however, demand planning for Amazon was treated like any other customer. Plans and actuals were lumped together with existing, traditional channels. Because the initial volumes sold through ecommerce were very small relative to the existing business, the performance measures did not highlight the challenges that the sales and marketing teams faced selling into the ecommerce channel.

When performance measures for ecommerce were separated and highlighted on their own, a very different picture emerged. Accuracy of the plan was significantly worse than what anyone expected. The client demand leaders started to dig in and answer the fundamental questions: Did we do what we said we would do? Was the impact consistent with what we expected? The answers put a spotlight on two critical issues. In some cases, promotional activities were not being executed because the salespeople lacked experience with online retailers. In other cases, promotional activities were being executed, but were found to be delivering poor results. Examining the ecommerce performance measures separately helped to equip the business leaders to act, address the issues, and make better decisions.

Put in the context of achieving business goals and objectives, demand plan performance measures are not limited to measures of accuracy and bias. A more holistic view of demand plan performance measures commonly includes revenue and margin, market share, efficiency and effectiveness of marketing activities, and achievement of strategic objectives. In fact, each of the most critical assumptions to the demand plan (recall the exercise from Chapter 7) will ideally have an associated performance measure.

This isn't to say that demand plan accuracy and bias aren't important. Bias is a critical demand plan measure. It objectively measures one of the most important characteristics of the demand plan—trustworthiness. Bias is defined as the plan being consistently overly optimistic or overly pessimistic compared to actual sales. Bias is evident when there is a clear pattern, consistently over time, in the difference between the demand plan and actual results. Every plan will have some degree of inaccuracy, but a believable plan should have no bias. In other words, there should be no pattern in the errors.

The bias measure, therefore, is a key indicator of whether a reasonable person should rely on the demand plan, prima facie. When history shows that the demand plan is usually biased, explicitly or implicitly, people naturally respond by compensating for the bias going forward.

This characteristic of human nature makes the measurement of demand plan bias relevant to the executive team and the CEO. As we discussed in Chapter 3, in order for an executive team to work together, participants must be able to share and trust each others' functional plans. Trust is a feeling. Just as we can't instruct someone to feel happy, we can't instruct someone to trust. The demand plan must first prove itself to be trustworthy for it to be trusted.

Consider the following examples depicted in Figures 12.1 and 12.2. In Figure 12.1, actual sales are always higher than planned, which is frequently called negative bias. Figure 12.2 shows that actual sales are always lower than planned, which is commonly termed positive bias.

In both cases, the accuracy of the demand plan could be high. It wouldn't matter though. The recipients of these plans—representing supply, financial, and senior leadership—most likely would not believe the plans at face value. It would be unreasonable to expect them to do so.

When a demand plan has bias, users of the plan often succumb to the temptation to create a more accurate plan than what was initially provided. They simply adjust the plan according to the historical pattern of bias. People without any knowledge of the plan assumptions, market dynamics, or sales and marketing plans believe they can create a more accurate plan by simply making a mathematical adjustment.

The tendency to adjust or override bias in a plan leads to an underlying problem. Creating something better can create a worse situation. Adjusting the plan downstream, such as a finance leader compensating for demand plan bias with a hedge or a supply planner creating his or her own adjusted version of the demand plan, creates a disconnect in the enterprise. The users of the

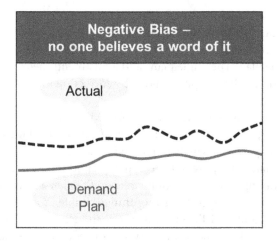

Figure 12.1   Example of Negative Bias. © Oliver Wight International, Inc. Used with permission.

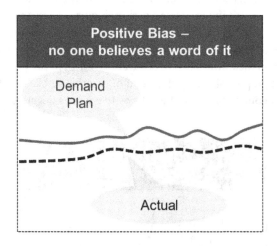

Figure 12.2   Example of Positive Bias. © Oliver Wight International, Inc. Used with permission.

adjusted demand plan may not understand how the plan has been changed or how those changes relate to the demand plan assumptions. All the effort to reach consensus on the plan has been systematically undone by these adjustments. When the demand plan is arbitrarily adjusted, the sales and marketing organizations often believe that it is no longer their plan. In their view, the plan is *owned* by whoever adjusted it.

A word of caution: I have seen companies attempt to force the recipients of the demand plan to adhere to it, despite obvious bias. It is usually a toothless edict. Recipients of the plan often resort to subterfuge rather than adhere to an unbelievable plan. They hide plans and adjustments, believing this behavior is secretly doing the company a favor by correcting for such obvious flaws in the plan.

As noted earlier, a plan without any bias will still have errors, but those errors will be impossible to predict by downstream users of the demand plan simply based on past performance. They will know that sales are just as likely to exceed the plan as they are to be less than planned (see Figure 12.3). Thus, there is no better option than to simply rely on the plan as it is.

To measure bias, I suggest keeping things simple. You do not need advanced analytics and statisticians to measure and eliminate bias. The drivers of bias are almost always behavioral. What is needed is a measurement that can be easily understood and acted upon by those individuals whose behavior needs to change to create trustworthy demand plans.

In my experience, a simple over/under measurement is easy to understand and is effective for driving focus and action. Figure 12.4 is an example showing the difference between the demand plan and actual sales for each brand, by month. Negative numbers mean that actual sales were more than the plan. Positive numbers mean the actual sales were lower than the plan. To the right of the table is a graphic showing the trend of positive versus negative months. Beside that is a count of the number of positive versus negative months.

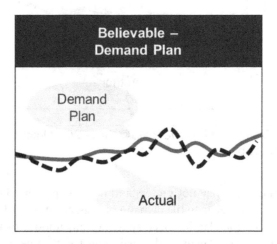

Figure 12.3 Example of an Unbiased Plan. © Oliver Wight International, Inc. Used with permission.

Brand	Jan	Feb	Mar	Apr	May	Jun	Trend	Over/Under
Brand A	-2%	-5%	-19%	-3%	-24%	-10%		0 / 6
Brand B	-23%	10%	-22%	24%	24%	15%		4 / 2
Brand C	18%	-10%	25%	6%	24%	-19%		4 / 2
Brand D	-16%	4%	11%	6%	-18%	-7%		3 / 3
Brand E	21%	13%	5%	7%	4%	8%		6 / 0
Brand F	-17%	-23%	23%	-12%	11%	-16%		2 / 4
Brand G	-14%	16%	18%	-16%	-10%	15%		3 / 3

Figure 12.4 Example of Demand Plan Bias Measurement. © Oliver Wight International, Inc. Used with permission.

Looking only at a single month, it is impossible to determine if there is positive or negative bias. There will always be some error, positive or negative. A pattern of bias only becomes visible by looking at the results over time.

In Figure 12.4 we see that sales of Brand A have been less than planned in six out of six months. A rational person would, if looking at the plan for July (the next period), believe that the plan is likely overstated. Conversely, sales for Brand E have been greater than planned for six out of six months. The same expectation would exist for Brand E, only in reverse.

The approach in Figure 12.4 is meant to reflect the same thought process that recipients of the demand plan will use when deciding whether to believe it. Remember, the objective is to create a demand plan that can be trusted. If a measurement is overly complicated and provides a different answer than what users' judgment would conclude, they may miss the point and draw an incorrect conclusion. A simple measurement with a clear implication equips a demand manager to work with the commercial organization in the Demand Review to recommend actions that will eliminate bias.

Bias can have a variety of sources, but they are almost always behavioral. Some typical behaviors that can result in bias include:

- Not wanting to deliver disappointing or bad news.
- Confusing plans with targets and trying to artificially force the plan to equal the target.
- Attempts to manipulate rewards systems.
- Human cognitive biases and overreliance on judgment.
- Attempts to secure constrained supply by manipulating the demand plan higher.
- Misaligned performance measures and lack of accountability.

For those reasons, it is best to measure demand plan bias at a level that corresponds with individual accountability, such as a brand, channel, or customer. This approach enables behaviors to be clearly, and factually exposed and addressed.

For example, a focus on bias only in total may not provide enough information to show the commercial side of the business how well they are performing and what needs to improve. When you measure bias by salesperson, it may tell a different story. Some salespeople are notoriously optimistic or pessimistic. These natural traits show themselves by measuring demand plan accuracy for each salesperson (also called sales plan accuracy). It is not unusual that sales plan accuracy for each salesperson could be accurate when measured for the total year; but month to month, it's a different story. It's common to hear salespeople say that the customer said they would buy in

February, but now they plan to buy in April. I've heard sales vice presidents challenge this explanation by asking, "When was the last time you talked to the customer?" Scrutiny of demand plan accuracy by salespeople inevitably helps them develop better discipline and follow-up, which frequently creates stronger relationships and trust with the customer.

This example highlights that addressing bias-generating behaviors may involve a wide range of solutions. There may be a need to address complex, structural issues within an organization. It may mean a leadership team has to commit themselves to not shoot the messenger and learn to accept visibility of gaps between the latest demand plan and the annual budget and then assign actions to close the gaps. It is a best practice to take concrete actions to close those gaps, rather than autocratically adjusting the plan to equal the annual budget.

In other cases, the solution to bias may involve the risks and opportunities that have been identified as part of the Demand Management process. Use of risks and opportunities in this fashion may require adjusting the approach for deciding what to include or exclude from the plan as a means of consciously compensating for an unconscious bias. When risks and opportunities are used in this way, more serious attention to the detail in determining whether risks and opportunities are likely to materialize will typically result.

For example, there may be a habit of putting bad news on the risks list rather than calling down the plan. Taking a hard look at the list and acknowledging the bias will create a more robust and truthful demand planning process.

In Chapter 7, we outlined several best practices for driving an assumption-based demand plan. Assumptions should be thoughtfully developed with sufficient detail to extract demand volume and timing. When assumptions are robust, bias can be linked to specific planning assumptions. In turn, root causes of the bias can be quickly identified. There may be weak or inadequate assumptions supporting a plan, or there may be one or two planning inputs that are driving bias (e.g., new products).

I noted earlier that measuring demand plan accuracy, in addition to bias, is also important. For most business leaders, however, measuring demand plan accuracy on its own is often meaningless. Knowing that your product line has an accuracy of 72 percent does not provide much indication as to whether that is good or bad, or if something should be done about it. Furthermore, there is no gold standard for demand plan accuracy. Demand plan accuracy is influenced by the type of products, where the products are in their life cycle, the condition of the marketplace, and the business strategy and goals for each market, product category, customers, and the overall business.

It is therefore important to understand how demand plan accuracy impacts the internal customers of the demand plan, the decisions they make, and the achievement of business goals and objectives, such as cost, customer service, and working capital. It also is imperative to make sure the accuracy metric fairly reflects the quality of the demand plan, and that it is not being gamed or manipulated. If demand plan accuracy is being used to incentivize performance in the organization, business leaders need to ask whether the right behaviors are being incentivized in order to instill trust in each other and work as a team, rather than incentivizing people to distrust, second guess, or act in a self-oriented manner.

In Chapter 6, we noted that there are many internal customers of the demand plan. Business leaders need to consider the decisions these stakeholders may make based on the demand plan in the context of how improving demand plan accuracy might deliver greater value to the business. This thought process helps ascertain the range of positive and negative impacts that variations in demand can have on decision making. For each of the internal customers of the demand plan, identify the decisions that they are making and then document the answers to these questions:

- What is the impact of selling more than in the plan? (Overselling)
- What is the impact of selling less than in the plan? (Underselling)
- At what level of detail and lead time are these implications relevant? (Brand? Customer? SKU?)

For example, let's look at the most straightforward activity—the manufacturing of finished goods. The implication of selling below plan is having excess inventory. Depending on the product, excess inventory may be strictly a working capital concern—the consumption of cash. It also may have profitability implications if the inventory has a short shelf life or is expensive to store. Conversely, the implication of selling above plan is likely to degrade customer satisfaction and often increases the costs of expediting (e.g., overtime, premium transportation, etc.).

There are other decisions that should be made based on the demand plan that are highly impactful. But, when demand planning has historically been a supply chain activity, these implications may not be appreciated—for example, communicating expected financial performance to the board of directors. Losing the trust and confidence of the board would undoubtedly have significant consequences, especially when asking the board to approve capital investments in order to improve the company's capabilities.

One lesson that often emerges is that different levels of accuracy will be acceptable to different internal customers of the demand plan. It is not always the case that a more accurate demand plan will lead to improved business results. The demand plan simply needs to be accurate enough.

As the implications of demand plan accuracy on decision making become clear, they provide clarity on how accurate the plan must be to qualify as *accurate enough* and also clarifies the potential return on investment from making improvements. Documenting the implications helps to develop a set of sources from which to calculate benefits of improved demand planning. These sources are called the costs of failure. Figure 12.5 illustrates example costs of failure related to the manufacturing of finished goods.

With the costs of failure outlined, a link or causal relationship between the incidence of failure (how often we oversell or undersell) and the magnitude of the cost can be established. Some links and costs are easier to identify than others. In my experience, a well-constructed business case should

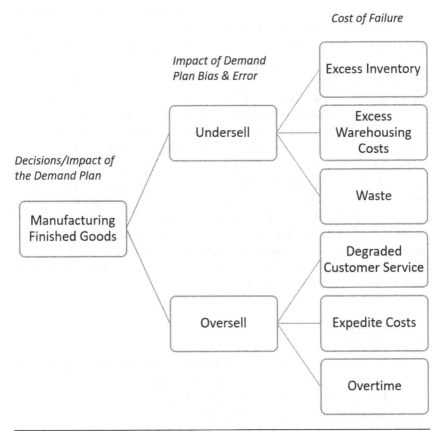

Figure 12.5 Costs of Failure. © Oliver Wight International, Inc. Used with permission.

clearly communicate the degree to which improvements can be confidently attributed to demand planning.

Through this exercise, it should become clear that *best-in-class* demand plan accuracy is an irrelevant concept. What matters is how your company uses the demand plan and the implications of demand plan accuracy on achieving your business objectives. Deciding what is *accurate enough* for your business and, consequently, the targets for demand plan accuracy that should be set, must tie back to a cost/benefit trade-off.

One way to think of it is that Olympic marathon runners complete a race in around two hours. Average casual runners typically finish in four and a half hours. If you were a casual runner, would it make any sense to set a goal of completing a marathon in two hours? Probably not.

The right approach is to take your current performance and establish a plan to improve it. Note that I used the word *plan*. A plan to improve accuracy, just like the demand plan itself, should be built on assumptions. Are you implementing new tools? New processes? New inputs? Hiring more planners? If you don't have an idea of what you will do to improve, establishing targets significantly beyond where you are today is an exercise in frustration.

The improvement plan should consider the costs to achieve those improvements balanced against the benefits that will be realized by the different internal customers of the demand plan. For example, making the demand plan more accurate at a SKU level may have no impact on the reliability of revenue commitments being made to the board of directors. It may, however, have an impact on the amount of safety stock that is held by the supply chain, and in turn, may lead to a reduction in working capital. Just remember, there is often more than one way to achieve an objective. As illustrated in Chapter 3, company-level goals such as improving margins can be achieved in many ways. Improving demand plan accuracy may be one of several options to evaluate as a means for achieving those goals.

SUMMARY

- Measuring performance is not about laying blame or punishment. Measuring performance is a way to continuously learn and improve.
- Performance measurements must first and foremost consider the goals and objectives of the business.
- Measure and eliminate bias—a demand plan that is not trustworthy will not be relied upon, and therefore, will have no bearing on decision making or business performance.

- Bias is behavioral—measure bias at the level where decisions are made so that you can use knowledge of bias to influence and drive better decisions about demand.
- Remember that demand plan accuracy is a means to an end. The acceptable level of error will depend on the decisions being made based on the demand plan.
- Establish a plan for improvement—know where you are today, what it will take to improve, and the expected impact of those improvements.

QUESTIONS TO ASK

- Who in your organization has demand plan accuracy or bias as a measure in their incentive plan?
- When demand plan accuracy or bias is reported, how often are the root causes clear and actions taken to resolve them?
- Are the people who are accountable for executing the demand plan appropriately measured on how well they execute it?
- What decisions are being based on the demand plan, and what are the business impacts of demand plan errors and bias?
- If improvements are warranted, what would it really take to accomplish them?

ENDNOTES

1. Philip Kotler. *The Father of Modern Marketing*. pkotler.org.
2. George Palmatier and Colleen Crum. *The Transition from Sales and Operations Planning to Integrated Business Planning: Practices and Principles, Second Edition*. J. Ross Publishing, Inc., 2022, p. 230.

CHAPTER 13

TRUSTED ADVISORS

In 2009, the Institute of Business Forecasting (IBF) surveyed businesses to find out where their demand planning functions reside organizationally. The answers they received were: Supply Chain, Sales, Marketing, Strategic Planning, Finance, Forecasting Department, and of course, Other. I can't think of any other function that is as widely dispersed in organizations as demand planning.[1] Either everybody wants it, or nobody wants it. Sometimes I'm not quite sure which it is.

In any case, the IBF survey finding validated what demand management experts at Oliver Wight had been telling clients since the mid-1990s: it may not make much difference where the demand planning function resides in an organization, provided there is a good process in place where all the functions work together.

All things being equal, the best option is for demand planning to report to the Sales or Marketing organization since that is where accountability for the demand plan must reside. It is vital to recognize, however, that demand planning provides value to so many different stakeholders in a business that there will always be a need for cross-functional trust and collaboration. I believe this is why demand planning varies in reporting structure so much more widely than most other functions.

To leverage the information that the demand planning organization provides for the rest of the organization, it must be trusted. The demand plan itself is usually not trusted on its merits alone. The people involved in developing and communicating the demand plan must be viewed as credible and trustworthy.

To create trust, the organization's leaders must acknowledge that demand planning is not just number crunching. Demand planners must work across functional boundaries to gather critical information. They need to be able to translate numbers, information, and analytics into the language of the business. They need to tell the story of the updated demand plan each month in a way that others will easily understand and use in decision making. To do so, demand planners must understand how the plan is being used across the business, and they should continuously seek to improve its usefulness. The demand plan will rarely be perfect—neither is a supply plan, or any plan for that matter. But demand planners must build sufficient credibility that the business leaders do not lose trust when the demand plan is imperfect.

The attributes described demonstrate that demand planners must be competent in skills beyond forecasting and analytics. They must be skilled in developing trusting relationships and collaborating well with others. Building trust involves more than just having the right answers. It requires being respected for judgment and business acumen.

In my experience, demand planners are too often viewed as administrative staff that enter forecasts into a planning system. This view is held by leaders and planners alike. The origins of this low expectation date back to the early days of Materials Requirements Planning when supply planners needed a forecast to drive the system. The story of the five monkeys experiment helps to explain why this view is still pervasive today.

In the story, five monkeys were put in a room. A ladder with bananas on the top rung is placed in the room. Each time a monkey climbs the ladder and reaches for the bananas, all the monkeys are sprayed with cold water. Over time, when a monkey climbs the ladder, the others pull him down to avoid being sprayed. Eventually, none of the monkeys would climb the ladder.

Then, one by one, each of the original five monkeys are removed from the room and replaced with a new monkey. When a new monkey tries to climb the ladder, the others pull him down. Even those who had never been sprayed with cold water pull the new monkey off the ladder. By the end of the experiment, none of the five monkeys would climb the ladder, and none of them had experienced being sprayed with cold water.

The view that demand planning is an administrative task persists in organizations because "that's just how it's always been done." I've worked with senior leaders who vehemently believed that demand planning should involve nothing more than a statistical forecast because that's the way it was done earlier in their careers. This view is reinforced by lowered leadership expectations of the value of demand planning, and by extension, the way that demand planning roles are structured and filled.

Take a moment to think about the demand planners in your organization. What does leadership expect of them? Would a Vice President of Sales, Chief Financial Officer (CFO), or Chief Marketing Officer actively seek out advice from the head of demand planning? Has the head of demand planning earned that trust?

Georges Tetegan was the Senior Vice President of Supply Chain for Irving Companies in New Brunswick, Canada. Oliver Wight had been working with one of their group companies to develop the capability of their demand planning team.

The demand planners reported to the supply chain function, and their job descriptions largely reflected supply planning activities even though they were expected to create sales forecasts. That was the way it had always been done.

When the business decided to improve demand planning and implement Integrated Business Planning (IBP), the expectation for demand planners shifted to developing much stronger relationships with the commercial teams. As this transition commenced, the demand planners asked what this new expectation meant for the team and their career paths. The demand planning team asked Georges a simple, but important question, "What do you expect from us now?"

In answering this question Georges consciously raised the bar. He didn't expect them to be great forecasters or analysts. He expected them to become trusted advisors. In a town hall presentation, he outlined the core elements of what he expected from a trusted advisor:

- Providing critical insight—having expertise in planning and a solid understanding of the business and being able to apply those skills to help business leaders make better decisions.
- Being disciplined—respecting the process, cadence, and people's roles and responsibilities.
- Demonstrating emotional intelligence—being transparent, listening, and separating logic from emotions.
- Having skin in the game—playing the long game, driving improvement, and recommending paths forward that are in the best interest of the organization.

Georges recognized that trust was central to what it would take for a demand planner to successfully support the commercial organization. Critically, he set high expectations. He chose to break free from "the way it had always been done" and establish a more progressive demand planning organization.

Georges' vision of a trusted advisor is not unique to demand planning. In the book *The Trusted Advisor,*[2] the authors suggest that the key to professional success is not just technical mastery of a discipline, but also the ability to build trust and confidence of the people with whom you work. The authors outline four characteristics of trust: credibility, reliability, intimacy, and self-orientation.

A *credible* demand planner has a firm grasp of the business. A demand planner does not need a crystal ball that can see into the future to be credible. They must, however, be able to understand and to speak to the drivers of demand. They must understand key business goals, objectives, and strategies. They must be cognizant of the competitive environment in which the business operates. They must be skilled in planning, and then critically be able to apply that skill to help business leaders make better decisions. As noted earlier, this means they must be skilled storytellers who are able to craft their message in a way that is relatable to a wide variety of different audiences and internal customers.

I often find that the most credible demand planners are the ones who have come from a sales or marketing background. Those demand planners are naturally better equipped to be able to speak about the business in terms that other commercial leaders will understand and trust.

A *reliable* demand planner is one who behaves consistently. As Georges noted in his townhall presentation, adherence to process is key. Making and keeping commitments, even as simple as facilitating the Demand Review (DR) process consistently each month, builds trust. This is why a key Oliver Wight Class A behavior is: "Do what we say we are going to do."[3] This doesn't mean that what we say will always make everyone happy, but it does mean that we won't consciously over- or under-promise. We keep the commitments that we make so that others don't have to spend time worrying about whether we will keep them.

An *intimate* demand planner is one who can create meaningful connections with others in the organization. Establishing intimacy requires emotional intelligence, which is the ability to understand and manage your own emotions as well as those of others. Demand planners rely on information and insight coming from a wide variety of stakeholders. Often their only means of gathering this information is through influence. These relationships should not be thought of as transactional. Many demand inputs and assumptions are subjective and qualitative, and as such, are best conveyed when there is a trusting relationship between parties. A demand planner must be able to recognize and adapt their approach to consider their own emotional state and the emotional state of others.

For example, a salesperson has been working to secure a new customer account for several months. Each month, the demand planner asks for an update on progress. Transactionally, the salesperson could simply respond with some basic information—perhaps simply confirming that the account has not yet been secured.

With a more intimate relationship between the salesperson and the demand planner, the discussion could easily go deeper. The demand planner might notice tension in the salesperson's voice while discussing the account. Instead of doggedly asking when the deal will close and what likelihood it is, they might instead ask, with sincerity, how things are going with the account. Responding to genuine interest and caring, the salesperson might reveal that they are struggling to convince the customer that their products are an ideal fit with the customer's application. That discussion could easily provide the demand planner with much more valuable information regarding not only the likelihood of the opportunity, but also the overall relationship with the customer. The demand planner might even be able to offer help.

A demand planner with *low self-orientation* is one who routinely puts the business first. This means that while working with cross-functional partners, there is a genuine belief that the demand planner is working toward shared business goals, and not only outcomes that will benefit the demand planner and how they are measured or rewarded.

When low self-orientation exists, a demand planner is not overly focused on operational metrics, such as demand plan accuracy, at the expense of the well-being of the business. Demand planners are often measured and incentivized based on demand plan accuracy. As we discussed in the last chapter, while demand plan accuracy is an important metric, demand planners should recognize that the metric is a means to an end. There are times when the best business decision might negatively impact a demand planning performance measure, such as choosing to support incremental sales within lead time. Demand planners with low self-orientation will not hesitate to support those actions when they are for the greater good of the company.

Stepping back from demand planning, take a moment to think about the people in your life whom you trust and turn to for advice. There are people whom you trust as service providers, such as doctors or therapists. There are people whom you trust in your personal life, such as close family members and friends. There are people whom you trust in your professional life, such as mentors or close colleagues. In every case, trusting relationships are built on the elements of providing credible insight, being respectful and reliable, demonstrating emotional intelligence, and having low self-orientation.

While all of these attributes are important, I believe one of the most challenging attributes, particularly in business, is the ability to have low self-orientation. In fact, I believe it is why demand planning teams tend to have such inconsistent reporting lines in organizations. When leaders become focused only on *their own* functional priorities, it can be difficult for their teams to work cross-functionally without being perceived as neglecting their function's own goals and objectives.

The perception of self-orientation is why consultants are often hired to provide coaching and guidance to companies. Consultants don't come with the stigma of being perceived as speaking for any one function. Consultants are more likely to be viewed as prioritizing the interests of the overall organization. Similarly, when mentorship relationships are established between two people in a company, it is a best practice for the mentor to be from a different function or department than the mentee. For advice to be trustworthy, it has to come from a place of caring primarily for the individual to whom the advice is being given. People naturally evaluate not only *what* information is being shared, but also *why* it is being shared.

I regularly observe problems caused by self-orientation. One example has continued to stick with me over the years. I interviewed sales leaders at a client company during the initial stages of an IBP engagement. I asked one sales director to describe the relationship with the demand planning team. He flatly responded that he "couldn't tell them anything." I have known salespeople who lacked the motivation to proactively share information, but this level of outright refusal was different.

The sales director told me that the demand planning team would be tattle-tales. Like children, they would "run and tell Dad what they heard." I asked for further explanation. The sales director said a salesperson might share some news with a demand planner that may have a negative impact to the demand plan and revenue outlook, such as the loss of a customer or actions by a competitor. Without full understanding of the situation, regard for the chain of command, or how this information would be received by the leadership team, the demand planner would quickly spread the news. The demand planner didn't stop to think about or ask whether the information was part of a bigger story. The sales director acknowledged that the demand planner believed she was doing the right thing. Demand planners were measured on the accuracy of the demand plan, after all.

His objection, however, was the motivation of the demand planning team. He felt that the demand planners were quick to spread information because it gave them a sense of power and an ability to act as if they had inside information. He believed that their self-orientation led them to prioritize being first to share a piece of news over considering the implications to the business. Bad news early is better than bad news late, but incomplete or misrepresented news can be even worse.

An important aspect of this example is that it centered around the *perception* of self-orientation. The demand planners certainly did not state that they were operating in their own self-interest. In fact, the demand planners were not even aware that the perception existed. When I spoke to the demand planners to understand their side of the story, they told me that salespeople were "unwilling to share bad news and face the consequences." They had no idea that their actions, or more important, the perception of their motivations, had contributed to the breakdown in trust.

The solution in this case started with leadership. The senior sales leader in the organization was one of the most gracious and trustworthy leaders I have worked with. My request of him was simple: "Don't shoot the messenger." Any fear of reprisal for sharing bad news would undermine any efforts to establish trust between the sales and demand planning teams.

We worked to bring the two teams together and identify common goals. We educated the sales team about the demand planning process and how it relied heavily on cross-functional information sharing. We educated the demand planning team on the sales management process and how salespeople were expected to bring solutions, not just problems to their work. We showed both teams how the two processes were codependent. Little by little, the two teams started to build trust with each other.

When I think back to my various leadership roles in industry, trust was not a dimension that was expected to be evaluated during performance reviews. People were most often measured on performance and/or their potential for future performance. It was up to me as a leader to set the expectation that trust was important, just like Georges Tetegan did.

The highest performing teams balance performance with trust. The two go together. Some of the highest performing organizations in the world use an approach for measuring and ranking employees that includes both trust and performance.[4] There is a clear distinction between trusting someone's technical skills and believing that they are trustworthy as an individual. Trust builds a team, whereas high performing individuals who are not trustworthy tend to be only looking out for themselves. Like the ice hockey example from Chapter 3, if a player is always going it alone, the team's performance will suffer.

As I have grown and evolved throughout my career, I have come to see the value of being trustworthy and having the ability to build trusting relationships. I have come to believe that trust is an expectation that must be set for the demand planning team, and then measured.

Consider the following scenario involving two demand planners. One has exceptional analytical skills and consistently provides well-researched insights and advice. Unfortunately, the cross-functional partners don't trust him/her because they can't relate to him/her and haven't built trusting relationships. The other tends to provide less sophisticated advice but is considered trustworthy by his/her cross-functional partners. Which one should receive a better performance rating? Which one should be groomed for career progression?

Setting the expectation for trust doesn't automatically make it happen. Luckily there are some simple ways to start building trusted cross-functional relationships. A sales or marketing leader could make it a point to invite the demand planners to the sales and marketing town hall meetings or off-site events. A demand planner could offer to take a sales director out for lunch to learn a little bit more about his/her challenges. They might discuss how the demand planner could help him/her to navigate those challenges. The demand planning team could offer to host education sessions and share with the commercial organization the ins and outs of the demand planning process. These examples are gestures *offering* support, and not requesting it. That's the first step in establishing low self-orientation. Each person must be willing to give in order to expect trust in return.

While soft skills are important, to trust and to be trusted, the soft skills need to be backed up with hard skills. The ability to dispense good advice, integrate information from various sources, and apply analytics are all hard skills that are important to demand planning. A hockey team made up of highly trustworthy individuals who can't skate wouldn't get very far (both literally and figuratively).

While building trust in technical skills might be easier to establish than building trusting relationships, trust must still be earned. Sports teams practice with one another to both demonstrate and improve their technical skills. Having a good reputation certainly helps, but people naturally put more faith in technical skill that has been observed. If I want to take my wife out for a nice dinner on our wedding anniversary, all other things being equal, I'm more likely to go to a restaurant that I've been to before and am certain will prepare a great meal.

In one conversation with a CFO on the topic of building up the credibility of a demand planning team, he drew on his whiteboard the diagram illustrated in Figure 13.1.

The premise in this illustration is the CFO's belief that the development of trust in the technical competency of a demand planner is a journey. It starts with being able to explain the past. If what caused results in the past cannot be explained, leaders are hesitant to accept a demand planner's prediction of the future. This might sound simple, but I regularly observe demand planners who are so wrapped up in statistical models that when I ask the question, "Why did we sell what we did last month?" they struggle to provide a good answer.

Planners will often focus on the second level of trust—predicting the future—without attempting to understand the past. I often find demand planners who are frustrated when others are unwilling to accept their predictions

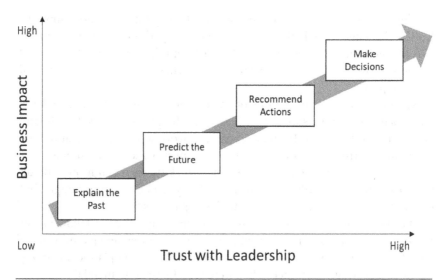

Figure 13.1 Trust in Technical Competency Is a Journey.

of the future. The truth is that they haven't earned the trust of their cross-functional peers in being able to explain the drivers of demand. The solution, almost paradoxically, is to spend more time understanding and articulating the past in the context of what will drive demand in the future.

Trust then develops further as a demand planner is relied upon for their predictions of the future—grounded in their understanding of the various levers that drive the business. When this level of credibility is achieved, a demand planner is sought out for advice. They are asked questions like, "What do you think the impact of this promotion will be?" or "What will happen to demand for our product if a competitor launches a similar one?" This credibility becomes advantageous since the demand planner is now engaged earlier in the process of providing feedback on the impact of commercial activities and external drivers that influence demand. They are also relied upon by the commercial organization and business leaders for their objectivity. This advice gives early visibility of how demand may materialize and leads to fewer surprises. In the end, better business decisions are made to help ensure that business strategies and goals are achieved.

With a solid track record of being able to translate assumptions into impacts and help generate more reliable predictions of the future, a demand planner becomes trusted to provide recommendations and alternatives that may be taken to achieve goals. Instead of being asked what will happen, a demand planner is asked, "What do you think we should do?"

This level of trust crosses a line from an advisory role to a leadership role. I often challenge my clients to assess the career path of a demand planner. Would you want the people who best understand the commercial levers and impacts in your business to move into supply chain, finance, or commercial leadership roles?

Recalibrating the expectations of the demand planning process and demand planners is not a simple task. There may be gaps in both soft skills and hard skills. In the case of Irving Companies, Georges set the expectation that a technically strong demand planning team must work on developing their soft skills. In my experience, however, the soft skills are much more difficult to develop than hard skills. Analytical capability can be taught or bought, but trustworthiness is more challenging to develop from scratch.

During the design of the DR process at one large client, a fellow Oliver Wight principal and I were faced with a dilemma. The demand planning team reported to the supply chain organization and few of the planners had any sales or marketing experience. They were seen by the commercial organization as the front end of the supply chain, and not a group that would provide trustworthy advice to commercial leaders.

My colleague and I were wrestling with who to recommend as the process leader for the DR. On the one hand, we wanted to elevate the role of the demand planning organization in its importance to the business. On the other hand, we knew that the soft skills were lacking with that team. The demand planning team had not yet earned the trust of the executives.

We asked the business unit leaders, "Who do you turn to for advice and guidance about future demand and generation of revenue?" Their answer was senior sales strategy leaders. The sales strategy leaders had deep commercial experience, were trusted, and would be better suited to prepare for and lead the DR meetings.

In this example, we had to identify the people in the organization who had the necessary capability to lead demand planning activities without constraining ourselves to existing job titles or functional reporting lines. This challenge wasn't unique to this client. I often find that the full breadth of demand planning capability in an organization spans multiple functions. I have recommended individuals from various functions including sales, marketing, finance, and strategy to lead in demand planning activities.

That being said, I do believe that leaving the leadership role of demand planning ambiguous is not a good long-term solution. In the previous example, my colleague and I recommended that the demand planners be made responsible as process leaders for the preparatory meetings leading up to the DR. That challenged the demand planners with elevated expectations of identifying and facilitating commercial discussions, but at a level that was not too far beyond their capability. It established routines where the demand planners and sales strategy leaders would work together. This approach provided an opportunity for the demand planners to observe and learn from the sales strategy leaders. They could see what it took to lead DR discussions at the business unit level.

Appreciation for this broader scope of demand planners being trusted advisors drives business leaders to rethink the career paths that lead to and from this role. It highlights the need in many cases to elevate not only the pay scale, but also the way demand planners are positioned to the organization. In my experience, the demand planner role should attract high-potential talent and should be a route to accelerate a career trajectory. Demand planning should not be a parking lot for the mediocre talent in the organization.

Elevating the expectations of demand planners takes time and commitment, but it is worth it not only for the organization, but for the individuals as well. My Oliver Wight colleague in the prior example likes to say that she measures her success not only based on client business performance, but also based on how many of the client's people whom she works with get promoted. That approach has paid dividends, as the individuals whom we coach often move on to leadership roles where they, in turn, leverage our support to strengthen their organizations. They transition from *trusted advisors* to *trusted leaders*, which is the subject of the next and final chapter.

SUMMARY

- It may not make much difference where the demand planning function resides in an organization, provided there is a good process in place where all of the functions work together.
- The people involved in developing and communicating the demand plan must be viewed as credible and trustworthy.
- Demand planners must be skilled in developing trusting relationships and collaborating well with others.
- Demand planners must demonstrate credibility, reliability, intimacy, and self-orientation:
  - A credible demand planner has a firm grasp of the business.
  - A reliable demand planner is one who behaves consistently.
  - An intimate demand planner is one who can create meaningful connections with others in the organization.
  - A demand planner with low self-orientation is one who routinely puts the business first.

- The highest performing teams balance performance with trust.
- While soft skills are important, in order to trust and to be trusted, the soft skills need to be backed up with hard skills.
- The development of trust in the technical competency of a demand planner is a journey that starts with being able to credibly explain the past before being trusted to predict the future.
- Soft skills are much more difficult to develop than hard skills. Analytical capability can be taught or bought, but trustworthiness is more challenging to develop from scratch.
- The full breadth of demand planning capability in an organization often spans multiple functions.

QUESTIONS TO ASK

- Is your demand planning team trusted by commercial leadership?
- Is the information provided by the demand planning team relied on by leaders in order to make commercial decisions?
- Have the expectations of trust and trustworthiness been established with your demand planning team?
- Under a broader definition of demand planning, which other functions are currently involved in demand planning activities?

ENDNOTES

1. Chaman L. Jain. *Fundamentals of Demand Planning and Forecasting.* St. John's University, 2019.
2. David H. Maister, Charles H. Green, and Robert M. Galford. *The Trusted Advisor.* Free Press, 2004.
3. *The Oliver Wight Class A Standard for Business Excellence, Seventh Edition.* John Wiley & Sons, 2017.
4. Simon Sinek, *The Infinite Game.* Penguin, 2019.

CHAPTER 14

CONCLUSION

I have had the opportunity to work closely with leaders from organizations of all different shapes and sizes. I've coached different leadership styles and personalities. One common trait that I've observed is that leaders who embrace trust always seem to outperform their less-trusting peers. Companies where trust is embedded in the culture attract the best talent, achieve their goals and objectives, and offer rewarding careers for their employees. Leaders who are both trusting and trustworthy spend less time politicking and more time leading. They are able to spend their time wisely, working *on* the business.

I hope this book has shown you how to develop demand planning processes that increase the probability of achieving company goals and strategies. I hope it has clarified roles. I hope it has created a better understanding of what it takes to develop and execute a credible demand plan. I also hope this book makes clear why it is necessary to trust your colleagues and their plans.

That being said, I regularly remind my clients that *hope* is not a strategy. Taking any number of learnings from this book and doing something with them is a choice. Becoming a trusted advisor and a trusted leader is a choice. Being vulnerable, sharing information, and trusting others are all choices. Breaking free from "the way things have always been done" is a choice. Each of these choices are for you, and not someone else, to make. Likewise, change is not something for someone else to do.

Developing trust and becoming trustworthy usually involves change. Change is hard, especially for leaders. It's no less difficult for company presidents to change their behaviors or ways of working than anyone else. In fact, it can be *more* difficult. Leaders go through change, both as individuals and as leaders. They must understand and accept what a change means for themselves while dozens of eyeballs are pointed at them, observing how they handle the change, and then expecting them to articulate what that change means for the rest of the team as well.

Dr. Gail Matthews, a psychology professor at Dominican University of California, led a study on goal achievement in 2015. She investigated how goal achievement is influenced by writing those goals down, committing to actions, and establishing accountability for those actions.[1] Matthews found that more than 70 percent of the participants who sent weekly updates to a friend reported successful goal achievement. Of those who kept their goals to themselves, only 35 percent reported successful goal achievement.

When I teach the Oliver Wight course on Demand Management, I wrap it up with a challenge to my students: (1) identify one or two things that they learned from the class that they would like to implement in their organization, and (2) write them down. Then I invite my students to share those goals with the class and with others in their organization. My experience has been consistent with the findings from Dr. Matthews' study. Those who commit to making changes and then share that commitment with their peers tend to have a much better track record of achieving them.

At the end of each chapter, I pose a series of questions to ask yourself about your current planning and decision-making processes. Your answers to those questions, combined with the insights gained from the chapters in this book, should form a good foundation for a path forward. I encourage you to identify the most significant areas of opportunity along with one or two things that you can do to address them. You have invested your most precious resource—time—in reading this book. Do not let that investment go to waste.

One question that I often receive from my students, particularly those who have a long list of opportunities written down is: Where should we start? My response is for them to start with the improvements that are within their control. For demand planners, brand managers, and financial analysts, tactical improvements can often be made. Tactical improvements, such as documenting assumptions or measuring demand plan bias, typically do not require significant cross-functional engagement. The most impactful improvements, however, must be embraced by executive leadership. As noted in Chapter 4, grassroots efforts to build trust and create cross-functional collaboration are rarely successful.

That is why this book has been written for an executive audience. Business leaders have a much broader ability to influence and impact the way the business is run. A business leader's list of improvements has the potential to unlock the tremendous value that demand management can bring to your organization. I know this because I have observed it time and time again with my clients.

For example, a business leader's list of improvements may include making a personal commitment to adopt a best practice behavior, such as being more transparent with gaps or eliminating bias from their plans. In other cases, it may be making a commitment to learning about best practices, which leads to changes in ownership and accountability for the demand plan and the demand planning process. Often the scope of demand management, in the eyes of the leadership team, expands. Formerly disparate processes become consolidated into one process for planning and managing demand. The role of demand planners becomes elevated and career paths are reconsidered.

In every case, when asked what my clients would do differently in the future, the answer is the same. They all wish they would have started sooner. The business value that is realized from better teamwork and, more important, strengthened *trust* is so significant that the best time to start is *yesterday*.

In the preface, I noted that the profession of Demand Management has evolved significantly over the past twenty years. My reason for writing this book was to address those changes in a way that is relevant for an executive audience. As I look toward the next twenty years and try to predict what will come, I firmly believe that the principles discussed in this book will remain relevant and will become commonplace.

We will undoubtedly continue to see advances in technology and analytics. Processes like Integrated Business Planning will continue to be broadly adopted. Evolution of these processes will continue as it always has. That being said, the one constant will be people. Companies are made up of people. Companies perform their best when people *trust* each other and can work together as a team.

ENDNOTE

1. Sarah Gardner and Dave Albee. "Study focuses on strategies for achieving goals, resolutions." Dominican University of California, 2015. https://scholar.dominican.edu/news-releases/266/.

APPENDIX A

ANALYTICS AND TECHNOLOGY IN DEMAND MANAGEMENT

As a company grows its portfolio of products and services, acquires new customers, and expands its points of distribution, the demand planning process increases in complexity. This complexity often grows at a pace where simply hiring more demand planners isn't the solution.

Tools, and in particular tools that provide statistical forecasting capability, are a common way to free up demand planners from many of the manual activities of data management and analysis. Some business leaders are also thinking more broadly about how to leverage analytics to help executives make better business decisions. Many other business leaders make investments in analytics and data science out of fear of missing out on the latest technology. They neglect to develop a solid understanding of how and where analytical techniques should be deployed and how the analytical information will give them more insight on the future of the business.

Regardless of your level of technical expertise or role in the organization, it is important to understand the different ways in which statistics can be leveraged in demand planning. There is plenty of evidence that proves analytics can be incredibly powerful. We benefit in our daily lives from analytical software applications such as artificial intelligence (AI) and machine learning. Tools that we take for granted leverage AI technology. Some examples include email spam filters, navigation applications, facial recognition, media and product recommendations, virtual assistants, and household items such as autonomous vacuum cleaners. You don't have to look farther than your doorstep for evidence of AI and analytics. Amazon relies heavily on data and analytics to predict consumer behavior, and it's happening on a massive scale.[1]

Achieving a level of reliance on analytics in your business that is akin to Amazon is incredibly difficult. The reasons are not technical, but behavioral. Amazon has a culture of trusting their algorithms. They rely on them implicitly. Developing that level of faith in an algorithm used by your business will usually take time to become deeply embedded in the company culture for planning and decision making.[2]

Advanced analytical models are far more *black box* than simpler analytical techniques. The inner workings of these models are not as broadly understood as those commonly taught in business school statistics classes.

I believe Dr. Sven F. Crone of Lancaster University said it best: "The more we talk about statistics to leadership, the less they trust us." It may have been a tongue-in-cheek comment, but there is a lot of truth in Crone's statement. If management overrides, bias, and other poor behaviors are frequent in your company's demand management process, these are symptoms of lack of trust and belief that the demand plan is not credible. The reasons for these symptoms—whatever their source—will need to be resolved before bringing in advanced analytical techniques based on AI or machine learning.

I recently worked with a large consumer products company that was spending an inordinate amount of time reconciling between two different views of demand. One view was created by the marketing department and was used as a basis for making financial commitments. The other was created by the demand planning team (which reported into supply chain) and relied heavily on statistics. While speaking with the executive team, I discovered that this problem was relatively new. Two years prior, there was only one demand plan—developed through a consensus process and ultimately owned by marketing. A study had been done showing that a statistical forecast would be more accurate. It was then decided, strictly based on accuracy, that statistical forecasting should be adopted as the new basis for the demand plan.

Two years later, the marketing team still didn't trust the statistical forecast. No one could explain how the statistical forecast was being developed or what it assumed. Marketing reverted to their less sophisticated, but explainable demand plan models—and the time-consuming effort to resolve the differences between the statistical forecast and marketing's plan.

The lesson here is that the executive team decided to rely on something before it was understood or trusted. The lack of understanding made following through with that decision impossible.

It is undeniable, however, that analytics should play an important role in demand planning. Many of my clients regularly manage demand plans for hundreds of thousands of products. Planning on that sort of scale is impossible to do manually with brute force alone. While there are a diverse and growing number of applications for analytics in demand planning, here are a few of the more common uses of statistics in demand planning. Each of these applications will be explained in more detail.

- Create a forecast at an aggregate (e.g., category, brand, or product family) or detail (e.g., item/customer) level
- Predict the mix of items within a family (disaggregation)
- Predict the impact of a cause-and-effect relationship (e.g., increasing price by X drives an impact of Y on volume)
- Establish a benchmark to identify outliers or elements of a demand plan that warrant further investigation
- Find and group items with similar demand patterns and behaviors

CREATING A STATISTICAL FORECAST

Most people envision using statistical methods to create a demand forecast. When creating a statistical forecast as part of a demand planning process, time-series modeling is a common approach. A time-series algorithm analyzes historical demand data segmented into periods of time, such as every month or week of the year, to generate a forecast of future demand.

Figure A1.1 illustrates two graphical examples of time-series forecasts. The solid line represents the history and the forecast, and the shaded areas represent the confidence intervals. The confidence intervals reflect an estimate of how much error there may be in the future forecast compared to history, and hence, the relative confidence in the projection. The wider the shaded area, the greater the likelihood of error compared to history.

You can see visually from the two examples that the demand history provided is the same, but two different algorithmic models, ETS and ARIMA, are used resulting in very different outputs. This highlights the importance of properly understanding different statistical models and selecting ones that are the most appropriate for a given circumstance.

The ETS algorithm is based on exponential smoothing and weighted averages. The newest history is given more weight in the calculation than the oldest history.

The ARIMA model considers the level (or average), the trend, and the seasonality of the historical demand data. Level represents the average value of the historical data. Trend is the direction (either increasing or decreasing) of the historical data. Seasonality represents variations in demand that historically occur in the same time period. The ARIMA algorithm mathematically decomposes these components from the historical data and then extrapolates the components into a future forecast for each time period. For the ARIMA model to yield the most accurate statistical forecast, at least two years (and ideally more) of historical data is needed to properly represent seasonality and trend.

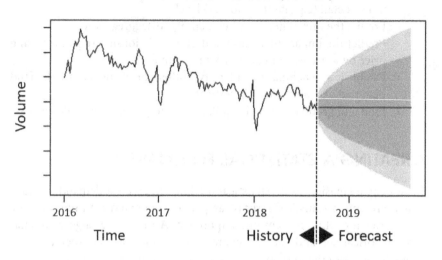

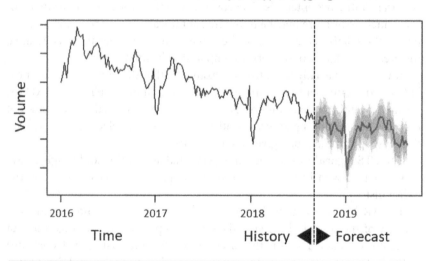

Figure A1.1   Examples of Time-Series Statistical Forecasts. © Oliver Wight International, Inc. Used with permission.

These algorithms, used to produce a statistical forecast, do what you might do intuitively—look for patterns in the history that can be expected to repeat in the future. In the ETS example only the average level of the historical data is considered. The trend (upward or downward) and the seasonal (repeating) demand patterns are not reflected in the forecast. In the ARIMA example all three components (level, trend, and seasonality) are incorporated by the algorithm.

Intuitively we would say that the ARIMA algorithm appears to produce a more accurate forecast of future demand. The forecast appears more believable because it incorporates all three components, including seasonality. A word of caution, however, as there are occasions where a clear pattern or seasonality may not be apparent or statistically significant in the historical demand data. In those cases, a straight-line, or average, forecast might be the best option. Statistical forecasting algorithms should not be judged on appearance.

In practice, software packages contain several algorithms. The software creates forecasts using the different algorithms and then selects the one that creates the most accurate future forecast based on the historical data. These tools take the history and split it into two parts—one part is used to train the model and the second part is used to validate it. The model is tested and benchmarked based on its ability to predict the results that it was not able to see during training.

The advantage of using software to create a statistical view of demand is the speed at which it processes, trains, validates, and produces a result. The software tool is much faster than what it would take a human being to perform the analysis and produce the statistical forecast.

Statistical forecasting techniques can and should be applied at different levels in the demand planning hierarchy. I often find organizations only run statistical forecasts at the lowest level of detail in a hierarchy (e.g., an item, or item/customer combination). That is the most challenging level—the patterns of seasonality and trend may be less evident at that granular level.

Take for example a retail product that comes in three different sizes. If that product is promoted every year, but the size that is promoted varies, the seasonality of that promotion will not show up in the item-level history. It will, however, show up at the product family level. I recommend trying time-series techniques at various levels in the hierarchy to find those levels where the algorithms perform best.

A statistical forecast is one view, or input, into the demand planning process. This is a best practice. These questions arise for demand planners: How much weight should be given to the statistical forecast input into the demand plan? How well does the statistical forecast represent the future? How accurate is it?

It is important to remember that a statistical forecast is only assuming that the future will be like the past. Without additional information or variables, a time-series forecast cannot predict an inflection point or significant change in trend. A demand planner must consider whether that assumption is valid. Just as we noted in Chapter 13, demand planners must first be able to articulate and explain the past before they can be relied on to make predictions of the future. This capability is very relevant when using a statistical forecast.

Using Figure A1.1 as an example, the ARIMA forecast assumes that the downward trend of sales will continue. To be confident in that prediction, it is important to understand why the downward trend of sales has existed in the past, and then agree that it makes sense for those same assumptions to continue in the future.

DISAGGREGATION—PLANNING THE MIX

Another common use of statistical forecasting is to predict the mix of items within a family. As discussed in Chapter 10, a family could be a group of items, customers, locations, etc. Particularly in large organizations that sell thousands of items, it is often impractical to manage the demand plan for each item manually. To attempt to do so would require planners to spend thousands of hours doing what statistical forecasting software can do quickly and cheaply.

When used to disaggregate, statistical projections are not used as a direct input into the demand plan. Instead, they are used as proportional factors. The demand planning tools deploy the proportional factors as an index to calculate the future mix of demand at lower levels in the planning hierarchy.

For example, suppose we have two items within a family. A demand planning tool may look at the last four weeks of sales history and determine that one item represents 30 percent of the volume and another represents 70 percent. That same ratio can be used in a forward projection to take a volume plan for the family and disaggregate (split) it across those two items. The demand planner would only have to manage the demand plan for the family. This frees up planners to focus on aggregate levels of the hierarchy, and consequently fewer forecasts to manage.

Because these lower-level forecasts are only needed to generate proportional factors, they often don't need to consider other influential factors like seasonality. They can often be very simple—for example, using a moving average of the last few weeks' actual sales. The seasonal pattern can be planned at the aggregate level, and the lower levels will inherit that seasonality as it is disaggregated down to them.

When using a statistical forecast strictly for disaggregation, the absolute volume of the statistical forecast does not end up reflected in the final output. The volume of the aggregate forecast being disaggregated is preserved. For this reason, when somebody tells me that they use statistical forecasting, I am always careful to clarify whether they are using it to create the forecast, to disaggregate the forecast, or both.

CAUSE-AND-EFFECT RELATIONSHIPS

Statistical techniques like regression are often used in planning to determine cause-and-effect relationships. For example, at some point, most organizations have considered the impact of changing the price of their products or services. When doing so, price elasticity is often calculated. Price elasticity represents the degree to which a change in price will drive a change in demand. Price elasticity is commonly determined with regression—evaluating historical data and plotting the relationship of influential factors such as the relationship of different price levels to demand volume.

Regression differs from time-series approaches in that the cause-and-effect relationship is independent from time. Regression will identify a relationship that is not dependent on timing. These cause-and-effect relationships, sometimes referred to as causals, can be combined with time-series forecasting to create a demand plan that considers trends as well as specific assumptions about the future. Time-series forecasts are used to form the basis of the plan, and causal models are added to or subtracted from the time-series forecast in order to model the impact of actions that are planned toward influencing demand in the future. Figure A1.2 illustrates an example of this technique. The statistical forecast shown is the same ARIMA time-series forecast from Figure A1.1. Adjustments have been made based on assumptions of future activities.

Examples other than pricing include the demand volume lift from promotions and advertising, the increase in volume from expanding distribution, and the increase in demand resulting from improving product quality. Depending on the amount of data that is available, causal models may be developed for these and many other factors that influence demand volume that could be considered in the plan.

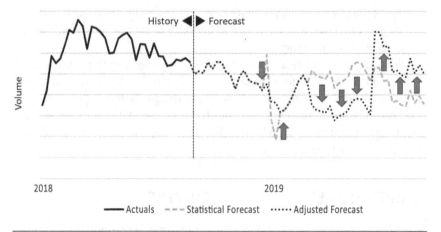

Figure A1.2   Example of a Statistical Forecast Adjusted with Causal Inputs. © Oliver Wight International, Inc. Used with permission.

BENCHMARKING

Statistical forecasts can be used as benchmarks or measuring sticks to help detect outliers or unusual plans. Figure A1.3 shows a statistical forecast that includes confidence intervals (the shaded area around the line). The confidence intervals tell us the range within which we are likely to see actual results, given the historical variability of demand. Demand results falling outside of those confidence intervals would be highly unlikely.

Even if a statistical forecast is not used as an input into the demand plan, a statistical forecast is still useful for evaluating the demand plan. It can be used, for example, to look for case time periods where demand volume is at risk of being outside the confidence intervals. When this risk is identified, time and attention can be focused on validating the assumptions behind the demand at these time points. Using a statistical forecast as a benchmark takes advantage of the fact that statistics are ruthlessly objective. The algorithms are not influenced by targets, incentives, or company politics.

FINDING AND GROUPING SIMILAR ITEMS

As discussed in Chapter 10, grouping items with similar demand patterns in a hierarchy is a best practice. Finding patterns and correlations in historical sales can not only lead to more accurate projections of demand but can

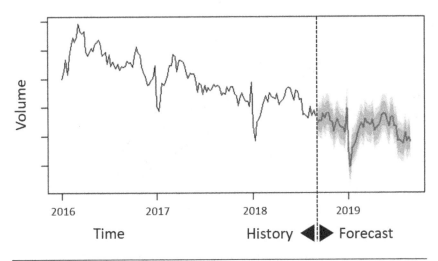

Figure A1.3   Example of a Statistical Forecast with Confidence Intervals.
© Oliver Wight International, Inc. Used with permission.

also guide commercial decision making. Seeing patterns can help to identify which products should or shouldn't be promoted together, for example. It is possible to see which products customers substitute when their preferred product is unavailable. This information is also useful when making product portfolio and pricing decisions. Many insights can be gained from identifying historical patterns of different segments of demand.

A good example of the insights that can be gained from this technique occurred while I was working with a toy manufacturer. I helped the client to assess the composition of their portfolio of products by looking at the relationship between demand volume and variability of historical sales of the products. We plotted the demand for all products in a graph with volume on one axis and variability on another (Figure A1.4). Each point on the graph reflects an individual product. The variability of each product is calculated to reflect the fluctuation of demand from month to month for that product. The volume of each product is calculated as the total volume sold of that product over the course of a year.

A traditional segmentation approach would be to divide Figure A1.4 into four quadrants and apply different forecasting techniques to each quadrant. Items with low variability and either high or low volume are often good candidates for statistical forecasting. Items with high variability tend to require

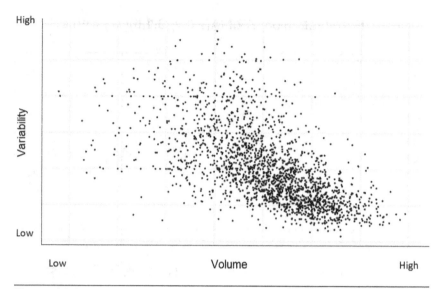

Figure A1.4 Demand Plotted by Volume and Variability. © Oliver Wight International, Inc. Used with permission.

more human intervention, such as collecting information about promotions or tenders. Items with high variability and low volume might be inherently challenging to plan and may require different strategies such as holding higher levels of safety stock or establishing longer customer lead times.

Upon further investigation we identified two very different types of products were being sold. Some products were considered *evergreen* and would be sold year after year. Others were seasonal products—here today, gone tomorrow. This was common knowledge to the sales and marketing teams, but that common knowledge was not being effectively translated into the demand planning process. The differentiation of these two types was not reflected in the product hierarchy.

By splitting the data into two groups, the distinctions and patterns became clearer. Evergreen products were better candidates for statistical forecasting— there was little variability in demand over each time period. Nearly all the difficult-to-plan products were in the seasonal group, which was not surprising since there were other influential factors that came into play during each season (see Figure A1.5).

A keen observer might notice that several products in the seasonal grouping have low variability as well. While that was true, the value in this exercise was not in achieving perfect segmentation or grouping. The goal was to group

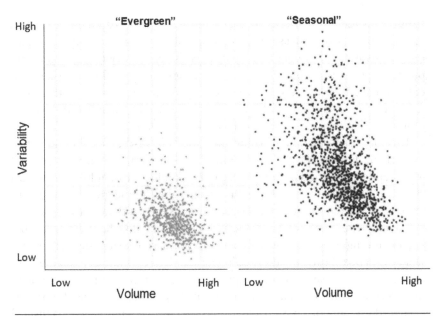

Figure A1.5   Demand Patterns of Different Groupings. © Oliver Wight International, Inc. Used with permission.

similar items so that we could not only improve our ability to plan, but also make better business decisions. For those reasons, the grouping of evergreen and seasonal products was useful. The variability differences between the two products could be easily and naturally understood. This understanding made it easy for the sales and marketing managers to appreciate why a statistical planning approach would be best used for evergreen products while other, more assumption-driven approaches would be needed for seasonal items. Consequently, subsequent forecasts were more trustworthy.

Consider an alternative plan of grouping all products with low variability. Such a group might include some evergreen and some seasonal products. That grouping would have little commercial relevance to the business because the approaches to developing, marketing, and selling evergreen and seasonal products are very different. It would be difficult to have a productive conversation with the sales and marketing team about a grouping of products that isn't meaningful to them.

The experience with the toy manufacturer involved intuition and perseverance that led to identifying a new dimension with which to view—and plan—those products. Within the field of machine learning, there is a type of algorithm referred to as *unsupervised learning*. This technique creates the freedom to identify patterns in data without applying parameters, such as specific goals or objectives, that might impede finding certain types of patterns. This method of data investigation is therefore very useful in demand planning. It helps to find different ways of grouping or clustering demand data to make it easier to identify seasonal patterns or cause-and-effect relationships. Unsupervised machine learning creates the potential to find new groupings that may never have been considered before.

Unsupervised machine learning promotes out-of-the-box thinking, particularly in industries with strong traditions in the way they market and sell to customers. The food industry is a good example. In this industry, standard category definitions for each product on the shelf at the grocery store have existed for decades (for example, cookies, crackers, snack nuts, frozen meals, powdered beverages, etc). Customers and suppliers alike have yielded to using a planning hierarchy based on age-old standard category definitions. So, what could possibly be the downfall? The standard definitions often don't reflect consumer behavior. For example, unsweetened iced tea may be grouped in an iced tea category. If a consumer wants to purchase a bottle of unsweetened iced tea, but none is available, would they buy sweetened iced tea instead or a bottle of water? The question is whether the consumer is looking for tea or an unsweetened beverage.

The iced tea example was shared with me as an example of how unsupervised machine learning can uncover new and interesting insights. In that case, the company wanted to know how and where they could promote their existing products to find new untapped market potential. They found they could position unsweetened iced tea as an alternative to bottled water which was a new way for them of thinking about the product at that time.

Unsupervised machine learning is not burdened with a predefined mental model of the world, in this case the retail grocery world. It will find patterns and clusters based on facts and data alone. The result of this type of evaluation can help rethink the way hierarchies, categories, and strategies are defined. It is also used to rethink the way products are positioned and promoted to consumers.

DEMAND PLANNING TOOLS AND TECHNOLOGY

There is a reason why the topic of technology is found at the end of this book. People become enamored with technology and neglect agreeing on the demand planning process itself, including ownership, accountability, and cross-functional collaboration and decision making. All aspects of the process should be defined and agreed to first, before deploying technology. Technology should be considered an enabler of the process. These are considered best practices.

If an organization goes down the path of implementing demand planning technology without first properly understanding what demand planning means and how the process should work in their environment, the results can be disastrous. I have, unfortunately, seen companies spend millions of dollars on software, only to have people continue to plan using spreadsheets. This phenomenon is not new. At one company, I learned the story of how they spent hundreds of thousands of dollars on a new mainframe computer system for their sales quotations department. One of the salespeople took the new mainframe terminal and put it on the floor under his desk. He could prepare quotations three times faster using a calculator, pencil, and paper.

Earlier, I shared an example of a client where most of the time and energy in the planning process was spent debating whose forecast was the right one. People became exhausted and frustrated. A consensus process existed in the past, but it had been scrapped after someone concluded that a piece of software could achieve the same level of accuracy while minimizing the time people spent planning and reaching consensus on the plan. Even though the software produced a forecast, the planners and managers struggled to adopt the statistically generated forecast as a plan they could commit to executing. Ownership of the forecast did not exist. Planners and commercial managers did not feel accountable for executing the forecast. They could not see or validate the assumptions (if there were any) that went into the statistical forecast and they felt the statistical forecast was not worthy of being used for decision making.

That being said, with the right understanding of best practices, technology can greatly simplify and improve the work that goes into demand management. I spent several years in information technology leadership roles, and to this day I still enjoy working with technology. I regularly help clients demystify different technology solutions. The currently available technology software solutions are quite powerful. I believe they will continue to evolve at a rapid rate. But always remember that there are no *silver bullets*. Technology alone will not create credible demand plans nor spur improvements in demand management.

The good news about technology is that the investment in big data tools has democratized data analysis. More and more people have access to the data and tools. The bad news is that data analysis has become increasingly more decentralized, and opinions and forecasts have proliferated. Without an agreed-upon process that defines roles, accountabilities, and how consensus and decisions are made, the return on investment in the tools is questionable. Esteemed publications, like *Harvard Business Review*, have documented that few data analysis and modeling experts even consider whether their models generate value for the business.[3]

Business executives and information technology professionals tend to forget that *models do not make business decisions*, even when analytics highlight possible business problems or opportunities. Top-rate demand planning teams are motivated to achieve business goals and objectives, not to push a number or a model.

Having said that, technology, when properly managed, contributes to an improved outcome for planning demand each month. Demand planning software applications, in fact, are a necessity as the number of products and customers grows. While I have certainly come across some truly amazing demand planning models built in Excel, it is neither recommended nor practical (even from a cost perspective) for most organizations to try to build detailed demand planning tools in-house. Highly capable demand planning solutions can be bought for a relatively low price to provide essential functionality that, when done manually, is difficult or error-prone. These tools include the following functionality that links directly with the best practices that have been outlined in this book:

- Aggregating and disaggregating demand data and plans—allowing a demand planner to work at multiple levels in the hierarchy and then reconcile those changes
- Creating statistical forecasts across many products and/or customers
- Taking *snapshots* to provide reporting on performance measures, such as demand plan accuracy and bias
- Integrating with financial planning and supply planning tools to enable seamless sharing of the demand plan with internal customers
- Integrating with transactional systems that are used by the people who are executing the demand plan (e.g., transacting sales orders)

A subset of demand planning tools that is also worth mentioning is a *demand sensing* tool. A demand sensing tool is designed primarily to manage demand in the near term. These tools leverage statistical algorithms to process large volumes of demand-related data to adjust and react to day-to-day changes in sales patterns. For example, a demand sensing tool might assess daily point-of-sale data and weather forecasts to realign the short-term demand plan on a day-by-day, location-by-location basis. These tools are most frequently used to optimize product distribution and the flow of inventory from manufacturing through to the end consumer. Demand sensing tools also play an important role in providing early warning where patterns in actual demand are deviating from planned demand. This is an important enabler for processes like Integrated Tactical Planning to be able to manage execution of the demand plan.[4]

When considering demand planning technology and tools, there is much to choose from. Those responsible for purchasing the tools should not treat the task like they are in a candy store. When evaluating a demand planning software package, pay heed to the following key considerations.

First, be clear as to the problem you are trying to solve and assess the solution against that problem. There will always be more bells and whistles than are truly needed, but sometimes the things most critical to your business aren't well supported. Consider the capability of the team that will be using the tools. For critical functionality, have your planners try it out. Some tools are far easier to use and configure than others.

Second, before investing, demonstrate or prove that the solution works, using your own data. If, for example, the goal is to improve demand plan accuracy—show it. Provide the vendor with a snapshot of your historical data and relevant inputs to the demand plan. Have them generate a plan. Before comparing the result with the actuals (which are known), have them present that demand plan to you. Would you have believed it? Remember, the tool not only needs to provide an accurate plan, but it should also generate the plan in a way that enables a demand planner to understand it and communicate it effectively. There is no sense in buying a new tool that is confusing to use or understand the output, and consequently, will be ignored.

Last, don't try to solve for process, behavior, or organizational problems with tools. In my experience, it will never work. If, for example, you struggle today with people overriding the plan, simply removing an override capability from the tool *without making adjustments* won't stop them from not wanting to use the plan. It would just further frustrate planners who would then have to figure out another way to force the override into the system. Accountability and behavioral problems require leadership and behavioral solutions.

LAKES AND WAREHOUSES

A multiple-input demand planning process requires gathering, organizing, and storing inputs (data) from multiple sources. Those inputs must then be converted to show how they impact the volume, value, and margin in the demand projections. In Chapter 7, I referred to collecting and storing assumptions in a virtual shoebox. As the amount of data collected increases in scale and complexity, it can quickly lead to a situation where the data exist, but not in a format or location that can be digested for planning.

Technologies like *data lakes* can help break down these barriers and open access to a wider variety of input data for use in planning. However, there are some important subtleties to take into account when considering how to best use data lakes.

Data lakes are essentially pools of raw data. There may be sales history, promotional plans, marketing plans, and financial plans in the same data lake, but there is no guarantee that the different types of raw data can be linked or connected without further processing. The processing that is required to make the raw data useful is often referred to as *schema on read*. This term means that the data are interpreted when they are read from the lake, as opposed to being interpreted when they are being written into the lake.

Data warehouses, by contrast, are structured for an intended purpose such as storing data for demand planning or financial reporting. Data are cleansed (detecting and correcting inaccurate records) and organized before they are put into the warehouse and do not need to be further processed or interpreted to be used as an output for a plan or reports.

In my experience, the technology behind these types of tools is straightforward. Computing power, storage capability, and network bandwidth have reached a point where there are very few functional technology constraints. The only questions are: (1) How much of each is needed? and, (2) What are the associated costs? The real challenge lies in harmonizing the data for use in planning. By harmonizing, I'm referring to the alignment of hierarchies and data definitions. What may seem simple on the surface may be quite complicated in practice. Here are just a few examples where harmonization might be challenging:

- *Product hierarchies*: A sales planning tool might group products by the way they are promoted. A financial planning tool might group products to provide consistent year-over-year financial reporting. A supply planning tool might group products based on how and where they are manufactured.
- *Time periods*: A financial planning tool might treat a *month* as a grouping of four or five weeks. A sales planning tool might treat a *month* as a calendar month. Syndicated point-of-sale data may be reviewed in four-week *quads* (13 per year).
- *Customer hierarchies*: A sales planning tool might group customers based on sales accountability. There may be an intermediary distributor

to which product is sold, and then distributed to end customers. In that case, a supply planning system may not be able to distinguish between the different end customers when all product is shipped to one destination.

A data lake will not automatically solve for these sorts of data harmonization challenges. It will, however, often shine a spotlight on the harmonization challenges and may create a platform for resolving them.

SUMMARY

If there is one point to emphasize from this appendix, it is that there are no *silver bullets*. Analytics and technology will not create credible demand plans on their own. That being said, it is important to cover the topics being discussed here that give an overview of what can be accomplished with analytics and technology—knowing full well that this is a subject that will undoubtedly continue to be developed. I hope it is apparent that analytics and technology must be operated and applied with trained hands. As the saying goes, "lies, damned lies, and statistics" can be used to support weak arguments if they are misunderstood or misused. I also hope that this appendix has demystified some commonly used (and misused) terminology in an approachable way—and perhaps even created an appetite to learn more.

ENDNOTES

1. A. Selyukh. "Optimized Prime: How AI and Anticipation Power Amazon's 1-Hour Deliveries." NPR, November 21, 2018. https://www.npr.org/2018/11/21/660168325/optimized-prime-how-ai-and-anticipation-power-amazons-1-hour-deliveries.
2. "How Well Does Your Company Use Analytics?" Harvard Business Review, July 29, 2022. https://hbr.org/2022/07/how-well-does-your-company-use-analytics.
3. Kaylan Veeramachaneni. "Why You're Not Getting Value From Your Data Science." Harvard Business Review, December 7, 2016.
4. Hozack et al. *Integrated Tactical Planning*. Wiley, 2021.

INDEX

Note: Page numbers followed by "*f*" refer to figures.